# How to Give a Damn Good Speech

By
Philip R. Theibert

CASTLE BOOKS

This edition published in 2005 by
CASTLE BOOKS ®
A division of Book Sales, Inc.
114 Northfield Avenue
Edison, NJ 08837

This edition published by arrangement with
Career Press
3 Tice Road
Franklin Lakes, NJ 07417

*How to Give a Damn Good Speech* © 1997 Philip R. Theibert.
Original English language edition published by Career Press

Library of Congress Cataloging-in-Publication Data

Theibert, Philip R.
How to give a damn good speech / by Philip Theibert.
p. cm.
        Includes index.
        1.   Public speaking. I. Title.

PN4121.T46      1997                          97-1337
805.5'—dc21                                   CIP


ISBN-13: 978-0-7858-2105-2
ISBN-10:  0-7858-2105-8

Printed in the United States of America

# Contents

## Introduction

# Let's Write a Great Speech

Someone once said it's easy to write a book. You keep notes on a subject and fill up a shoebox with them. When the shoebox is full, you have a book.

I'm not sure it's that easy, but it did get me thinking. After all, during my 15 years as a professional speechwriter for CEOs, political figures, and other top officials, I have accumulated not a single shoebox, but drawers and file cabinets of speechwriting materials: helpful tips, attention-getting leads, spellbinding anecdotes, ice-breaking jokes, inspiring stories, and fascinating statistics. It occurred to me that these materials could be valuable to all those of you who find yourselves in a position to give a speech.

In other words, I believed I had a *book* in all those files! Well, it wasn't quite so simple as carting my materials off to a publisher. You'll be pleased to know that I've carefully sifted through my notes and culled the very best to share with you. I selected the best advice, the best openings, the best stories, the best facts—so that you can make yours the *best* damn speech you can give.

### Part 1: Preparing a Great Speech

The first part of the book will explore the basic components of a good speech. It goes beyond the basic "tell them what you're going to say, say it, tell them what you said," and includes the crucial elements that must be laid on top of that foundation to ensure an outstanding speech.

I offer concrete examples to back up each point. In fact, let me point out that the best speeches also include strong examples to illustrate an idea, to make the information stick in the audience's minds.

I have included four speeches at the conclusion of Part 1. I dissect each speech, step-by-step, to show you how and why they're effective.

Finally, a worksheet at the end will help *you* develop your next speech.

## Part 2: Outstanding Tips for Speeches

I realized, after completing Part 1, that I had barely touched upon the "tricks-of-the-trade" or successful techniques that professional speechwriters use. I added Part 2, featuring 100 valuable tips.

## Part 3: Fantastic Openings

The toughest part of writing a speech is *starting* a good speech. I have, and I'm sure you have too, struggled many times for that perfect "ice-breaker," a clever, entertaining way to open a speech, to connect with the audience, and to establish goodwill. Part 3 contains 100 great openings that you can use or modify for any speech.

## Part 4: Great Stuff to Use in Your Speeches

Timing is vital to a good speech. In some quarters, it's also called pacing. The average speech lasts about 15 to 20 minutes. That's a long time for anyone to sit and listen. You can't keep hitting your audience over the head with serious stuff. Every now and then, you have to let your audience take that psychological pause by throwing in a good story that will let them relax.

And that is what Part 4 is all about. Here are many great anecdotes and stories that you can use to weave into your speech to provide that psychological pause.

## Part 5: Great Quotations

There's something about a third-party endorsement that gives you credibility. I can tell my wife that the engine is going to fall out of the car and she will doubt me, knowing that I have the mechanical ability of a fish. But a mechanic can tell my wife the exact same thing and she will believe him. Why? He's a qualified outside expert who knows what he's talking about. By reinforcing my opinion, he made me look smarter.

Wouldn't it be great if every time you gave a speech you had someone standing behind you, a famous historical figure, a world-renowned expert, or someone the audience holds in awe? Of course that won't happen. But the second-best thing can. You can quote a respected person and imply their endorsement. Part 5 contains 250 great quotations you can use in your speech (of course, not all at once.)

## Part 6: Almanac

Finally, in keeping with the underlying philosophy of this book—to give you everything you need to write a good speech—I have attached an almanac. It contains funny, interesting, important stuff that happened on specific days. I include several entertaining facts for each day of the year. This is great material, much like the quotes and anecdotes, that you can weave into your speech to reinforce important ideas.

## Who Will Benefit from This Book?

If you have to get up and convince people to do something—buy a product, support your project, donate to your charity, join the PTA, vote for a candidate, invest in your business—then this book is for you.

If you are running for office, convincing personnel to invest in saving bonds, breaking bad news to employees, encouraging your congressmen to support an idea, appealing to a company to move to town, accepting an award or honor, telling an audience how to do anything—then this book is for you.

If you are a boss, business owner, CEO or department manager; if you are an entry-level employee aspiring to move ahead in the corporate world; if you are a public relations professional, a committee chairperson, an officer in a community volunteer organization; if you are a teacher, a camp counselor, a scout leader—then this book is for you.

In fact, if you find yourself in any situation in which you must speak before a crowd larger than one—and almost all of us do—then this book is for you.

In short, if you want to be the best you can be at public speaking, at selling yourself and your ideas, this book will prove to be a bargain at any price. It is an investment in the fundamental cornerstone of any endeavor—your ability to communicate ideas.

# Part I

# Preparing a
# Great Speech

I am amazed at the number of books that make writing a speech sound like a very complicated subject. Talk to enough "communication consultants" and you might think you need a Ph.D. in linguistics to compose even the most basic speech.

Believe it or not, in just a few short pages, I am going to give you the basic elements for preparing any speech—the blueprint, if you will.

## The Basics of a Good Speech

By the way, as we go through this first chapter, keep in mind this basic advice, handed down from generation to generation: "Tell them what you are going to say, say it, then tell them what you said." Those words of wisdom reflect the bare bones that any speech hangs on.

### 1. Identify Your Topic and Goal

The first thing I want you to do is consider this question: *What is my speech about?* Then answer that question in one sentence. For example:

- I want the audience to know our company must make cutbacks in order to avoid going out of business.
- I want the audience to support United Way by volunteering or giving money.
- I want the audience to vote for adding a new art program in our school.
- I want the audience to understand how our product can increase company revenues.

Answering this key question sets up your whole speech. Don't even bother trying to prepare your speech unless you're clear about the topic and your purpose. What are you trying to accomplish?

Note that in the examples given, the topic and goal are quite specific. For instance, in the first example, the speaker addressed a necessary action—cutbacks—

rather than just talking about industry problems. It's important, when identifying your topic and goals, to be as focused as possible.

## 2. Write Your Opening Line

Now that you know what your speech is about, write your opening line. Tell the audience what you are going to talk about. Here again are a few examples:

- Today, I want to talk about the tough times our company is facing and the key steps we will take to solve these problems.

- Today, I want to enlist your help in making the United Way a stronger organization.

- Today, I am going to talk about why an art program is important for our school system.

- Today, I'm going to tell you why we are excited about our new product—the handyman's helper—and why you should be excited, too.

Let me clarify that this opening line will not necessarily be the first sentence in your speech. But to begin the process of developing your talk, you need a strong anchor—and what better anchor than the topic and goal?

## 3. Identify a Few Key Points

Okay, now you know what you are going to talk about. What key points will you make about it? Get three to four cards. (A good speech should not have dozens of key points, or you'll lose your audience—three or four ought to be plenty.) Put a key point on each card. Here's an example:

Today I want to talk about the tough times our company is facing and the key steps we will take to solve these problems.

1. We have lost 50 percent of our customers due to increased competition.

2. We will relocate our offices to reduce rent.

3. We will take away all perks ranging from company cars to country club memberships.

4. Taking these steps means we can avoid layoffs—provided we see financial improvement within six months.

## 4. Support Your Key Points

Now put key point cards on a table. Put a card *underneath* each of those cards. This card will contain the key messages you will use to back up your key points. An example:

**Key Point One:** We have lost 50 percent of our customers due to increased competition.

**Backup:** This puts us in a bad economic situation. We have lost $100,000 in revenues, while our overhead has not decreased. In other words, our revenues have been cut in half, our overhead hasn't.

**Key Point Two:** We will relocate our offices to reduce rent.

**Backup:** We are currently in a high-rent district of town. This is nice for image, but our customers rarely stop by. In fact, 90 percent of the time we go to them. Although it might make your commute longer, we can cut our rent in half by moving out of the city into Porksville. We will start this move on September 22.

**Key Point Three:** We will take away all perks ranging from company cars to country club memberships.

**Backup:** If we are not making money, we cannot spend money. Thus we must look for ways to quit spending money. The easiest and the least painful way to accomplish that right now is to eliminate several perks. We will, beginning next month, eliminate all car allowances and country club memberships, and reduce the amount of health insurance premiums we pay on your behalf.

**Key Point Four:** Taking these steps means we can avoid layoffs—provided we see financial improvement within six months.

**Backup:** I know these cost-cutting measures do not make you happy. But by taking these measures we do not have to lay off any employees. And if we can continue to cut costs and increase revenues within the next six months—which means working harder to attract new customers and cross-sell existing clients—we can avoid having to lay off any employees.

## 5. Wrap It Up With a Summarizing Conclusion

So now you've told them what you are going to talk about. You've talked about it. Now it's time to tell them what you said. An example:

I have told you that our revenues have been cut in half. I have told you what steps we will take, right now, to deal with that problem. I have also told you there will be no layoffs. Are there any questions?

# Beyond Basic—To a Damn Good Speech!

Now we are going to move onto the next segment and tell you how to turn that "good" speech into a great speech, how to go beyond the basic outline, how to weave important concepts, so your speech can reach the next plateau.

## 1. Acknowledge Your Audience

As I explained earlier in this chapter, you want to start your speech in a way that grabs the attention of the audience and introduces your topic. You will discover 100 such openings in Part 2 of this book.

But another purpose of the introduction is to welcome or acknowledge your audience in a positive way. Everyone likes to hear nice things said about them. So does your audience. So start off with a friendly and complimentary welcome.

That's exactly how Norman R. Augustine, president and CEO of Lockheed Martin, started this speech before the Red Cross:

"It is indeed a great honor to be with you here today to help kick off this 1996 Conference on Volunteerism.

"I have been asked to speak with you this afternoon about volunteer leadership. This is a subject with which you are abundantly familiar—after all, you are the ones who lead what in many people's opinions is the greatest volunteer service organization in the world. You are the ones who help lead the efforts of 1.5 million volunteers. You are the ones who day in and day out lead the way into situations rife with challenge and hazard. As one volunteer noted, 'The Red Cross goes places that everyone else is trying to leave.'"

Note how this quote is taken from a member of the Red Cross. If you respect what your audience has to say, they will listen to you with more respect.

Here's another example: Kenneth T. Derr, chairman of the board and CEO of the Chevron Corporation, also knows the value of letting the audience know they are admired and appreciated. In a speech to the Desk and Derrick Clubs, he began not with a joke but with this bit of sincere appreciation:

"I'm very proud to be speaking to you today. Throughout my career, I've found Desk and Derrick members to be a great source of knowledge on oil and energy industry trends and issues. And the reason for this is clear.

"Your association has been dedicated to promoting personal education, professional development, and continuous learning since 1949. Your motto, "Greater Knowledge—Greater Service," really does describe the outlook of all the Desk and Derrick members I've known.

"More importantly, it's a philosophy that will serve you as individuals—and the companies you work for—well into the next century.

"In fact, our goals are a perfect fit with a subject that's captured my interest and attention in recent years, and they are at the heart of what I want to talk about today. And that is the need for the people in my company—and in any company for that matter—to be part of a learning organization."

Notice how the speaker uses this appreciation of his audience to segue very smoothly into his main topic.

## 2. Take a Moment to Define Your Terms!

Before we had children (we call this period of our marriage BC—Before Children), my wife and I went on a cross-country trip in a Honda car. One day we met another couple walking along a creek at a campground. We started chatting and discovered we both were driving Hondas.

But then it got a little weird. The other woman asked, "Don't you find it's tough to pack stuff?" My wife replied, "It's a bit cramped, but we do okay." Then the other woman said, "How about those bugs, don't they drive you crazy?" My wife looked at her curiously.

Well, by this time, I had figured out that while we were talking about our Honda automobile, the other couple was talking about a Honda motorcycle. Yet neither my wife nor the other woman ever realized they weren't sharing the same experiences. About two minutes later, they both walked away, very satisfied that they had bonded and had a nice conversation.

No harm done, of course. But if you are addressing a crowd of important people, and they are giving you 20 minutes of their precious time, you better make sure that they understand exactly what you are talking about. In short, define your terms.

As you prepare to give your speech, are there any terms you must define for your audience? Don't assume that you and your audience will agree on the same definitions. Clarify up front what your terms are and what you mean when you use those terms.

Educator Fritz Hinrichs very carefully describes what he means by "classical" for his audience.

"The word 'classical' or 'classic' is used in many contexts and often without specific meaning: Classic Coke, classical music, classic rock. However, classical usually means something that, through time, has proven worthy of our respect and interest. In music, the work of certain composers has been recognized as worth saving, while that of others, though popular in its own time, has been tossed into the dustbin of history. The same is true of books. Some books are more worthy of study than others because of the profundity and clarity with which they express the ideas they contain...."

You don't have to get fancy when defining your terms. Service is a concept that we have all heard *ad nauseum*. But what is service? Notice how Robert Williams, assistant vice president of Travelers Home Equity Service, defines the term for his audience through the use of short examples and a quick story:

"Service is getting served at Dunkin' Donuts within seconds after you sit down...with a smile...and a clean mug...and a genuine thank-you when you get your change.

"Service is a store clerk—maybe at one of the famous Nordstrom's department stores—who tells you they don't carry your brand but if you'll wait a minute, she'll run down the street and get it for you.

"Not long ago, a telemarketer in our office got a call from the United Way asking if anyone could help a deaf man get some information about a mortgage. As luck would have it, our man had deaf parents. He promised to return the call the next day when he could bring his teletype from home—a machine that translates spoken words into print so deaf people can read it. Nobody told Orlando Barnabei to do that. But somehow he understood that service is more than being polite on the phone and giving out correct information. Service is getting inside the skin of a customer, to find out what they expect."

So remember. Don't expect the audience to have the same definition that you have. Define your terms carefully so there is no misunderstanding!

## 3. Clarify Your Qualifications

After you have bonded with your audience by saying something nice about them, answer the questions about *you* that have been raised in their minds. Who are you and why are you qualified to speak to them? After all, they're going to be sitting in the chair for 15 to 20 minutes listening to your words of wisdom. Are you really worth listening to?

In the first few minutes of your speech you must establish your credibility. Don't be afraid to emphasize your credentials.

But didn't I get a great introduction? Why should I repeat what my introduction says? Sure, the person who handled the introductions might have given you a glowing introduction. But right away, you are making a basic mistake that many speakers make. You are assuming the audience was listening. Wrong!

The introduction is like a commercial before a television show. The audience is just waiting to get through it until the show begins. Which, by the way, is you.

So how can you establish your credibility? You might use a bit of self-deprecating humor. Here are two examples:

"Tammy, in her introduction, introduced me as an expert. Well, we all know that an expert is anyone with a briefcase who is more than 20 miles from home. But I do have more than 10 years of experience studying the mating habits of polar bears and have made 10 trips to the frozen north to study polar bears in action."

"A schoolboy once wrote that Socrates went around giving advice, so they poisoned him. I am well aware of the danger of giving advice, but let me assure you I can give some tips on remodeling your home. I have run my own construction company for 20 years and, believe me, I know what works and doesn't work in remodeling...."

Let's look at some of the ways other speakers have established their credibility. Louis J. Freeh, director of the FBI, was giving a commencement speech at the Catholic University of America. He had to assure the audience that he wasn't a political appointee with no real world law experience. He did this in his straightforward way.

"I became an FBI agent in 1975—and mostly investigated organized crime cases in New York City. It was among the most rewarding assignments I ever had as an FBI agent—what I considered a real contribution to the public's well-being. I later served as a federal prosecutor and then as a federal judge before being appointed by President Clinton, 20 months ago, to a 10-year term as FBI director.

"It has been in part exhilarating as we strive to better protect the public from harm. But these 20 months have also been at times been filled with pain and tragedy. For example, we have deployed hundreds of agents to Oklahoma City and elsewhere to investigate the bombing that took so many lives at the Alfred Murrah Building on April 19th.

---

"This week—Police Week—I have joined with the FBI family and with law enforcement officers around the country to mourn the agents and police officers who were slain in the line of duty during the past year. In all, 76 brave men and women...."

If you have "been there, done that," your audience will be impressed. A combat veteran is much more believable talking about the horrors of war than someone who has never fought. We all have our personal battles we fight and out of personal battles come our feelings, insights, and beliefs. If you can share a story with your audience that shows you have fought that battle, been in that conflict and emerged with experience and insight, they will be willing to listen to you (of course, this method may not work with teenagers—very few voices of experience do).

I remember writing a speech for a CEO of a major energy company to a group of teachers who were teaching English as a second language. He had no idea what to tell them. He complained to me that he had no expertise in education and he had no experience in dealing with Hispanic students.

In the course of our conversation, I discovered this very executive didn't speak English until he was in first grade. He had grown up in an Italian family, and on the first day of school he was surrounded by kids who all spoke this foreign language, English.

It dawned on the executive that this was a story the ESL teachers could identify with. He could talk from his experiences as a stranger in a strange land, surrounded by a foreign tongue. He used the story and it went over great!

Commissioner Bob Williams, who heads the Administration on Developmental Disabilities, is disabled himself. He convinced the audience that he knew what he was talking about with these words. (A fuller text of this speech appears toward the end of this chapter.)

"I want to put this in a very personal as well as an historical context, that each of you will not only understand, but many will have experienced first-hand yourselves....

"As increasing numbers of individuals with significant disabilities throughout our nation have done, I have beaten the odds society stacks up against us—prejudice, stereotype, and continuing discrimination...there are those of us who will always remember, and remind others of a much different time. In the early 1960s, for example, children with cerebral palsy who drooled, as well as those seen as mentally retarded, were legally barred from attending most public schools in my home state of Connecticut....In the early 1970s, I remember asking the Special Education Director of my town, point blank, why I couldn't go to the same school and take the same classes as my brothers and sisters. His reply was just as point-blank and matter-of-fact. He said the reason why I couldn't go to regular classes was that I couldn't speak clearly enough...."

James N. Sullivan, vice chairman of the board for Chevron Corporation, had to talk to an audience of crisis management professionals. Instead of telling them that he was a big shot and therefore knew all about crisis management, he did something much better—he told them a personal story:

"Well, I am in senior management, but I started 37 years ago as an entry-level refinery process engineer in the chemical industry and over the years I have lived crisis management.

"Back then, we used to say that if you could keep your head while those about you were running around in panic—well then, you obviously didn't understand the situation.

"But I did learn the value of keeping your head. I learned, first hand—maybe too many times—what it means to face a 3,000-pound hydrogen-hydrocarbon leak from the business end of a fire hose with the thought, 'If this goes wrong I won't even know about it.'

"And, believe me, I know that a lot of things can go wrong. In the late '70s I was the operations manager of the Richmond Refinery when we had a flash fire that, thankfully, didn't seriously hurt anyone.

"But it kept us busy all weekend, and when I had finally gotten home and opened a beer I got a call from our public affairs guy wanting me to come back to the refinery to explain to some TV reporters what happened. It must have been a slow news day. So I did, reluctantly.

"Later, when I turned on the set for the 11 o'clock news, there I was explaining that the cloud of black smoke the citizens of Richmond had seen earlier that day really wasn't dangerous, at the same time the camera slowly zoomed in for a close-up of the sign behind me that read 'Safety First—No Accidents.' "

Establishing your credibility doesn't have to take a lot of time. It can be done in one simple paragraph. That's exactly what Richard Lidstad, 3M vice president of human resources, did when he delivered a speech at the Carlson School of Management, University of Minnesota.

"I was asked to speak to you today because I have always felt a strong, personal link to the University of Minnesota. My bachelor of science was from the university, more years ago than I'd like to remember. My relationship with the university has been strengthened over the last few years, partly because I have been a part of the Executive Mentoring Program for MBA students."

## 4. Address Audience Biases

Every audience brings a set of assumptions with them. For example, for many years, I wrote speeches for a big utility company that had a number of nuclear power plants. It was no surprise that most people walked into the company auditorium believing that nuclear power was nasty stuff that would make you glow if you got within two miles of the plant. Thus, the audience came in with a preconceived notion that the speaker was going to try to convince them that nuclear power—what they knew was bad—was good. The challenge for the speaker, and for me as the speechwriter, was to address their biases before they were even willing to listen.

Many of our beliefs about many subjects ranging from crime to the state of the American family come from the media. Thus, to dispel myths, sometimes the best approach is to use the media as your medium. That's exactly what Bob Armstrong, an assistant secretary for the Department of Interior, did when giving a speech to the National Cattleman's Association:

"Range reform has not been an easy experience! When we introduced our proposal almost a year ago, there were widespread predictions of doom and gloom. Let me just take a moment to read you two quotes from the press over the past few months:

" 'Today, range reform is all but dead.' (*Salt Lake Tribune*, March 13, 1995)

"'Rangeland reform totally rewrites the rules of the game. Ranchers certainly dislike it. But more than that, there's panic.' (*Idaho Statesman*, July 16, 1995)

"And that's some of our better press!

"Despite all this, August 21, 1995—the day on which the new regulations were implemented—has come and gone. I think a comment in the August 21 *Grand Junction, Colorado Daily Sentinel* sums up best what actually happened on that date:

" 'The earth did not yawn yesterday and swallow the rural communities of the West. Reports of raining frogs remained nonexistent west of the 100th meridian. And the rivers hereabouts are still filled with water, not blood.'

"Today is January 29 and I'd like to take some time to talk about why there are still no frogs or blood. I want to talk about why range reform is working and why it's attracting support from public land users, including stockmen, throughout the West."

Note that in this speech, Mr. Armstrong took the media coverage, poked fun at it, then came out with the truth, supported by the media, that he wanted his audience to be aware of.

## 5. Tell Them What You Are Going to Talk About!

Morris K. Udall, the former Arizona senator, once began a speech with these six simple words. "I'm here to talk about crime."

Bingo! That's how you can segue into your topic. Once you've welcomed the audience, established your credibility, and addressed biases, don't waste any time—tell the audience your main point. I don't care if it's about crime, how to improve a product, how to reduce teenage pregnancy, how to lose weight. Stand up in front of your audience and say, "I am here to talk about _____."

This is a very crucial part of the speech. Most people make one very basic mistake when they give a speech. They forget the audience is listening to them! I know that sounds obvious, but it is a very important point.

The audience is not reading your speech. They cannot go back and review parts of it they missed. You must clearly establish what you are talking about. You must tell the audience simply, "This is what I'm talking about. These are my three key points."

This is not the time to be cute or clever. In a few short paragraphs, you are giving the audience a clear road map of where you are taking them. You are giving them an outline of exactly what you are going to talk about.

Here's how Rick Belluzzo, an executive vice president for Hewlett-Packard, told the audience what he was going to discuss:

> "I was given responsibility for HP's combined computer activities just a little over a year ago. Today, I'd like to do three things. First, I'd like to describe the vision of pervasive computing HP has been working toward for many years now. Then I'd like to show how that vision plays out in the strategies we are pursuing today in our four customer segments. I'll close with some comments about the nature of HP and what you might expect from us in the future."

Boom, boom, boom. Nothing fancy there. Mr. Belluzzo laid out the facts; he told the audience where he was taking them.

Robert E. Allen, chairman and CEO of AT&T, also told the audience exactly what he was going to talk about:

> "I want to convince you: That Californians have a big stake in opening up this last and greatest bastion monopoly in the telephone industry to real competition.
>
> "I want to convince you: That you have an opportunity to set the pattern for the country and in fact the world.
>
> "And that if you do, you'll play an important role in boosting California's economy and competitiveness."

Note that while Mr. Allen was telling the audience what he was going to talk about, he also told them how his points would benefit them.

Following is a classic example of "tell them what you're going to tell them." It is an excerpt from the first fireside chat by President Franklin D. Roosevelt. (For you trivia buffs, it was given on March 12, 1933.)

> "I want to talk for a few minutes with the people of the United States about banking—with the comparatively few who understand the mechanics of banking, but more particularly with the overwhelming majority who use banks for the making of deposits and the drawing of checks.
>
> "I want to tell you what has been done in the last few days, why it was done, and what the next steps are going to be.
>
> I recognize that the many proclamations from state capitals and from Washington, the legislation, the treasury regulations, etc., couched for the most part in banking and legal terms, should be explained for the benefit of the average citizen. I owe this in particular because of the fortitude and good temper with which everybody has accepted the inconvenience and hardships of the banking holiday. I know that when you understand what we in Washington have been

about, I shall continue to have your cooperation as fully as I have had your sympathy and help during the past week."

By now you have probably noticed that some of the top leaders in the nation don't beat around the bush. They tell the audience exactly what they are going to tell them. Also, you have noticed that they explain this very simply and quickly. It only takes a minute or less to outline your speech for the audience. In fact, Kenneth T. Derr, chairman of the board and CEO for Chevron, took two sentences to sum up his talk:

"I'm here today to suggest that we take more active and aggressive steps to *change* the perception we're 'part of the problem.' In particular, we need to look at how we *formulate* environmental solutions, how we *package* them, how we gain *support* for them, and how we *communicate* them to stakeholders."

Well, at this point I know I'm in danger of violating the cardinal rule of speechwriting. *When the horse is dead, get off.* That means that once you've made your point, don't belabor it; move on. But at the risk of belaboring my point, I want to give one more example.

This summary statement is from Joseph Dionne, CEO of McGraw Hill:

"As your program suggests, I'd like to direct my remarks today to the special challenges and opportunities that confront our organizations in the international marketplace. So for my part this afternoon, I'd like first to focus on the expanded potential for world trade and economic development as a result of these recent events.

"Next, turn to the aspect of trade that is dearest to me and my company— but also should become part of your own trade vocabulary—the transfer of information around the world.

"Finally, I'd like to suggest what our nation and our companies must do to safeguard and protect and, therefore, optimize our role in this new world order."

Well, by checking in on how business leaders organize their speeches, we discover there are no fancy tricks. The speeches are divided into three to five main points. At the beginning of each speech the executive says, "Look here, folks, these are the main points I will cover. They are...."

Audiences appreciate this kind of approach. You have revealed exactly what to expect from the speech and where the speech is going. And, believe me, if top executives use this approach, it will work equally well for you. Always remember, you are not writing a mystery. Tell the audience exactly where you are going. The audience will then know exactly what to listen for.

## 6. Tell the Audience Why They Should Care

Now that the audience knows why *you* care, you must tell them why *they* must care! Telling the audience why they should care about your topic doesn't have to take up hours. It can be accomplished in one minute.

For example, James D. Wolfensohn, president of the World Bank, spoke at the United Nations Fourth World Conference on Women in China in 1995 and introduced his speech, "Woman and the Transformation of the 21st Century," with this short story:

> "Back in June, as I made my first trip as president of the bank, the first country my wife and I visited was Mali in West Africa....While we were there, a baby was born—a girl. I have thought often of that little girl and the life ahead of her.
>
> "Her chances of going to school are no better than one in four. She will likely be stunted in her growth due to chronic malnutrition. Around the age of six, she will probably suffer genital mutilation, brutally. When she marries, probably at a very young age, she faces two decades of childbearing. And her chances of dying during childbirth are terrifyingly high—about 1 in 20. She will be expected to grow most of her family's food, but be the last to sit down at a meal. She will be responsible for educating and taking care of her children, but will have to walk miles a day to gather firewood and water. And if she subsequently works for a wage, she is likely to earn a third less for doing the same job as a man.
>
> "If our meeting here is to have any real meaning, it must hold out a vision of a new and better world for that little girl."

Reed Hundt of the Federal Trade Commission uses a similar approach in a speech before a group of technology experts. He makes sure they know why their work is so important and what advanced technology in their children's schools can mean to them personally.

> "Those of you who are parents, like me, think how different life would be if you could exchange e-mail with a teacher as easily and frequently as you do with your colleagues at work. No more notes in bookbags or lapses of months between parent-teacher conferences. Think about your child being able to download a project at home so that you could work on it together. No more gulf between the way you work and the way your children learn."

## Putting It All Together

So far, we have discussed several important components of an effective speech and techniques to make these components powerful. Now let's break here to look at an example that incorporates each of these techniques. Raymond W. Smith, CEO of Bell Atlantic, gave this speech at the Philadelphia Education Summit on February 27, 1997:

> "I want to thank Mayor Rendell, Council President Street, and Ernest Jones (Greater Philadelphia Urban Affairs Coalition head) for giving me a chance to talk about a subject near and dear to my heart.
>
> "Of course, when the mayor calls, he doesn't give a guy much choice."

Notice how the speaker thanks certain individuals, acknowledging his audience, while incorporating an ice-breaking humorous remark.

"By the way, I was interested to read David Boldt's preview of my speech this evening in his column in Tuesday's *Inquirer*. According to David, I'm here to-night to tell you 'about the marvelous educational things that can be done with computers if one happens to have an infinite amount of money.'

"I wish that were true, because that would be a much easier speech to give than the one I signed up for...."

Here, the speaker address addresses and deflates a popular myth.

"I do believe the *children* of Philadelphia can be educated to become the knowledge workers of the 21st century—in part, through the intelligent appli-cation of technology. But I also believe the answer to our educational crisis *lies as much in the heart as in the head....*

"Tonight, I'd like to talk about the challenges facing all of us interested in the future of public education."

Here, the speaker identifies the focus of his speech.

"I'll be speaking as a CEO of one of the leading communications companies in the world, who's wondering where the employees of the future will come from.

"I'll be speaking from my experience with education task forces and hands-on projects, which has given me some ideas about what works and what doesn't when it comes to educational reform."

These comments help establish the speaker's credentials.

"And I'll be speaking as a citizen, a father, and a grandfather—which means that I share your passion to give our kids a foothold on the future."

By bringing his comments back to the audience, he is justifying to them why it is important that they care.

## 7. Back Up Your Points With Stories

Business writer Tom Peters once observed, "People, including managers, do not live by pie charts alone—or by bar graphs or three-inch statistical appendices to 300-page reports. People live, reason, and are moved by symbols and stories."

Indeed, your audiences will be moved by the stories you use to illustrate your ideas. What may have been a dry fact or a vague concept to them springs to life and gains dimension when you present a story—whether a personal experience, a famil-iar anecdote, or a recent news event.

Let's see how good stories can be used to back up your key points. Betsy Bernard, president and CEO of Pacific Bell Communications, gave a speech about the impor-tance of the Internet. Note the three key points she makes, then note how she tells a story to back up each point.

"The Internet will help people:

- Streamline operations.
- Enter new markets.
- Be more human.

"Story number one: A year ago, the state of Florida issued a report on water quality. You could have a paper copy mailed to you—for $122. Or, you could download a copy from the Internet. Free. Four thousand people did. The state gladly picked up the cost of distributing those copies—23 cents for the lot, the figure. The cost of electricity.

"Story number two: Two years ago, a young woman named Monica Lopez opened a little shop in Pasadena to sell gourmet hot sauce. One variety's called Jamaican Firestorm. Another, Endorphin Rush. The name of the shop is 'Hot, Hot, Hot.'

"One morning, as her husband, Perry, was opening the shop, along came a college student who'd been assigned to create a Web Site as a class project. He asked if he could use their shop as his subject. Perry said, 'Why not?'

"A couple of months later, they turned up the site. In less than an hour, here came the first order—*from Tel Aviv*. Then one came from England. And ever since, 'Hot Hot Hot' has been, well, *hot, hot, hot.*

"Third and final story: I know a man in his 40s who recently subscribed to electronic mail. One of his first correspondents was his college-son. At first it was messages like 'Test. Did you get this?' Then it went to borrowing money on-line. But pretty quickly, they started talking about things they'd never talked about face-to-face, or on the phone. Good, constructive, candid things.

"These three simple stories represent just the beginning of the most important modernization in history...."

## 8. Back Up Your Points With Facts

You don't need to overwhelm your audience with facts. But when you make an important point, try to back it up with a relevant statistic your audience can relate to. Note how First Lady Hillary Clinton uses a key fact to back up her call for universal health insurance in this example:

"The upcoming debate over how we will provide universal coverage for every American is not just about insuring the uninsured, although that is the highest moral imperative. Those who have no access whatsoever have to have a right to security. But the debate is also about the many millions who are currently insured, but without any certainty as to what their insurance will look like next year.

"Every single month 2.25 million Americans lose their insurance—2.25 million. Now, some may only lose it for a week, some may lose it for three months, some may lose it for a year or more. But that number of Americans every month is rendered insecure."

Backing up your points with impressive research shows you know your stuff. That's exactly what Stanley Eitzen, professor of sociology, Colorado State University, did:

"The other aspect of culture I want to address briefly is the messages of the media, particularly those from television, the movies, and advertising. These media outlets glamorize, among other things, materialism, violence, drug and alcohol use, hedonistic lifestyles, and easy sex. The messages children receive are consistent: They are bombarded with materialism and consumerism, what it takes to be a success, the legitimacy of violence, and what it takes to be 'cool.' Let me illustrate the power of the media.

- Three-year-olds watch about 30 hours of television a week. By the time an American child graduates from high school, she or he will have spent more time in front of the tube than in class.

- Between the ages of 2 and 18, the average American child sees 100,000 beer commercials on television.

- Young people see some 12,000 acts of televised violence a year. A study by the University of Pennsylvania's Annenberg School of Communication revealed that children watching Saturday morning cartoons in 1988 saw an average of 26.4 violent acts each hour (up from 18.6 per hour in 1980). Two of the conclusions by the authors of this study were that: (1) children see a mean and dangerous world in these cartoons where people are not to be trusted and disputes are legitimately settled by violence; and (2) children who see so much violence become desensitized to it.

"The powerful and consistent messages from television are reinforced in the movies children watch, as well as the toys that are made for them, and the computerized games such as Nintendo that so many find addicting.

"Given these strong cultural messages that pervade society is it any wonder that violence is widespread among the youth of this generation? Nor should we be surprised at children using sex, alcohol, tobacco, and other drug use as ways to act 'adult.'

"Moreover, we should not be puzzled by those youth who decide to drop out of school to work so they can buy the clothing and car that will bring them immediate status."

Be careful: When backing up your points, don't just throw the statistics or research at your audience. Translate your findings into human terms. Notice how Alexa McDonough, leader of Canada's New Democratic Party, did that:

"Medicare—one of Canada's proudest achievements—is in serious danger. The Liberal government in Ottawa has cut health care by 40 percent! Brian Mulroney, in his wildest Fraser Institute fantasies, never dreamed he could get away with that. But Jean Chretien's done it.

---

"This budget, the one where Paul Martin said the era of cuts was over, slashed another $2 billion from Medicare. And yet somehow they could afford to give tax credits for Canadians with $600,000 worth of property in the U.S. The Liberals subsidize the wealthy, but cut health care for the sick.

"That's why we need more New Democrats. These cuts aren't just abstract numbers. They are real hospital beds, real clinics, real operating rooms, real nurses. And they're hurting real people. As I stand here today, Mr. Harris is closing hospitals in Toronto."

Also note that your statistics can *introduce* an important point. They can be used like this:

"In the five years just past, 143 companies have disappeared from the Fortune 500.

"Not just one-third—but near enough to deliver a powerful message: Change now or be changed forever."

Here's another example from Hans Decker, vice chairman of Siemens Corporation. Note that he begins with the sobering facts, then explains the implications at the end:
"Consider this:

• Almost 30 percent of the high schools offer no course in physics.

• Seventeen percent offer no course in chemistry.

• And an incredible 70 percent offer no courses in earth or space science. That's 70 percent!

• Right now, only 7 percent of America's high school seniors are adequately prepared to take a college-level science course.

"Seven percent! That doesn't leave much of a talent pool for the future, does it?

"These inadequacies put American business at a serious disadvantage in the international marketplace. Go up to some typical 13-year-old American students, and ask them to do a simple two-step math problem. Only 40 percent of them will be able to solve it. But, go up to a comparable group of Korean children, and 78 percent of them will be able to solve it.

"And, this isn't an isolated example. If you compare U.S. students with those from other nations, you'll find they rank among the bottom in calculus, algebra, and biology.

"And, if you think these statistics are sobering, wait 'til you look at the problem among America's minorities. Blacks and Hispanics earn only 8 percent of all bachelor's degrees in science and engineering, and only 4 percent of all Ph.D.s.

"Now, just to put this in perspective. By the year 2020, minorities will make up the majority of all students in the United States. So, we need to ask ourselves: Who will be running our businesses?"

## 9. Back Up Your Points With History

Another good way to back up your points is to use relevant examples from the past. Here's how Troy A. Eid, executive director of National Information Infrastructure Testbed, Inc., did exactly that:

"The history of information technology is littered with individuals who tried to predict the future but failed, and of visionaries who succeeded where few would tread.

"Here's what Western Union had to say in 1882 about Alexander Graham Bell's proposal to build the first municipal telephone network:

" 'Bell's proposal to place his instrument in every home and business is, of course, fantastic in view of the capital costs involved in installing endless numbers of wires....Any development of the kind and scale which Bell so fondly imagines is utterly out of the question.'

"A more recent example is the cellular communications industry. When AT&T first started selling cellular telephones in the mid-80s, it predicted a total U.S. market of 900,000 phones. Today, nearly 20 million Americans own cellular phones; usage has nearly doubled since 1992, and 14,000 new customers are signing up every day as rates continue to fall.

"It's one thing for AT&T to underestimate the potential of its own customers to buy its own products. But what if the U.S. Congress had adopted a national industrial policy a decade ago? Using AT&T's own market statistics, the Federal Communications Commission might well have concluded that cellular technology was a luxury item and given that share of the electromagnetic spectrum to other, more promising technologies."

## 10. Build Strong Transitions

Your audience needs you to guide them along the road of your speech. They need to know when a new turn is coming up. Transitions serve as road signs in your speech, warning your audience when you plan to steer in a new direction. Like road signs, these transitions alert your audience to pay attention.

Common transitions include:

- First, second, third...
- Why should this matter?
- Where do we go next?
- Why is this crucial?
- To illustrate the point...
- On the other hand...
- For example...
- Let's take a closer look...
- But more important than that...

- Therefore...
- Now a key point is...
- Let's begin with...
- Now let's turn to...
- Let me wrap this up with two key ideas...
- Now, let's move onto the next key idea...
- The point is...

## 11. Wrap It Up

As we've discussed earlier in this chapter, the best way to conclude your speech is to tell your audience what you told them. In other words, you need to summarize your speech into a tidy ending for your audience. Note how this conclusion sums up the speaker's main points and closes with a call to action:

"Today, I have talked about our organization, Helping Children Through Therapy. There are children out there with strokes, cerebral palsy, and other serious problems. Yet they cannot get therapy because their insurance will not pay for it and their parents can't afford it. I have shared some of these children's stories with you. I have told you how Helping Children Through Therapy has funds to help some of these children, but not all of them. I have told you why your help is so important.

"Please just don't leave here tonight. Fill out a pledge form by the door or leave a business card and we will contact you. Thanks."

Another way to conclude your speech is to end with a quote that expresses your key idea. Here's how The Honorable John Dalton, Secretary of the Navy, did it:

"Let me end with a quote by Franklin Delano Roosevelt. He wrote that, 'The only limit to our realization of tomorrow will be our doubts of today. Let us move forward with a strong and active faith.'

"These may have been, in fact, FDR's last written words; he died that same day, nearly 52 years ago. I am moved by the simple power of the statement; it captures the essence of the man and his generation. Yet these words also offer appropriate advice to a Navy and Marine Corps—and a nation—preparing to meet the challenges of a new millennium."

Here's another example, by writer William Bennet, who combines a few techniques for concluding his speech. He restates the main premise of his speech then closes with a story, a quote, and a call to action:

"We should be bold and aggressive on this issue and on other issues—things like partial-birth abortion; the overreaching judiciary; drug use; China; and other issues. And remember: In this town, politics is like a football game. There are no time-outs. You are either on offense or on defense. And right now, we're playing too much defense.

"Let me conclude: Pericles said the secret of democracy is courage, and he was right. What was done in Philadelphia a little over two centuries ago was the greatest political idea ever struck off by the mind of man. Not since ancient Athens had there been such sheer intellectual brilliance assembled at a single time and place, and with such consequence. We cannot forget that we are the inheritors of a precious legacy. Our Constitution is the most imitated political document in history. But it is not written in the stars that this noble experiment in self-government is guaranteed to continue. It depends on us. And so we need to summon ourselves again to noble and courageous purpose.

---

" 'In our youth, our hearts were touched by fire,' Justice Holmes once wrote, 'and we learned at the outset that life is a profound and passionate thing, and the only thing to scorn is indifference.' Our task today is to scorn indifference, apathy, and cynicism, and to get on with the job of protecting this great nation, this inestimable jewel, what Lincoln called this last, best hope of man on earth."

Another good way to conclude is to leave the audience with key questions that you want them to remember. The key questions are a good way of reinforcing the key points you covered. Here's how E. Gerald Corrigan, chairman of International Advisors, Goldman, Sachs & Co., did that:

"To conclude, we in the United States, together with the community of nations, are faced with a rare opportunity to shape our future in a manner that holds out the potential for peace and prosperity on a scope and scale unprecedented in history. To a very large degree our success in this venture will depend on how we manage our economic affairs over time and how well we cope with the especially daunting problem of adverse shifts in income distribution. For the most part, we know what needs to be done and we know how to do it. Thus we are faced with four critical choices:

"First, will we have the discipline to avoid the mistakes of the past?

"Second, will we have the vision to adopt and stick to policies that will produce the optimal results over the intermediate and longer term?

"Third, will we have the patience to stay the course when the inevitable setbacks occur in the short run?

"Fourth, will we have the courage to stand tall against those who would undermine openness and freedom in economic and political affairs?

"I for one am optimistic that the answer to all of these questions can be in the affirmative. For that reason, I also believe that a more secure new world order rooted in the supremacy of the individual and the genius of freedom is within reach."

Sometimes speeches are an opportunity to brag about your success and to encourage people to support your program as it goes forward. If that is the case, don't be shy: In your conclusion, brag about what you have accomplished. If you don't tell them, who will?

Here's how Canada's Honorable Diane Marleau, Minister of Public Works and Government Services, did her "bragging":

"Our goal was to get out of a business that could best be handled by the private sector. In doing so, we knew that we had to protect the Government of Canada's investment, and the investment of hundreds of employees who have made CCG what it is today. We have achieved this.

"I am very impressed with how smoothly this team was able to tackle the many challenges that arose throughout the process. I know the path to privatization was not easy. You have made history and as a result of your professionalism and hard work, you ensured the transfer was a great success.

"This transaction is a major milestone for both the Government of Canada and the private sector. It reinforces our commitment to Canadian taxpayers to get the best value for CCG.

"But most important, it has reinforced our commitment to CCG employees to get them the best possible deal with such a highly respected Canadian company.

"I wish you all the best for the future. Congratulations on a job well done!"

## 12. Include a Call to Action

Your audience has just sat through a 20-minute speech. So what? What should they take home? What do you want them to do? Telling them how to help is a powerful closing. Here's an example from Mike Dombeck, acting director of the Bureau of Land Management:

"Think about the past few years. The BLM, conservationists, and the livestock industry spent much of their energy and resources debating grazing legislation.

"Imagine the possibilities if such resources were committed to working together, to healing the land, to building bridges of respect and understanding. Because when we look beyond the harsh rhetoric, a simple truth becomes clear. All who care for the health of public lands—be they environmentalists or ranchers—share the common goals of protecting open space and rangeland health. No responsible livestock operator believes unhealthy rangelands are good for business. No reasonable conservationist finds subdivisions and ranchettes in the best interest of fish and wildlife conservation.

"We need your help to improve our knowledge of both the ecological and social systems we manage.

"We need your help to better understand how social and demographic changes are affecting local communities and public land use.

"We need to get out of Washington and work through Resource Advisory Councils, watershed coalitions, and community organizations to begin the healing of our lands and waters, and communities.

"But the people in this room cannot do it alone. We will not be remembered for our reorganizations or regulations. Our effectiveness begins and ends with how well we work with people on the land. The only way we can deliver healthy, diverse, and productive ecological systems is by working with people on the land."

## 13. Conclude With the Beginning

End where you started. One way to do this is to refer back to the title of your speech. Edith Cresson, a European Common Market commissioner, did it this way:

"Finally, let me draw your attention to the subtitle of our paper 'Inventing Tomorrow,' which is highly symbolic: 'Europe's research at the service of its people.' This is the essence of our research policy. In view of the manifest needs and aspirations, the rationale of European research on the eve of the twenty-first century must be to benefit its citizens. It must, therefore, become more transparent and visible than before with regard to the direction in which it is heading, it must be carried out more simply and it must produce more efficient results. I am confident that it can do all of these, and so demonstrate to the people the full extent of what the European Union can accomplish for them."

# Let's Examine Some Speeches

We have covered some important points in this first chapter. But writing a good speech involves piling technique upon technique. Another good way to learn the important techniques of writing a speech is to walk through a few and to analyze the techniques different speakers have used. Following are some sample speeches. Read them a couple times and you will be amazed at the techniques you pick up. I have highlighted several important techniques in each speech.

## Speech #1

### Adaptive Skills: Seven Keys to Developing Top Managers
### Jerry Yelverton, Executive VP and COO, Entergy Operations

"Today, I'd like to share seven key concepts that I feel are vital to developing excellent managers."

*The speaker immediately identifies—and quantifies—his topic.*

"But first, I think we must frame our discussion by looking at the environment we expect managers to work in. Managing a nuclear facility has never been easy; it demands great technical and great people skills. Being a nuclear manager has always meant pleasing a variety of constituents, from top-level managers to boards of directors, from internal employees to outside regulators."

*Here, the speaker offers the audience important background on the subject.*

"Now we are throwing competition into the mix. *The Wall Street Journal* is already saying nuclear plants will close down because they can't compete. In fact, a recent article stated deregulation will cause 20 of the nation's 109 nuclear plants to shut down prematurely."

*Note the use of a well-known publication to establish credibility to the speaker's claims.*

"Where does that leave our managers? What kind of environment are they working in? On one hand we're telling them to emphasize safety; on the other hand we're telling them to cut costs. That means they must make tough decisions around the allocation of resources. They must lead people who might be angry, upset, people who are not getting what they want and people who are making sacrifices to get ready for competition.

"Having noted this schizophrenic environment that nuclear managers are working in, the question arises, what important skills must managers develop to keep their sanity and to lead their employees?

"Of course, they must have top-notch technical skills. That goes without saying. But more and more, we must focus on developing the adaptive skills of our managers.

"Adaptive skills? Let me quickly explain: The difference between an adaptive problem and a technical one is simple. There are problems that are just technical. I'm delighted when a car mechanic fixes my car or a doctor gives me penicillin and cures my sinus infection. Those are technical solutions.

"But adaptive problems demand another set of skills. Installing a new company culture into a nuclear plant is an adaptive problem. There's no clear-cut technical solution. It's a challenge that is going to require people in the plant to change their values, their behaviors or their attitudes. They must be leaders, motivated, inspired."

*The speaker defines his terms, so that the audience stays with him.*

"To further demonstrate the importance of adaptive skills, consider this: We manage a variety of plants at Entergy and we have analyzed other nuclear plants around the country. And in all the successful plants, we found one vital ingredient—managing people.

"As we looked at all the plants around the country, we realized that it was not a matter of plant design, or how it was built or how old it was. Because if you look around the country at the whole nuclear fleet, you see the top performers are a real mix: different regions, different vendors, different vintages. So it all comes back to the people operating them. And that all comes back to how well managers can motivate and inspire people."

*The speaker has backed up his point with research and example.*

"Perhaps Jack Welch, CEO of General Electric, explained it best when he said, "The world of the '90s and beyond will not belong to managers or those who make the numbers dance, or those who are conversant with all the business and jargon we use to sound smart. The world will belong to passionate, driven leaders—people who not only have an enormous amount of energy but who can energize those whom they lead."

*The speaker further establishes his point with the endorsement of an expert.*

"Now, let me share seven key philosophies that I think are valuable in developing managers with excellent adaptive skills.

"The first key to developing a good manager is move him around. Don't keep him in the same department. The individual must be tested in different roles. In other words, if he's just been in operations and that's all he's seen, that's a very narrow focus.

"Sure, his management style may be successful in that one area. But you must pull him out and put him in other areas and situations that require him to stretch. It's incumbent upon you to force that person into roles he's not familiar with."

*The speaker effectively transitions into his main topic, the seven key philosophies, and he also pulls in the title of his speech here.*

"The importance of moving people around was reinforced when we interviewed 120 of Entergy's top leaders. And guess what? The number-one factor in their success was this: They had a variety of experiences in different functions, business units, companies, and even countries."

*Note how the speaker backs up his first point with research:*

"These experiences were not your typical assignment either. These were high-risk, high visibility assignments. They were multifunctional and focused on solving a crisis or a smoldering situation.

"By the way, something else stood out. The sooner this happened in their career, the better.

"It's also interesting to note that many times, top leaders didn't wait for the assignment to come to them. They were proactive and they threw themselves in.

"What benefits did our 120 leaders gain from these experiences? The benefits included: They developed a better understanding of how the whole business operates; they better understood the impact of their decisions on the rest of the organization; they were able to transfer best practices to new areas; they learned how to lead in a variety of situations; plus they developed strong networks inside and outside the company....

"There are people who say, 'I don't like working for this guy.' I don't care if you like him or not. You have to look at what you can learn from him as an individual. Look at the attributes you don't like and say, 'I'm never going to do some of those things.'

"Quite honestly, I have taken some attributes from people that I thought were terrible managers, but there was some real merit to some of their management styles."

*At this point, the speaker quickly goes through six more key points. Let's skip ahead and pick up some other techniques.*

"Let me introduce my sixth point with a quick story. Once when Muhammad Ali was flying, the flight attendant came over and asked him to fasten his seatbelt. Ali told the attendant, 'Superman don't need no seatbelt.'

"She replied, 'Champ, Superman don't need no plane.'

---

"The point is there are very few supermen out there and we all make mistakes. No one is perfect. But the manager who succeeds is the one that learns from mistakes.

"Or in the words of former Vice President Dan Quayle: 'I have made bad judgments in the past. I have made bad judgments in the future.'"

*Note how a humorous quote towards the end of the speech loosens the audience up and puts them in a pleasant frame of mind to better accept the ending.*

"My seventh and final point. I mentioned earlier that we interviewed top leaders at Entergy to see what made them successful. One other topic stood out on the list we developed. A leader had to have strong personal values."

*Notice how the speaker broadcasts his last point.*

"But the thing our leaders mentioned most was this: If you don't follow through on your promises, everything else is irrelevant.

"Let me leave you with these thoughts: The environment that our managers face is changing. Competition is adding a whole new spin to it. For our plants to be competitive, for our employees to follow us, our managers must develop important adaptive skills.

"They must learn important lessons: the importance of moving from site to site, the importance of working under many managers so they can pick and choose from the best; the importance of grooming their own replacements, the importance of mentors and honest feedback.

"We must give our managers true responsibility at an early stage, so they can succeed or fail on their own. We must teach them—don't manage your career, just manage what you're supposed to manage. Above all: Managers, if they are to be true leaders, must be willing to accept responsibility, admit to mistakes, learn from those mistakes and move on."

*In the previous three paragraphs, the speaker gears up for the close, summarizing his main points.*

"That's a rather long list, but all of these skills must be engrained in our managers. Only then can they move away from being mere managers to being leaders.

"Living in difficult times can be a tremendous advantage. It's like a natural athlete who doesn't have to work that hard, versus Michael Jordan, who got cut from his high school basketball team and then worked harder. Adversity can present an opportunity for people to grow and for people to build a truly creative and effective organization."

*The speaker uses an illustrative example to keep the attention of the audience.*

"Finally, let me close with one of my favorite quotes from that great American philosopher Reggie Jackson. During his baseball career, someone once asked Reggie what made a great manager. I think we can all learn something from his response.

"Reggie said, 'I'll tell you what makes a great manager: A great manager has a knack for making ballplayers think they are better than they are. He forces you to have a good opinion of yourself. He lets you know he believes in you. He makes you get more out of yourself. And once you learn how good you really are, you never settle for playing anything less than your best.'

"I think if we can concentrate on developing the adaptive skills of our managers, the so-called soft-stuff, we will have managers that can live up to Reggie's definition of a great manager."

*The speaker used a quote to support his idea and reinforce his close.*

## Speech #2

### Achieving America's Greatness
Edwin Lupberger, chairman of the United States
Chamber of Commerce and CEO of Entergy

"What I'd like to do today is talk about America. The ideas that have enabled American greatness as well as the principles and values that will enable America to succeed in the future."

*The speaker identifies the topic of his talk.*

"You know, something nice and easy—not what Madison Avenue would bill as a light subject.

"But it is the right time for this discussion. It's a presidential election year and we've already seen a lot of different ideas thrown around. And if not now, when?

"People like to argue about crime, decline of the family, drugs and particularly political rhetoric. I'm not sure—maybe politics has become our national sport. If so, it's time to be more than a fan. We may make some pretty important choices and, with luck, we can take some steps in the right direction for a change.

"But rather than dive into the details, I'd like to step back and look at the broader picture, because one of the more interesting debates underway is whether Americans should feel good about themselves...or bad.

"There have been a number of news stories over the last couple of months painting a pretty bleak picture of America. Some of this comes in the wake of corporate downsizing, and generally expresses the view that Americans are anxious, depressed, and uncertain. And no doubt some of them are. A lot of industries are going through restructuring, including my own—the electric power industry."

*The speaker offers background to the subject.*

"This involves pain and distress for individuals and families both. You don't want to discount that for a second."

*The speaker expresses sympathy toward audience feelings.*

"But is pessimism really the prevailing view of most Americans? Are we really down on ourselves?"

*Note how he uses key questions to frame the crux of his speech.*

---

"Paul Samuelson, a well-respected economist who has been around for a number of years, has some thoughtful things to say on the subject. He has written a new book called *The Good Life and Its Discontents,* and he says that if pessimism exists it may be because 'we confuse progress with perfection.' "

*Note the reference to an expert to give credibility to his viewpoint.*

"We came out of the second World War convinced that we could create the final American utopia. And now we're dismayed that perfection-on-earth hasn't arrived.

"He concludes that we were wrong the first time—and we're wrong now. We've gone from too much optimism to too much pessimism.

"In the United States, he argues—and I agree with him—that things are much better than they seem, or, at least, as they are portrayed in the press. Today, Americans are richer and freer. Modern communications and technology, from jet travel to computers, have been liberating.

"We can go more places. Be ourselves more readily. Explore more possibilities than ever.

"Still, we see a constant, unremitting drumbeat of national self-abuse raising even basic questions of whether the American dream still exists.

"Well, I was thinking what if you had been on a different planet for the last 10 years? And when you returned, you asked what had been happening? And someone replied, 'Well, they kicked over the Berlin wall. The Soviet Union fell apart. Eastern Europe has gone capitalist. China is working on it. South America has embraced democracy. We reopened our embassy in Vietnam. Nelson Mandela is president of South Africa—and America is the only economic and military superpower in the world.'

"Now, if you heard that, would you stand there and say, 'Well, there goes the American dream'? Probably not."

*The speaker sets up a hypothetical situation to illustrate his point and grab the attention of the audience.*

"You might even conclude that American values of freedom and liberty and human rights had prevailed. And you'd be right. You certainly wouldn't feel pessimistic about America's prospects.

"Well, maybe, just maybe, Americans are shaking it off and the pessimism, to the extent that it exists, is losing steam.

"The Yankelovich company, a highly regarded, pulse-taking polling firm, has been doing a major survey of attitudes, beliefs and social values every year since 1971. And the latest one concludes there are big changes occurring in America's value system."

*The use of outside experts and statistics backs up the speaker's ideas.*

"In recent years, Americans, faced with stress and frustration, gave up on notions of progress and improvement both personal and social and started looking for villains—someone to blame it on. People wanted things to change for the better, while fearing what change might bring. In other words, people wanted things to change yet remain the same.

"According to this new study, we may have turned the corner—stopped kidding ourselves—splashed on some cold water and begun to enter a new era. Americans seem to be leaving behind *distrust* and *denial* and returning to a more *positive* spirit of creating *possibilities* for the future. Americans *recognize* the *realities* of our society but they yearn to trust again, to find breathing room, to take charge and be responsible, to give up the finger-pointing and start looking for solutions."

*Note the use of alliteration to create a rhythm and emphasis, and get the audience's attention.*

"Well, if this is so, if Americans are ready to recapture the future in a positive and realistic way then it is more than good news. It's great news.

"And in this effort...I am here to say...they will find an ally in the U.S. Chamber of Commerce. The Chamber is premised on optimism. It knows no other way. It believes in Americans. It believes in the power of freedom. It believes in the potential of enterprise.

"That's all enterprise—big, small, and everything in between. And the Chamber, generally speaking, believes that the less restraints on Americans and their enterprise, the more we will accomplish together.

"I'll give you one big example—about as big as they come: the national debt. Here again, there's good reason to think that Americans have had enough. They realize that a society that cannot match its resources with its desires is a society without much of a future. We can't continue operating our country on a credit card.

"Americans like things that work. And when they see a national government drowning in red ink, promising the sun, the moon, and the stars but delivering much less, their patience runs out. That's what is changing things now.

"All around the world, the verdict is in. *Big* government has been a *big* flop. There's a *better* way and the *better* way goes by the name of freedom. I refer to political *freedom*, but also to economic *freedom*. The two are inseparable. Two sides of the same coin. You cannot long have one without the other."

*Note repetition of key words in italics to create an attention-getting rhythm.*

"In the long run, we cannot be true to America by being fearful. We must believe in the strength of our ideas and our ability to prevail....We can be more than an "amen chorus" to the balanced budget effort. We can be a voice. A powerful, authoritative voice. We can talk about the business side of the equation.

"Personally, I think just having a sympathetic congressional majority is a meager ambition. I dream of 535 die-hard entrepreneurs occupying the seats of the Senate and the House because that's when we will get lower federal spending, smaller deficits, fewer regulations, less paperwork, lower taxes. And more emphasis on individual freedom and responsibility. We've certainly made progress already.

"But all of these measures are part of a larger effort, a means to an end. The ultimate goal is a free, happy, resourceful, and vital America where hope and opportunity have a healthy home."

# How to Give a Damn Good Speech

*Note how he reinforces the goal they are all striving for.*

"Yes, we have allies within the business community. Yes, we have allies now in Washington.

"But this is a game without a buzzer. We don't just win a couple of fights and go out and have a beer. This is about the kind of America we live in and the ideas that drive it.

"To succeed, and I mean succeed over the decades ahead, we are going to need more allies. And to do that we will have to sell the principles and values of enterprise, better known as capitalism, to America.

"Not to the people who are in business. They know. They understand. And they believe.

"What I am saying is that we're going to have to recruit allies in this generation and the next.

"Right now there are tens of millions of Americans working out of their homes. That's lots of Americans who have to pay both ends of Social Security. Who have to pay taxes quarterly and set aside at least 50 percent of everything they earn to cover their tax bill. Who are trying very hard to make it on their own and who are asking for nothing more than the opportunity to succeed. They are natural allies of our cause.

"There are also tens of millions of Americans whose earning skills have expired. Who have neither the education nor the training to financially survive, much less succeed, in a knowledge-based economy."

*Note how he goes beyond saying "we have to recruit allies." He gives the audience specific details on who these allies may be.*

"Our challenge is to inspire more Americans with the promise and excitement of enterprise so that all of us, to the greatest extent possible, share in the power of our system.

"But first we must tend to the business at hand—and curb our free-spending ways."

*Note as the speech draws to a close, he repeats the main themes.*

"Because if we don't, by the year 2000 interest payments on the national debt will exceed defense spending. By the year 2002, Medicare will be bankrupt. And by the year 2012 entitlements will consume all tax revenue. Not some—all.

"This amounts to a self-inflicted wound, and we must heal it."

*After repeating the theme, he reinforces it with the strongest facts yet, these facts are the last ones the audience will remember and retain.*

"I believe we will. The one common characteristic of American *success* is *confidence*. And if America is moving toward a new agenda to a new sense of possibility where we feel confident in ourselves and confident in each other, then there will be no stopping us. We'll be entering a new economic territory, uncharted waters.

"But was it any different for our ancestors? They believed in America's capacity to move forward, its principles and values, and they were willing to live with risks knowing that life's better when you challenge the future and make something new, something wonderful.

"That's what the Chamber believes. That's what I believe. And if we can sign up a few more believers, look out."

*The speaker concludes with an upbeat ending underscored by optimistic vocabulary. Also note how the word "believe" opens and closes this section of the speech, setting it apart.*

## Speech #3

### The Boys of Pointe de Hoc
Ronald Reagan, Pointe de Hoc, Normandy, June 6, 1984 (40th anniversary of D-Day)

"We're here to mark that day in history when the Allied peoples joined in battle to reclaim this continent to liberty."

*The speaker identifies for the audience the subject of the speech.*

"For four long years, much of Europe had been under a terrible shadow. Free nations had fallen, Jews cried out in the camps, millions cried out for liberation. Europe was enslaved and the world prayed for its rescue.

"Here in Normandy the rescue began. Here the Allies stood and fought against tyranny in a giant undertaking unparalleled in human history.

"We stand on a lonely, windswept point on the northern shore of France. The air is soft, but 40 years ago at this moment, the air was dense with smoke and the cries of men, and the air was filled with the crack of rifle fire and the roar of cannon.

"At dawn, on the morning of the 6th of June, 1944, 225 Rangers jumped off the British landing craft and ran to the bottom of these cliffs. Their mission was one of the most difficult and daring of the invasion: to climb these sheer and desolate cliffs and take out the enemy guns. The Allies had been told that some of the mightiest of these guns were here and they would be trained on the beaches to stop the Allied advance."

*The speaker offers some background to the situation and in doing so paints a vivid picture for the audience.*

"The Rangers looked up and saw the enemy soldiers—at the edge of the cliffs shooting down at them with machine-guns and throwing grenades. And the American Rangers began to climb. They shot rope ladders over the face of these cliffs and began to pull themselves up. When one Ranger fell, another would take his place. When one rope was cut, a Ranger would grab another and begin his climb again. They climbed, shot back, and held their footing.

"Soon, one by one, the Rangers pulled themselves over the top and, in seizing the firm land at the top of these cliffs, they began to seize back the continent of Europe. Two hundred and twenty-five came here. After two days of fighting only 90 could still bear arms."

---

# How to Give a Damn Good Speech

*Note the use of descriptive language to recreate the scene.*

"Behind me is a memorial that symbolizes the Ranger daggers that were thrust into the top of these cliffs. And before me are the men who put them there."

*Note the nice use of "behind" and "before" to give paragraph balance:*

"These are the boys of Pointe du Hoc. These are the men who took the cliffs. These are the champions who helped free a continent. These are the heroes who helped end a war."

*Each word leading from boys to the final heroes builds up the prestige of the moment.*

"Gentlemen, I look at you and I think of the words of Stephen Spender's poem. You are men who in your 'lives fought for life...and left the vivid air signed with your honor.' Forty summers have passed since the battle that you fought here. You were young the day you took these cliffs; some of you were hardly more than boys, with the deepest joys of life before you. Yet you risked everything here."

*Note how the poem is nicely weaved in adding to the drama of the moment.*

"Why? Why did you do it? What impelled you to put aside the instinct for self-preservation and risk your lives to take these cliffs? What inspired all the men of the armies that met here? We look at you, and somehow we know the answer. It was faith and belief; it was loyalty and love.

"The men of Normandy had faith that what they were doing was right, faith that they fought for all humanity, faith that a just God would grant them mercy on this beachhead or on the next. It was the deep knowledge—and pray God we have not lost it—that there is a profound moral difference between the use of force for liberation and the use of force for conquest. You were here to liberate, not to conquer, and so you and those others did not doubt your cause. And you were right not to doubt.

"You all knew that some things are worth dying for. One's country is worth dying for, and democracy is worth dying for, because it's the most deeply honorable form of government ever devised by man. All of you loved liberty. All of you were willing to fight tyranny, and you knew the people of your countries were behind you...."

*The speaker first asks, then answers the questions, summarizing the entire philosophy of the nation.*

## Speech #4

### Life long Wellness and Disability
Bob Williams, commissioner, Administration on Developmental Disabilities,
Administration for Children and Families, U.S. Department of Health and Human Services

"Thank you. I am pleased to be able to meet with you today. You know, the last time I appeared before so many physicians I was around 12 and stripped down to my skivvies. I thought about coming in similar attire today. However, Federal ethics rules and Tuesday's election results tell me that discretion is the better part of valor."

*The speaker acknowledges his audience and connects with them through humor.*

"Seriously though, I appreciate the chance to address you this morning on the topic of life-long wellness and disability and to enlist your help in what many of us view as an increasingly critical challenge."

*Here, the speaker tells the audience the topic of his talk.*

"To many, if not most Americans, the two concepts of good health and disability seem to be the exact opposites of each other. This is not only true of the general public. Many individuals with disabilities, our families, and professionals have internalized the same point of view—that true good health is something which is out of reach of individuals with disabilities, and that the onset of illness and secondary disabilities is something to be expected—a natural part of having a disability.

"We must challenge this kind of thinking, not just on the part of professionals, family members and the general public, but, most importantly, in the hearts and minds of those with disabilities, because that is where it is having its most damaging and lasting effects."

*The speaker addresses a commonly held belief and dispels it, suggesting specific actions to take.*

"Learned helplessness is the greatest crippler anyone can experience. Many people with developmental and other disabilities have learned to be passive, have learned to view themselves as helpless—especially where questions of their own health and well-being are concerned. I do not think anyone of us with a disability is completely immune from such feelings. Why? Whether we were born with our disability or acquired it, most of us have come to live life viewing our health as something immutable—as just one more thing that is beyond our control.

"Growing up with cerebral palsy in the '60s and '70s, one of the central messages that I think I and most others with my same disability learned was that cerebral palsy was a static condition. That is, in the vernacular of the day, cerebral palsy was not something that got worse. Implicit in this same message, however, was the idea that if cerebral palsy did not get any worse, it certainly did not get any better either."

*The speaker shares a personal experience with his audience, thereby establishing his credibility.*

"In many ways, therefore, we were taught that our health and our disabilities went hand in hand. Society, our doctors, our parents, and others all told us the same thing: Our health and disabilities were inextricably linked and, therefore, were well beyond our power and influence to change or control.

"This thinking is encouraged by a culture which tends to define good health as the absence of sickness, injury or disability.

"Together the medical community and the disability community have the opportunity and the responsibility to begin to question and challenge this thinking, by fundamentally redefining what we think of as true health in our country."

*In this paragraph, after setting the stage in the previous ones, he moves into his main message of working together.*

"Good health is much more than the absence of sickness, injury or disability. True health is really about having the ability, assistance, and support to achieve greater choice and control in life. Even today, at a time when others are developing a sense of control and mastery over themselves and their environment, far too many children and young people with disabilities often learn to perceive themselves as helpless and powerless."

*The speaker defines his terms.*

"Technology can and must be a powerful force in making such perceptions fall by the wayside, both in the eyes of others and, most critically of all, in the eyes and spirits of children with disabilities themselves.

"Certainly this was true in my own childhood. In fact, to state the obvious, I would not be here at all if I had not had access to my very first piece of assistive technology some 30 years ago—an IBM electric typewriter. I was 7 at the time. I learned years later that my teacher did not believe I would ever learn to read. I am convinced that if I did not have the typewriter, that perception of my teacher would have become a self-fulfilling prophecy, which means I would have become like 50 percent of my contemporaries with cerebral palsy who, despite their typical intelligence, now face significant difficulties with reading, writing, and comprehending much of the printed word."

*The speaker again resorts to a personal story to back up his point. Note how he weaves relevant statistics in.*

"What implications does all this have for increasing access to assistive technology today? I think it has several. First and foremost, it implies that increasing access to assistive technology is very critical in schools, colleges and in other learning situations."

*The speaker asks a key question to draw the audience's attention to a crucial point.*

"Learning is not a passive act. It is a very active one, one that requires a great deal of communication and feedback. Once again, had I not had a typewriter, I am not certain that I could have ever convinced my teacher or others that I could learn to read. As Ann McDonald, an Australian woman who spent most of her first 20 years on the back ward of an institution has written, 'Unless others support individuals with communication disabilities to jump outside of our current means of expression, there is no way we can do so.'"

*The speaker uses another personal story of another person who has been helped by technology.*

"Having had a typewriter is one of those things that enabled me to make the jump, and not just in convincing others that I could learn to read, but, equally important, if not more critical, in enabling me to see that reading and writing had a real purpose, had a real consequence in my life. That, for me, is what makes technology assistive."

*The speaker uses an example to explain the term "assistive technology." Note how he keeps building on typewriter story.*

"Having access to assistive technology as well as to the training and ongoing support it takes to master its use is critical. In fact, for many people with cerebral palsy and other significant disabilities, having this access is often the only thing that can begin to tear down the age-old walls of myths and stereotypes regarding people with disabilities.

"Having access to such technology and support is, therefore, a critical prerequisite to leading a full life. It is not, however, the only one or the most important prerequisite. The process starts with expectations.

"Let me offer an illustration, again from my own life and that of my family: My parents had a knack for doing things *with* me, rather than for me. They made me believe I had a say in controlling my life. One reason I felt this way had to do with the "twenty-question" style we developed for communicating. Not only did we use it to enable me to let my parents and my four brothers and sisters know what was on my mind, my parents also insisted that my doctors, therapists, and teachers use it, as well.

"I will always remember this one incident in particular: I must have been 11 at the time. We had been sitting in the waiting room of the Children's Hospital all that day. When we finally got in to see the staff, it was nearly five o'clock. But my mom knew I had a question I wanted answered. So she had a world-famous neurologist and his grand entourage figure out and then answer my question. My question was why, if I had been seizure-free for three years, I was still on Dilantin.

"After that day I never took Dilantin again, nor did I ever have another seizure. However, the most lasting lesson I learned from this was that of my own power to influence my life and future. Other young people need to learn the same lesson. I dare say that many physicians could likewise profit from taking the same lesson to heart in their practice...."

*He closes the story with an important point relating back to fighting helplessness:*

"Right now, however, I am very much of an exception, an exception to some extremely important rules in our nation. I say this with little pride, and a great deal of outrage, outrage that my friend Vi went to her grave without ever getting the assistive technology, training, or ongoing support she needed to effectively express herself. Outrage that such technology, training, and support is still seen as a luxury rather than as the necessity it is for millions of people with disabilities, and outrage that, as a nation, we continue to spend an estimated $240 billion each year to keep people with disabilities needlessly dependent.

---

"Furthermore, I hope that you share in those feelings of outrage. Your and my job is not to come up with a few more exceptions, but to change the rules of the game entirely. Thank you."

*The speaker concludes his talk with a strong sense of outrage to motivate the audience to action.*

## Now It's Your Turn!

It's almost time to move on to Part 2, which presents idea after idea on how to improve your speech. But before we leave this section, study the following worksheet section and use it to help develop your next speech.

## Worksheet for Developing Your Speech

1. Do you know what your topic is? If it has been assigned to you, are you clear on the expectations of the person or organization who has invited you to speak? If you are responsible for coming up with a topic, have you given thought to an appropriate subject? Have you focused your topic rather than trying to cover too broad a subject? Jot down, in one or two sentences, your topic.

_____
_____
_____
_____
_____

2. Have you identified the three or four key points you want to make during your talk? List them here.

_____
_____
_____
_____
_____

3. Have you identified what information you want to use to back up your points? Have you considered using other experts, statistics, personal experiences, and history to back up your arguments?

_____
_____
_____
_____
_____

4. Do you know your audience? Are you aware of their feelings on the subject you will be discussing? Are you familiar with any biases or preconceived ideas they may have? Is there anything special you need to acknowledge about them? Anything you can say to give them a pat on the back?

_____
_____
_____
_____
_____
_____
_____

5. Do you have a good idea for an opening? Would you like to open with a joke? A personal anecdote? Some startling statistics? Give this some thought (turn to Part 3 for some creative ideas to get your juices flowing), and jot down some of your ideas here.

_____
_____
_____
_____
_____
_____
_____

6. Do you need to define any unfamiliar terms for your audience? Jot these down, with definitions, here.

_____
_____
_____
_____
_____
_____
_____

7. What are your qualifications for talking about this topic? What makes you a credible authority? Write down as many reasons as you can think of.

_____
_____
_____
_____
_____
_____
_____

8. Do you have any personal stories or experiences you can share with the audience on your topic that will support your credibility and illustrate the points you want to make? Write them here.

_____
_____
_____
_____
_____
_____
_____
_____

9. Might your audience hold some biases or misconceptions that will affect their acceptance of your ideas? Identify them—and address how you hope to dispel these biases—here.

_____
_____
_____
_____
_____
_____
_____
_____

## Now Outline Your Speech

**I am here to talk about:**

_____
_____
_____
_____
_____
_____
_____
_____

**I will cover these three/four main points:**

_____
_____
_____
_____
_____

**You should care about these points, because:**

_____
_____
_____
_____
_____
_____

**My first point is:**

_____
_____
_____

**I will back this point up with:**
Facts:_____
_____
_____
_____
_____
_____

**Personal story or anecdotes:**
_____
_____
_____
_____
_____
_____
_____

**I will use these quotes to reinforce my point (numerous quotes may be found in the quote section later in this book):**
_____
_____
_____
_____
_____
_____
_____
_____
_____

**My second point is:**
_____
_____
_____
_____

**I will back this point up with:**
Facts:_____
_____
_____
_____
_____

**Personal story or anecdotes (An anecdote to cover your point may be found in Part 3):**

_____
_____
_____
_____
_____
_____

**I will use these quotes to reinforce my point (numerous quotes may be found in the quote section):**

_____
_____
_____
_____
_____
_____

**My third point is:**

_____
_____
_____
_____
_____

**I will back this point up with:**
**Facts:**_____

_____
_____
_____
_____
_____
_____

**Personal story or anecdotes (An anecdote to cover your point may be found in Part 3):**

_____
_____
_____
_____
_____
_____

**I will use these quotes to reinforce my point (numerous quotes may be found in the quote section):**

_____
_____
_____
_____
_____
_____
_____
_____
_____
_____
_____

**My conclusion:**
**I will tell the audience to remember these main points:**

_____
_____
_____
_____
_____
_____
_____

**Finally, I would like my audience to take these actions:**

_____
_____
_____
_____
_____
_____
_____
_____

# Part 2

# 100 Tips for Outstanding Speeches

In this section are even *more* secrets, tips, and techniques for putting pizzazz into your next speech. Included are more than 100 great ideas to choose from. Many are from great speeches given by well-known personalities and political and business leaders. It's always best to learn from the best—so these examples will show you how top speakers get their messages across.

In addition, when you find an example without attribution, you'll know that it is one from a speech that I have written—or an example I created to illustrate a helpful tip.

Study all these tips and I'm sure that before long, you'll be using a tip here and a tip there to pack more punch in your next speech!

## 1. Use Fragments to Add Impact.

Although your English teacher probably tried to discourage you from writing in sentence fragments, these short, incomplete sentences certainly add emphasis to key thoughts and ideas. Take a look at this example:

"Our customer evaluates us at a glance. A snapshot. Good-bad. Pass-fail. It's exciting. Interesting. Challenging. And, yes, even fun. Are there risks? Uncertainties? Dangers? Sure. You bet. Competition is often chaotic and unpredictable."

## 2. Use Alliteration.

When words start with the same sounds or letters, that's alliteration and it's a good way to accent your ideas. Following are familiar phrases from two of America's most powerful speakers.

"Let us go forth to lead the land we love."—President John F. Kennedy

"My constituency is the desperate, the damned, the disinherited, the disrespected, and the despised."—the Reverend Jesse Jackson

## 3. Repeat a Word or Phrase at the Beginning of Successive Phrases, Clauses, or Lines.

"We shall not flag or fail. We shall go on to the end. We shall fight in France, we shall fight on the seas and oceans, we shall fight with growing confidence and growing strength in the air, we shall defend our island, whatever the cost may be, we shall fight on the beaches, we shall fight on the landing grounds, we shall fight in the fields and in the streets, we shall fight in the hills. We shall never surrender."
—Winston Churchill

"...But if we're willing to put our hearts and minds and bodies to the challenge, we can create hope.

"Hope for those who might aspire to become engineers, attorneys, teachers, or entrepreneurs—not just basketball players or rap stars or street hustlers or drug dealers.

"Hope for those who, right now, see that their chance of spending time in jail is greater than their opportunity to spend time in college.

"Hope for young women who see that their chance of having a high school pregnancy is greater than their chance of getting a high school diploma.

"Hope for young inner-city men who see that their chance of dying from a gunshot is greater than their chance of living in a decent neighborhood in a house of their own."—Alan Page, an associate justice of the Supreme Court of Minnesota

## 4. Repeat the Same Word or Phrase at the *End* of Successive Clauses.

"In 1931, 10 years ago, Japan invaded Manchukuo—without warning. In 1935, Italy invaded Ethiopia—without warning. In 1938, Hitler occupied Austria—without warning. In 1939, Hitler invaded Czechoslovakia—without warning. Later in 1939, Hitler invaded Poland—without warning. And now Japan has attacked Malaya and Thailand and the United States—without warning."
—President Franklin D. Roosevelt

## 5. Create a Rhyming Effect With Short Phrases.

"Thy kingdom come, thy will be done."

## 6. Oppose or Contrast Ideas or Words in a Balanced Construction.

"Not that I loved Caesar less, but that I loved Rome more."
—Shakespeare, *Julius Caesar*

## 7. Show Your Connection to the Place at Which You're Speaking.

"I was thinking as Joe Nye introduced me that I spent a lot of time on the Harvard campus when I was a Wellesley student (laughter), and I spent a lot of very anxious hours racing back to Wellesley when there used to be curfews, and then I had the very odd experience of following my daughter around as she has visited campuses, including Wellesley's and Harvard and feeling very much older than I ever had before.

"But it is a great honor for anyone in any capacity to be on the Harvard campus and to know that for so many years, so many centuries now, this university with all of its constituent parts has helped to lead our country and the world as we've attempted to make sense of the changes that we have confronted."

—First Lady Hillary Rodham Clinton

## 8. Show a Connection Between the Past and the Present.

"In a famous 1837 lecture at Harvard, Ralph Waldo Emerson asked his audience, 'If there is any period one would desire to be born in, is it not the age of revolution, when the old and the new stand side by side, when the energies of all men are searched by fear and by hope, when the historic glories of the old can be compensated by the rich possibilities of the new?'

"Like Emerson, we, too, live in an age of revolution: In politics, with the ending of the Cold War; in economics, with the dramatic growth in global trade; and in technology, with the continuing explosion of information systems. Today, we are living Emerson's desire in a revolutionary era of rich possibilities, an era when our energies are searched by fear and by hope. Our hope is symbolized by the success of democracy around the globe, by the growth of new global trade relationships, by the expansion of global communications, and by the explosion of information.

"Indeed, in this revolutionary new era, the term 'closed society' is rapidly becoming obsolete. Even those states that still desire isolation find it increasingly difficult to achieve. Indeed, it is impossible to achieve if they want to reap the benefits of the global economy, as China discovered during the Tiananmen Square crackdown, when they could not control the fax machines and modems."

—William J. Perry, Secretary of Defense

## 9. Take Control: Shape the Debate With a Simple, Understandable Question. Make It a Question Your Audience Can't Say No to.

"Today I want to ask a very simple question: Do you want to take a chance that your child will be a parent at age 12? Or 13 or 14? Of course, your answer is no. But if we all agree we don't want our kids to have kids, then why are we fighting over sex education?"

## 10. Make Your Point With Different Sources That Say the Same Thing. Tie the Last Example to the First.

"As St. Paul reminds us in Hebrews 12, we live our lives within a cloud of *witnesses*. In our earthly journey, we encounter and come to know hundreds, perhaps thousands, of our fellow human beings, and each one of them, affects us in some way or another and to varying degrees.... My late friend Russell Kirk, who was always

mindful of civilizational *witnesses*, quoted St. Augustine as saying, 'There are no dead,' presumably meaning that human voices are never truly extinguished...."
—Anthony Harrigan, former president, U.S. Business and Industrial Council

## 11. Create a Complex.

"Do we have the Sleeping Beauty Complex? If so, what will it take to wake us up?"

"We have the Eeyore Complex. Nothing is ever quite right."

## 12. Change the Tone of Your Language. Note How This Goes from Erudite Language to Common Language.

"Our tragedy today is a general and universal physical fear so long sustained by now that we can even bear it. There are no longer problems of the spirit. There is only one question: When will I be blown up?"
—William Faulkner, American writer

## 13. Ask a Key Question, Then Answer It.

"How do I know your homes are vulnerable to burglars? Because I was one. I was the guy who got past your impenetrable alarm system and walked away with your stereo system, TV, and VCR while you were on vacation."

## 14. Paint a Vivid Picture.

"For President Reagan, not an effusive man in private, walking through row after row of the parents and families of those who died on the USS Stark, and women clinging to him crying until his shirt was soaked and his suit wrinkled; his eyes red and swollen, his clothes stained with tears and makeup and lipstick, and yet he embraced every mother in that hangar...."
—Marlin Fitzwater, former press secretary to President Reagan

"You want to know what is wrong with drinking? Go visit my friend Tom and you'll find the answer to that question. The stench of urine in the hallway will stun you immediately as you enter. You'll have to wait a minute in that dark hall as your eyes get accustomed to the darkness. You see, all the windows have been boarded up. As your eyes adjust, you'll notice the scratching sound of things scurrying across the floor and wonder whether they're cockroaches or rats. Then, you'll hear a cough—and notice Tom huddled in a pile of blankets on the floor."

## 15. Take the Seven Deadly Sins and Recast Them for Your Industry or Audience.

"Television news is committing seven deadly sins. They are imitation, predictability, artificiality, laziness, oversimplification, hype, and cynicism."
—Andrew Hayward, CBS news president

## 16. Use Statistics to Lead Into a Joke.

"McDonald's has sold more than 75 billion hamburgers. They know that because they're on their fourth pound of hamburger."

"One-fifth of the people are against everything all the time."—Robert F. Kennedy

## 17. Abuse Statistics.

According to *The Journal of Irreproducible Results,* one of the most entertaining magazines around, pickles may be hazardous to your health. Approximately 99.9 percent of cancer victims have eaten pickles at some time in their lives, according to the publication. As have 100 percent of all soldiers, 96.8 percent of all communists, and 99.7 percent of anyone involved in car and air accidents. And, perhaps most frightening of all, of those born in 1839 who ate pickles, none are alive today."

"Statements made by the majority leader are all right so far as they go. But it is like the man who fell off the 20th floor of a building. As he passed the sixth floor, a friend shouted to him, 'Mike, so far you're all right.' "—former Senator Everett Dirksen, during a budget debate in which he grew frustrated with majority leader Lyndon Johnson's use of statistics.

## 18. Bring Statistics Down to Earth.

"There's an old saying, 'Tell people there are more than 300,000 billion stars in the universe and they will believe you without question. Tell them a porch railing has wet paint on it and they have to touch it to make sure.'

"Well, let me give you some facts and figures that are very believable."

## 19. Use Statistics as a Scare Tactic.

"Our children face a health crisis that is getting worse. One-third more 8th graders and one-quarter more 10th graders are smoking today than four years ago. One out of five high school seniors is a daily smoker."

"Nearly 177,000 persons in the United States are living with AIDS today. There are more than 501,000 reported cases of AIDS around the world. Ten to 12 million people around the world are estimated to be infected with the AIDS virus but have yet to become symptomatic."

## 20. Give the Audience a Quiz.

"Let me give you a simple quiz: If every sesame seed on every Big Mac hamburger ever sold was worth one dollar, would the total pay off the national debt?

"The correct answer, according to McDonald's as reported in *USA Today,* is no. McDonald's has dispensed 2.49 trillion seeds (178 on each of 14 billion Big Macs) in 25 years. The national debt is $4.23 trillion."

## 21. Talk About the Speed of Progress.

"The new communications and information technologies have themselves doubled and tripled the flow of innovation. It took almost 30 years to get TV out of the laboratory and into the living rooms of America. By comparison, fiber optics went from theoretical concept to nationwide networks in little more than five years.

"Gifted and creative people—the men and women behind today and tomorrow's inventions—are no longer limited by manual labor, nor bogged down by the inability to deal with thousands or hundreds of thousands of variables quickly. I wonder how much farther a great mind like Edison would have gone, if he had had today's electronic tools."

—Alfred C. Sikes, chairman of the Federal Communications Commission

## 22. Move from Broad Focus to Narrow Focus.

"To this point, I've spoken from a *global* perspective. Now I want to narrow my view to what's going on here at home...and to what is the most challenging part of our business.

"Had I been told 10 years ago, that the power business in this country would enter a free unregulated market, I would have said, "No way!"

## 23. Introduce Your Conclusion With George Bernard Shaw.

"George Bernard Shaw, the famous Irish-born playwright, once said, 'The greatest problem in communication is the illusion that it has been accomplished.'

"Today, I want to make sure that my ideas were communicated. I don't doubt your ability to learn—I doubt my ability to teach. So let me quickly review the three main ideas."

## 24. Use the U.S. Post Office to Illustrate Employee Commitment.

"To get people to follow you, you have to show them why, *what* they are doing is important. Consider your local mail carrier. He is not delivering mail. In the back of his mind, he knows he's doing something more important. He knows the Inscription on the United States Post Office in Washington, D.C., reads 'The Meaning of a Letter.'

'Messenger of Sympathy and Love
Servant of Parted Friends
Consoler of the Lonely
Bond of the Scattered Family
Enlarger of the Common Life
Carrier of News and Knowledge
Instrument of Trade and Industry
Promoter of Mutual Acquaintance
Of Peace and Good Will'

"What are your employees doing? Whatever it is, show them the importance of it!"

## 25. Dig Up Epitaphs to Make a Point.

"We women have always worked hard. For instance, here's an epitaph on a gravestone in England.

Here lies a poor woman who always was tired,
For she lived in a place where help wasn't hired.
Her last words on earth were, Dear Friends, I am going
Where washing ain't done, nor sweeping, nor sewing.
'And everything there is exact to my wishes,
For there they don't eat; there's no washing of dishes....
Don't mourn for me now, don't mourn for me never,
For I'm going to do nothing forever and ever.'

"That was written many centuries ago, yet today many claim that women work harder than ever. They not only put in eight hours a day at the office, they go home and put in another eight hours washing and working around the house!"

## 26. Illustrate Teamwork.

"A watch might be designed in Switzerland, have its electronic parts manufactured in Japan, have its timekeeping module assembled in Hong Kong, its watch case produced in the U.S., its face produced in Japan, and its final assembly completed in the Virgin Islands before being sold in the U.S. A brand name which formerly represented the perceived excellence of Swiss or American craftsmanship now stands for managerial excellence in coordinating labor and logistics in many nations to assure high standards of quality and service."
—Russell M. Moore, writer, *Marketing News*

## 27. Use a Limerick to Launch Your Topic.

"There was a young lady named Bright
Whose speed was far faster than light;
She set out one day
In a relative way,
And returned home the previous night."
—Henry Reginald Butler, British writer

## 28. Use Examples to Stress the Importance of Quality Control.

"You've all heard the statistical exercises showing why 99.9 percent accuracy is not good enough. If it were, we'd have to accept:

• Eighteen major plane crashes each day around the world.

• Doctors operating on the wrong patient 500 times each week.

• 17,000 pieces of mail lost by the U.S. Postal Service every hour.

• Your heart skipping 864 beats a day.

"Those statistical exercises hit us where we live in banking because of the sheer volume of transactions we handle every day. If 99.9 percent were good enough, First Union would make an error on 4,140 checking or savings account statements every month."

"Now, let me stress that we do not make that many errors, but you get the point: 99.9 percent is definitely not good enough. The amazing thing is that up until several years ago, we hadn't focused on the implications of not reaching 100 percent."

—John R. Gorgius, president, First Union Corporation

## 29. Use a Poem.

"The hand of the parent writes on the heart of the child the first faint characters which time deepens into strength so that nothing can efface them. In that regard, an unknown poet wrote *The Heart of A Child*, and it goes like this:

'Whatever you write on the heart of a child
No water can wash away
The sand may be shifted when billows are wild
And the efforts of time may decay
Some stories may perish, some songs may be forgotten
But this graven record-time changes it not.
Whatever you write on the heart of a child
A story of gladness or care
That heaven has blessed or earth defiled
Will linger unchangeable there....' "

—Joseph Hankin, president of Westchester Community College

## 30. Use a *Bad* Example.

"If I wanted to cite a badly led corporation, I could think of no better example than Springfield Nuclear Power. Springfield Nuclear is best-known for its most famous employee, the bumbling everyman Homer Simpson of television's hit animated show, *The Simpsons*. But the reedy, slit-eyed CEO, C. Montgomery Burns, is the perfect caricature of the bad, old corporate leader."

## 31. Drown Your Audience in Numbers.

"There are currently 21 trillion pages of paper stored in file drawers across the U.S. In a typical work day, U.S. businesses generate 600 million pages of computer output, 235 million photocopies, and 76 million letters. Combined, these documents are multiplying at an annual rate of 20 to 22 percent. The amount of stored information is doubling every four years. It costs approximately 25 cents annually to retain a paper document on file."

—J. Raymond Sutcliffe, vice president and general manager of Business Systems Division of Eastman Kodak

## 32. Use Statistics to Illustrate Customer Dissatisfaction.

For those of you who find yourselves in a position to give speeches in the business world, your topic may often be customer service or customer satisfaction. In that case, you'll find the following statistics may be helpful to weave into your speeches.

"In a survey to determine why customers stopped doing business with service organizations, the Federal government learned that 3 percent of the customers moved away; 5 percent developed other friendships; 9 percent left for competitive reasons; 14 percent were dissatisfied with the quality of the product; and 68 percent stopped because of an indifferent attitude from the owner, sales rep, manager, or another employee."
—Printing Industries of Northern California

- The average business will hear nothing from 96 percent of unhappy customers who receive rude or discourteous treatment.

- Ninety percent who are dissatisfied with the service they receive will not come back or buy again.

- Each of those unhappy customers will tell his or her story to at least nine other people, and 13 percent of those unhappy former customers will relate their stories to more than 20 people.

- Additional research indicates that for every complaint received, the average company has 26 customers with problems, six of which are "serious" problems.

- Only 4 percent of unhappy customers bother to complain. For every complaint we hear, 24 others go uncommunicated to the company—but not to other potential customers.

- Of the customers who register a complaint, between 54 percent and 70 percent will do business again with the organization if their complaint is resolved. That figure goes up to 95 percent if the customer feels that the complaint was resolved quickly.

- 68 percent of customers who quit doing business with an organization do so because of company indifference. It takes 12 positive incidents to make up for 1 negative incident in the eyes of customers.

—White House Office of Consumer Affairs by the Research Institute of America

## 33. Use Cartoons as Examples.

"It's a little like the old cartoon in the *New Yorker* magazine: The king is seated on his throne after just reading a message from the battlefront. At his feet, the cowering messenger is held by two of the king's guards. Whereupon the king says to the guards: 'Don't kill him. This news is neither good nor bad. Just take him outside and rough him up a little.' "

## 34. Wow Them With an Amazing Fact.

You can grab your audience's attention with the use of "believe-it-or-not" bits of information. Launch your speech with such a fact or scatter one or two in the middle of your speech to shake them awake. Consider these bits of titillating trivia:

- If your office chair has casters on it, and you sit in it five days a week, the chair travels about eight miles a year.
- In 1988-89 the United States produced more than 73,000 MBAs compared with fewer than 6,000 in 1962-63.
- During its first year, the Coca-Cola Company sold only 400 Cokes.
- Dr. Seuss's first children's book was rejected by 23 publishers. The 24th publisher sold six million copies.
- During his first three years in the automobile business Henry Ford went bankrupt twice.

## 35. Read Extensively. Great Books Have Great Quotes.

"We are at a time with many parallels to the early 1930s, when people did not recognize the changes that were taking place. That's what Thomas Wolfe was writing about in his book, *You Can't Go Home Again.*

"Wolfe said that the leaders of the nation 'did not know that you can't go home again. America had come to the end of something, and to the beginning of something else.' "—Richard M. Rosenberg, chairman and CEO of BankAmerica Corporation

## 36. Tell Them a Fairy Tale.

Fairy tales comtain many truths that can be used to explain business, politics, or even sports. For instance, the tale of the emperor and his new clothes might be used to illustrate hhow senior management gets into trouble because no employee is brave enough to acknowledge the truth. Or the story of the three little pigs and the big bad wolf might be a metaphor for the importance of building a solid business foundation.

## 37. Look in Training Manuals for Speech Ideas.

Whether a corporate guide published by your company, or the manual for a particular industry, training manuals often harbor a treasure of great guidelines that could be used in your speech. These 11 principles of leadership appear in the *Guidebook for Marines* published by the United States Marine Corps:

- Take responsibility. If you wish to lead, you must be willing to assume responsibility for your actions as well as those of the people who report to you.
- Know yourself. Be honest when you evaluate yourself. Constantly seek self-improvement.

- Set an example for others to follow. The manner in which you conduct yourself is more influential than any instructions you may give or any discipline you may impose.

- Develop your subordinates. If you are confident of your own abilities, then you must also believe in the competency of your subordinates.

- Be available. Be sure that employees clearly understand their tasks. Stay aware of their progress and the problems they are encountering, but do not take any initiative away from them.

- Look after the welfare of your employees. Know their problems, and make sure that they receive all appropriate help and benefits that they need.

- Keep everyone well-informed. Rumors only cause undue disappointment and unwarranted anger. Make sure that people know that they can always look to you for the truth.

- Set goals that are achievable. Setting unrealistic goals creates frustration and hurts morale.

- Make sound and timely decisions. If you think that you have made a bad decision, have the courage to change it—before it is too late.

- Know your job. Stay abreast of current events in your field. Do not look back to the way things were done in "the good old days."

- Build teamwork. Train employees so that they understand the contribution that each one makes to the entire effort. Insist that everyone pull his or her share of the load. When something goes well, celebrate it.

## 38. Use a Single Word to Shock.

"In ancient Athens everyone was expected to participate in civic life and take an interest in government. They had a word for a businessman who did not involve himself in public life. The word was 'idiot.'"

## 39. Exaggerate to Get Your Point Across.

"The president of MIT gave me this. That little device, which is one-fourth the size of a postage stamp, has 70—seven-zero—electric motors on it. It was a micro-miniaturization project at MIT designed to prove that they could build very, very tiny engines....In the future doctors may be able to perform heart surgery on an out-patient basis by having the doctor cut a very tiny hole in your leg and dropping in your own personal 'roto-rooter.' It would run around for a while, come back out and say you are fine, and you'd go home. Now that's just a bit fanciful...."
—House Speaker Newt Gingrich

## 40. Speak in Common, Everyday, Conversational Tones.

"I was lucky enough to work with Bill Cavanaugh, one of the great leaders in this industry, and he taught me the importance of saying, 'I screwed something up.' You learned very quickly with Bill. He wants you to admit if you screwed it up—that was reinforced through my career.

"I still remember my first experience with Bill. I was down at Grand Gulf and he came down and we had some things screwed up. He wanted someone to stand up, say, 'It was mine, I take responsibility for it.'

"And when you did that, he would say, 'You are going to fix it.' He just wanted to make sure that someone would acknowledge it was broken, that somebody was responsible for the problem.

"There's a real lesson there...admitting accountability, admitting you didn't do it right. That's a tremendous lesson. One of the parts of growing as a manager is to be able to say, 'I screwed it up.' "—Jerry Yelverton, vice president of Entergy Operations

## 41. Use a Universally Beloved Person or Symbol as an Example.

In the following example, the speaker attempted to convey how government regulations can frustrate those with the best intentions.

"In the winter of 1988, nuns of the Missionaries of Charity, an order led by Nobel laureate Mother Teresa, were walking through the snow in the south Bronx in their saris and sandals to look for an abandoned building that they might convert into a homeless shelter. They came to two fire-gutted buildings on 148th Street and, finding a Madonna among the rubble, thought that perhaps providence itself had ordained the mission. New York City offered the abandoned buildings at a dollar each, and the Missionaries of Charity raised $550,000 for the reconstruction. For a year and a half, the nuns then traveled from hearing room to hearing room, presenting the details of the project to city government officials. Finally, in the fall of 1989, the project won approval.

"Providence, however, was no match for the law. After they had begun reconstruction, the nuns were informed that the building code required an elevator in every new or renovated multiple-story building. It would add $100,000 to the cost, and the law couldn't be waived, even if the elevator didn't make any sense. Mother Teresa and the nuns gave up. They didn't want to devote that much extra money to something that wouldn't really help the poor."—Philip K. Howard, attorney

## 42. Use Short Words.

"Small words can be brief, crisp, terse—go to the point, like a knife. They have a charm all their own. They dance, twist, turn, sing. Like sparks in the night they light the way. They are the grace notes. You know what they say the way you know a day is bright and fair. Small words move with ease where big words stand still—or, worse, bog down and get in the way of what you want to say. There is not much, in truth, that small words will not say—and say quite well."—Joseph Ecclesine, writer

## 43. Use Short Sentences to Set Off More Complex Sentences.

"Leaders innovate. They create. They make things happen. They shape their environment. Managers tend to focus too much energy on administration. They want to do things right, rather than do the right thing."

## 44. Use Personal Pronouns.

Particularly when referring to statistics or describing a broad or general situation in your industry or in the world, try to make it more personal for the audience by using "we" or "you" instead of "they." Here are some examples:

"As huge a market as the United States is...as blessed as we are by natural and man-made sources...as much as we continue to hold a lead in high technology ...and, as important as we are as the main pillar of defense in the world—it is clear we no longer enjoy the clear-cut leadership of the post-war era.

"We are the world's largest debtor nation.

"We are staggering under a federal budget deficit—financed by Japan and others."
—Robert E. Allen, CEO of AT&T

## 45. Repeat and Recycle a Phrase.

"America isn't great because of miles of open prairies. It's great because people broke their backs to bust the sod and grow food.

"America isn't great because of a few industrial geniuses. It's great because of the thousands who fired the furnaces and forged the metal.

"And America isn't great because of a piece of paper called a Constitution. It's great because people fought, and bled, and sometimes die...."
—Lee Iacocca, CEO of Chrysler

## 46. Vary Your Verbs.

Avoid repeating the same tired verbs in your speech. A talk about corporate growth, for example, becomes dull and plodding if the speaker keeps referring to "growth" rather than sprinkling in "expansion," and "development." Here's an example of verb variety—how many can you count?

"But I have also learned that suffering confers no privileges. It all depends on what one does with it. And this is why survivors, of whom you spoke, Mr. President, have tried to teach their contemporaries how to build on ruins, how to invent hope in a world that offers none, how to proclaim faith to a generation that has seen it shamed and mutilated. And I believe, we believe, that memory is the answer, perhaps the only answer."—Elie Wiesel, Holocaust survivor, author and speaker

## 47. Create a Memorable Metaphor By Using a Word Beyond Its Strict Sphere.

"I listen vainly, but with thirsty ear."—General Douglas MacArthur

---

## 48. Eliminate Conjunctions Between Coordinate Phrases, Clauses, or Words.

"We shall pay any price, bear any burden, meet any hardships, support any friend, oppose any foe to assure the survival and the success of liberty."
—President John F. Kennedy

"But, in a larger sense, we cannot dedicate, we cannot consecrate, we cannot hallow this ground."—Lincoln's Gettysburg Address

## 49. Use an Understatement That Speaks More Loudly Than an Exaggeration.

"War is not healthy for children and other living things."

"One nuclear bomb can ruin your whole life."

"Reports of my death have been greatly exaggerated."—Mark Twain.

## 50. Give a Familiar Saying a Surprising Twist.

"There but for the grace of God—goes God."—Winston Churchill

"If a thing is worth doing, it is worth doing badly."—G. K. Chesterton

## 51. Use Elvis. He Always Gets a Laugh.

"Well, I know you have to be very cautious about making predictions. Especially when you predict where things are going to be five years from now. For example, in 1973, there were 457 Elvis impersonators in America. In 1993, there were 2,736 Elvis impersonators in America. If this trend continues, by the year 2000 one out of four Americans will be an Elvis impersonator."

## 52. Play With Familiar Slogans.

"Our city is nearly bankrupt. It's gotten so bad that critics now refer to Washington as a work-free drug place."

## 53. Examine a Popular "Buzz Word" That Pertains to Your Topic.

"Today I want to talk about company culture. We hear all the time that we need a strong company culture. I disagree. A strong company culture, although it is the latest buzz word, is the last thing this company needs. A strong company culture says, 'This is the way we do things around here'—and that gets you into trouble.

"The American auto companies in the 1970s had strong company cultures but they were inflexible. They were used to doing things the same old way, the way their strong company culture dictated...."

## 54. Give Life to a Historical Figure.

"(The Unknown Soldier) was standing as though at attention—tall, straight, and very still. He was obviously a white man, yet the shadow of his helmet, under the stars, made his face look like that of a colored man. He told me, later, that he had been born on a farm in the middle West. His voice, as he talked, had the broad and cultivated accent of Boston. He had enlisted from New York, so he said, and his name, which I could not hear very distinctly, seemed to be a Jewish name. He was a queer blend of persons and place, this Unknown Soldier. All I could be sure of was that he was an American.

" 'Hello, buddy,' he exclaimed, as he emerged now distinctly from the darkness and sat down upon the tomb, with a peculiar kind of radiance about his person. He seemed to shine, as though from a light within; yet there was no light cast into the darkness, and the night seemed as heavy as before.

" 'Are you surprised to see me?' he continued.

" 'Well, I am just a bit,' was my reply. 'I came up here because I thought I would like to be alone and do a little thinking about you and this war business, and all the rest.'

" 'Yes, I thought so,' he said in a voice still far away, and yet very near. 'And I thought perhaps you might like to talk with me, for I know something about this war business.' "—John Haynes Holmes, Unitarian Minister

## 55. Employ a Sudden Change of Tone to Get Your Audience's Attention.

"Good evening. As you can see by the attendees, this is a special night.

"Special because we are here to honor those who, through innovations and inventiveness, have made major contributions to Ford Motor Company's technological leadership.

"Tonight is special, also, because spouses are with us. Here is your chance to prove that you really are as smart as you've been telling your mate you are. And here's an opportunity to explain all of those extra hours at work and in the den at home with a—'See, I told you I wasn't goofing off.' "

—Lou Ross, vice chairman and chief technical officer of Ford Motor Company

## 56. Incorporate a Brief Prayer (a Politically Correct One, of Course).

"But I've got to tell you I've been both a parent and a graduate...and parenting took more of my thoughts...more concentrated learning...more money...and a greater emotional toll...than any sheepskin I've earned.

"Most of the parents will understand when I tell you that I spent many days encouraging my kids to be independent...and many nights whispering the parent's prayer: 'Dear God don't let them hurt themselves. Help them fly, but don't let them fall.' "—Donald E. Petersen, chairman and CEO Emeritus, Ford Motor Company

## 57. Introduce Your Speech With Words of Wisdom.

" 'Each leaf is the tree,' Lao Tzu said 2,000 years ago. To understand the importance of one humble leaf and how it functions in balance with the tree is to perceive the entire tree and how it is a small, yet integral, part of the unity in a grander order.

"Western science is finally confirming this ancient Chinese wisdom. Scientists now say that each cell of a leaf contains the genetic pattern for the entire forest. Each part is a complete representation of the whole.

"At Ford, we have long believed that should also be true of the 10,000 parts of a great car."—Vaughn Koshkarian, president of Ford of China

## 58. Carry Your Analogy Throughout the Speech.

"Last Thursday, I described the American form of government as a three-horse team provided by the Constitution to the American people so that their field might be plowed. The three horses are, of course, the three branches of government: the Congress, the Executive, and the Courts. Two of the horses are pulling in unison today; the third is not. Those who have intimated that the President of the United States is trying to drive that team overlook the simple fact that the President, as Chief Executive, is himself one of the three horses.

"It is the American people themselves who are in the driver's seat. It is the American people themselves who want the furrow plowed. It is the American people themselves who expect the third horse to pull in unison with the other two."

—President Franklin D. Roosevelt, in one of his popular fireside chats

## 59. Bracket a Particularly Pertinent Thought With a Repeating Statement.

"A university is a community of scholars. It is not a kindergarten; it is not a club; not a reform school; it is not a political party; it is not an agency of propaganda. A university is a community of scholars."

—Dr. Robert M. Hutchins, former president of the University of Chicago

## 60. Take a Serious List and Throw in One Funny Item.

"Today I want to share with you the eight key steps you need to take toward a successful corporate career:

1. Always show up for work before your boss does.
2. Volunteer for high-profile assignments.
3. Always keep learning. The knowledge you need to do your job today will be outdated next year.
4. Learn how to give speeches and presentations.
5. Give your employees credit.
6. Take responsibility when things go wrong.

7. Never wear a striped shirt with plaid pants, unless you are an engineer.

8. God is in the details. Don't ever forget that.

"Okay, I was joking about the stripes and plaids. It's okay to mix them—especially if you're a computer programmer. But leave off the pocket protector."

## 61. Share a Childhood Experience to Connect With Your Audience.

"I come from a large family. There were eight of us children living in a one-room shack with my parents. My father always worked hard to provide for us, but it was an uphill battle. He was a seasonal railroad employee. And he was an Indian, which meant he was always the last hired and the first fired.

"One year, it was getting on toward fall. My dad had been off working for some time, and my mother ran out of money to buy food. So she rounded up all eight kids, and we headed out into the woods to pick bittersweet berries. We picked for hours. Then we put the berries in baskets and hung them in one of those little roadside stands that our people had set up along the highway running through the reservation. We sat out there all the rest of the day and sold those berries. And when we were done, my mother had enough money to buy us a little food.

"She didn't ask for anyone's help. She didn't go and beg for a handout. And she never took welfare. She told me then—and she still tells me today—that she would never take anything she hadn't worked for.

"That's what I learned from my mother. And that's what we're trying to do today at Mille Lacs. Someday the casinos may close down. But the values that we're instilling in our children—work hard, get an education, get a job instead of trying to get something for nothing—those values will last forever."

—Marge Anderson, chief executive of the Mille Lacs Band of Ojibwe

## 62. Tell a Vivid Story From Your Work Experience.

"Let me finish today with my story. I am a general surgeon. I have removed cancerous lungs. I have removed cancer of the throat, larynx and voice box, tongue, jaw, and gums of hundreds of patients whose faces I will never forget. I have watched the tears roll down the faces of my patients and their families as I have told them of their cancer. I have heard their words of regret for not overcoming their addiction to tobacco. So, I must tell you I had great difficulty one year ago watching seven leaders of the tobacco industry raise their hands and swear before this nation and God that they do not believe nicotine is addictive.

"Who knows, they may honestly believe that. But I have raised my right hand with a scalpel too often not to know—they are dead wrong...."

—Randolph Smoak Jr., trustee of the American Medical Association

## 63. Use Dialogue in Your Speech.

" 'Dad, I don't see what the big deal is about marijuana. It's not so bad.'

" 'What? Why, marijuana is *illegal!* You'd better stay away from it!'

" 'But why is it illegal?'

---

" 'Because, Son, it's addictive and there's an old saying: Never pick up what you can't put down.'

" 'So...you worry about me getting addicted to things.'

" 'That's right. It's not healthy to be addicted to anything.'

" 'But, Dad, what about the coffee you drink every morning.'

" 'That's different. I need it to get going.'

" 'And the cigarettes you sneak when Mom's not around.'

" 'Now, wait a minute. I just do it to calm down occasionally.'

" 'And the six-pack you put away every Saturday. Why is it okay to be addicted to beer but not weed?'

" 'Not the same thing. And, besides, I'm not addicted!'

"Well, you get the point. It's hard for us to tell our youth to stay away from substances like marijuana when we consider our own addictive behavior."

## 64. Poke Fun at Yourself or Your Company.

"...To be cited as an outstanding international executive in a town where companies like McDonald's and Motorola wrote the book on international trade is a tribute that is truly humbling. Humbling is something at Disney that we encourage.

"It reminds me of an experience one of our young American Disney executives had when he was opening a new office for us in London and wanted to impress his new British secretary. As she entered the office, he was speaking on the telephone and said, 'Why, of course, your majesty, think nothing of it. You can call me anytime. See you soon. Regards to Prince Philip.'

"Then he hung up and said, 'Oh, hello, Miss Brown. Did you want to see me?'

" 'I just wanted to tell you sir,' said the secretary, 'that the men are here to hook up your telephone.' "—Michael Eisner, CEO/chairman, Walt Disney Company

"...I'm a Baptist minister. And you know Baptist ministers take at least 30 minutes to clear their throat. Especially in the African-American tradition. Secondly, I'm a former college professor and you all know that it takes a college professor 45 to 50 minutes to make a point. That's why the classes run that long. And then if you've been watching C-SPAN and watching the national debate in the United States Congress, you know that members of Congress talk and talk and never make their point.

"And so tonight you have a combination of Baptist preacher, former college professor, and a former member of Congress. I hope that you can stay here until midnight with me as we deliberate the great issues of our time."

—William Gray, president of the United Negro College Fund

## 65. Tell Them What You're *Not* Going to Tell Them.

"I'd like to start by telling you what I am not going to say about our education system and what needs to be done to fix it. First of all, I am not going to suggest that a new, big budget federal program is needed to fix the system's problems—just in case you were wondering. And I am not going to recommend that turning the schools entirely over to community control will do the job either.

"I am not going to suggest that we hire more teachers in order to lower the student-teacher ratio. Nor will I advocate that we impose higher standards, or create an examination that students must pass in order to graduate from high school.

"I am not going to spend my time extolling the virtues of vouchers. Nor am I going to call on business to create more mentoring programs.

"Some of these are not bad ideas. But at this point, they're the equivalent of slapping duct tape onto the Hindenburg after it's already burst into flames. They're fixes for the system we have now. And I believe that we need to create a completely new system...."—Richard L. Measelle, managing partner of World Wide Arthur Andersen Consulting

## 66. Use Surveys to Back Up Your Ideas.

"The questions that were asked of the Chicago inner-city students follow:

- Should students have the freedom of speech in the classroom (i.e., should they be able to talk when they wish)? 59 percent said no.
- Should students be allowed to use abusive language in the classroom? 74 percent said no.
- Should students be allowed to use informal slang (street language) in the classroom? 71 percent said no.
- Should students have the right to argue with their teacher? 81 percent said no.
- Should students who continually disrupt class be expelled from school? 60 percent said yes.
- Should students who use drugs and alcohol in school be expelled? 56 percent said yes.
- Should students who sell drugs in school be expelled? 56 percent said yes.

"Do these responses surprise you? I think so! Here is ample evidence that those poor children recognize that the answer to their dreams is in education...."
—Benjamin H. Alexander, president of Drew Dawn Enterprises

## 67. Tell Your Audience How Many Points or Ideas You Will Cover.

You'll help your audience follow along if you announce to them in the beginning of your talk how many ideas you plan to cover. Then, as you reach each new idea, remind the audience where you are in the sequence. For example, "Now, let's talk about the second reason we should support...." Here are two examples of this technique in action:

"Today, I'm going to focus on three aspects of the employee issue. First, the overall mood of America today and how it affects the workplace. Second, the need for a new attitude in the workplace. And third, the need for better balance between our work and personal lives."—Thomas White, president of GTE Telephone operations

"I'd like, very briefly, to touch upon three topics today: I want to speak first about having realistic, rather than utopian, expectations—because in my judgment, far too much boosterish propaganda surrounds the subject of the information highway.

"Second, I'd like to pose a question: What benefits do we want from the information highway?

"Third and finally, I'd like to suggest that if we care about having the information superhighway lead toward a more humane and civilized culture for all of us, there is a logical ramp onto the information highway nearby—a familiar and effective institution—which can point us in the right direction."
—Ervin S. Duggan, CEO of Public Broadcasting Service

## 68. Set Your Audience Up With a Story They Think They Know the Answer to.

"Dr. Cooperrider conducted a study in which two separate groups of people tried to improve their bowling skills. Both were videotaped as they bowled.

"For the first group, the instructor pointed out their weaknesses and concentrated on helping the team work through them.

"In the second group, the instructors pointed out strengths, helped the team analyze what made them strong and offered suggestions on how to apply that strength to other aspects of the game.

"So what do you suppose happened? If you're like I was when I first heard that story, you're probably saying, 'Oh. I know—the first group got worse and the second group got better.'

"Well, that's not the case. The first group improved. The traditional approach to problem solving does work."—Thomas H. White, GTE Telephone Operations

## 69. Use Old Stories to Make a New Point.

"There is a story of a wealthy man who called his servant in and told him that he was leaving the country for a year and that while he was gone, he wanted the servant to build him a new house. The wealthy man told him to build it well, and that when he returned, he would pay all the bills for material and for his labor.

"Shortly after the employer left, the servant decided that he was foolish to work so hard, so he started cutting corners and squandering all the money he saved. When his master came back, he paid all the bills, and then asked the servant, 'Are you satisfied with the house?' When the servant said that he was, the master said, 'Good. Because the house is yours. You can live in it the rest of your life.'

"As a supervisor, I ask you: Are you motivating the motivators to build the kind of houses that they (or you) would be happy to live in for the rest of their (or your) life? Despite your encouragement, despite your incentives, despite the trust that you have developed, are they cutting corners and squandering money? Making you or your department look bad?"—Richard Weaver, a professor in the Department of Interpersonal Communication at Bowling Green State University

## 70. Bring to Life Little-Known Historical Facts.

"One might think that the signers of the Declaration of Independence, those men who built the foundations of our country, might have been blessed with good fortune following their momentous commitment to our democracy. Here's what happened to them:

"Nine signers died of wounds or hardships during the Revolutionary War. Five were captured or imprisoned, in some cases with brutal treatment.

"The wives, sons, and daughters of others were killed, jailed, mistreated, persecuted, or left penniless. One was driven from his wife's deathbed and lost all his children.

"The houses of 12 signers were burned to the ground. Seventeen lost everything they owned."

## 71. Use Historical Trivia in the Context of Modern Problems.

As they say, the more things change, the more they stay the same. Your audience may be surprised to know that the problems we believe are plagues of the modern world were suffered by society since ancient times. Here are some tidbits you may want to incorporate in your talk:

- Athenian philosopher Socrates assailed earlier generations for destroying the forests and landscape.
- Julius Caesar, frustrated with traffic congestion, dust, and noise, banned all wheeled vehicles from Rome during daylight.
- Titus Livius (Livy), a Roman historian, objected to greedy self-indulgence, moral rot, failure to save income, and slipping standards of conduct.
- Aristotle criticized young people as thoughtless, unmindful of parents, and unruly in school.
- Xenophon, a Greek historian, complained of litigiousness clogging the courts.

## 72. Turn to Gandhi for Words of Wisdom.

Mohandas Gandhi compiled "The Seven Blunders of the World," a list of mistakes that he claimed lead many people and societies astray. This is a good list to use whenever you are talking about any problem that affects your community.

1. Wealth without work.
2. Pleasure without conscience.
3. Knowledge without character.
4. Commerce without morality.
5. Science without humanity.
6. Worship without sacrifice.
7. Politics without principle.

## 73. Use Familiar Names to Illustrate Your Key Points.

"For the last year, three black males have dominated the nation's focus on race. They are O.J. Simpson, Louis Farrakhan, and Colin Powell. Each in his own way fed America's appetite to live vicariously and to shrink from confronting our racial reality.

"Each said something different about the state of race relations in America. They allowed white Americans to either ridicule, demonize, or idealize black Americans. The O.J. case conveyed an almost irrevocable division between blacks and whites feeling he was guilty before and after the trial. Louis Farrakhan allowed whites to attack the messenger rather than confront the part of his message about the desperate conditions in much of black America. Colin Powell permitted white America to fantasize that an answer to our racial divisions amounted to no more than, 'We like you; you do it for us.'"—Senator Bill Bradley, New Jersey

## 74. Use Current News Stories.

"It is tough to survive in today's society, especially without skills. In fact here's a story that proves that:

"*The Wall Street Journal* chronicles the plight of such workers in the boom town of Branson, Missouri, which has become a popular tourist destination as a mecca for fans of country music. Don Mullins moved to Branson in 1993 with his wife, two unemployed sons and their wives and children. They could not afford the security deposits or utility down payments that would have been necessary to rent an apartment, so all 11 family members continued to sleep in a 28-foot trailer for most of a year. At the time the story was written, members of the family held down five jobs. They had five children and about five square feet per person. The newborn baby slept in the sink."

## 75. Raise the Alarm.

Too many businesses get into trouble because they become complacent. Sometimes it is your duty to be blunt, to tell them what is really happening. Following are two examples:

"Your industry is in trouble and my message today is that your industry needs a communication strategy based on both a credible message and credible messengers. To succeed you must change public attitudes by clarifying that gold and indeed all mined resources are essential to a safer and more prosperous society. You must also mount a more intense campaign through the interest group world of politics."
—Fred L. Smith, Jr., president of Competitive Enterprise Institute

"The winter of 1995-96 will be remembered for more than the historic blizzard that struck the northeast or the cold that enveloped the midwest. It will be remembered by those in the retailing community as a defining moment; when the brutal realities of change finally hit home; when they could no longer ignore the fact that consumers boldly rejected their offerings. When the glow of the Christmas shopping season took on firesale proportions.

"But sadder than the paltry sales and even more paltry profits was the predictability of it all. For as early as 1990 consumers have been telling us—at first quietly, whispering it, then louder and louder, until reaching thunderous proportions this past December—that they have changed; that they have other priorities; that they are smarter and more discerning shoppers than their parents and grandparents. That they will take advantage of every retailing opportunity and weakness presented to them, and then, with fickle abandon, move on. That they will not be toyed with.

"But many in the retailing community were unwilling or unable to listen or understand. Many continued to do business as usual and wondered why, as the 1995 holiday season approached, they were helpless, seemingly unable to reach their customers, unable to entice them to shop.

"By December 1995, retailing in the United States was truly on the brink of fundamental change, and only by understanding the nature of that change will it survive and prosper into the next millennium.

"And that's what I'm here to talk about today: The new millennium and the consumer...."—Wendy Liebman, president of WSL Strategic Retailing

## 76. Use the Rule of Seven.

Seven seems to be an effective number for rules, points, lists, and ideas. (Note, *The Seven Habits of Highly Effective People,* the Seven Wonders of the World, etc.)

"I recently read a study which identified 64 essentials of good character—the personal dimensions we should discover and develop throughout our lifetime. I'm not going to talk about all 64, but I would like to discuss *seven* personal characteristics which I believe are essential to our development. They include:

1. Recognizing opportunity
2. Making choices
3. Developing focus
4. Practicing daring
5. Having confidence
6. Constant learning
7. And having a philosophy of life."

—Catherine B. Ahles, Macomb Community College

## 77. Show the Audience Why You Are Exactly Like Them. This Helps to Establish a Common Bond.

"It is a pleasure to be with you this evening, among fellow business people. I say fellow business people because running an NGO is like running a business. I have to make a payroll every two weeks. I have a board of directors scrutinizing our balance sheet. I have to make risky investments. I know there is no sure thing. The only real difference between you and me is that you can get your banker to cover a bad year. A nonprofit can't afford to have a bad year."—C. Payne Lucas, president of Africare

## 78. Start With Something Shocking.

"Good morning, everyone. I believe that 5-year-olds should get behind the wheel and drive. They should pilot mini-submarines among exotic sea creatures. They should travel to distant planets. And they should hang out with characters named Frogmella, Clump the Grump, and Dave the Wave.

"Now you may be wondering whether I lost not just my money but my marbles at the roulette table. But when I think about computers, I think of their power to transport the imaginations of the very young."—Eckhard Pfeiffer, president and CEO of Compaq Computer Corporation

## 79. Start a Series of Paragraphs With *And.* This Shows You Are Piling Problem On Top of Problem.

"...And it also means something else. It means that we are in a much more competitive environment. It used to be it was the folks in the rust belt and the snow belt fighting with the folks in the sun belt. We were always jealous of what they were doing down in Houston and down there in Florida.

"And they were taking our jobs from, you know, Massachusetts and Pennsylvania. The textile jobs down to North Carolina and South Carolina.

"And we were always jealous about someone taking jobs from the Midwest down to the Southwest or out to the West Coast. That's no longer the issue anymore. Now those jobs are offshore.

"And so what we're seeing is competition that comes from strange places. The Pacific Rim countries, countries that in my generation we never thought too much of, but now they have tremendous economic strength and power. They're standing on the stage with America.

"Before there was America and, yes, the Soviet Union. But now today in the Pacific Rim, there's Japan, there's South Korea.

"And Lord only knows what's going to happen when China gets its act together, which it rapidly is doing. Attracting even American industry to build automobiles. Low-cost workers, millions of them, that will be producing goods and services.

"And then you look to Europe and you see an expanding common market. A group of countries that have broken down all the barriers. Talking about a common currency, a common political organization, and working together as one gigantic market to compete in the global village.

"And that's really a major challenge."
—William Gray, president of the United Negro College Fund

## 80. Identify Yourself, Your Organization, or Your Cause.

Don't assume people know why they're listening to you—even if it seems obvious. Take time to introduce yourself, identify your organization, or clarify your cause.

"It's really a pleasure to have this opportunity to be here with you, discussing the Disabled American Veterans—the DAV. Our staff members do much more than simply counsel veterans and their families concerning veterans' programs. They help veterans and their families file claims for all veterans' benefits provided under federal, state and local laws.

"They function as attorneys-in-fact for the veterans and families they represent. NSOs assist them in filing claims for VA disability compensation and health care, pension and death benefits, employment and training programs, Social Security disability benefits, VA educational benefits and many other programs."

—from a DAV boilerplate speech

## 81. Build a Story From an Everyday Experience.

"...I was waiting for a bus a few days before Labor Day. I live in a neighborhood that is a 'have' street in a sea of 'have nots.' And this 'have' couple, an upscale young couple, very handsome indeed. He had the latest issue of *The Wall Street Journal* neatly wrapped under his arm. She had the latest issue of *Vanity Fair*. And they were a beautiful couple. And I couldn't make conversation with them.

"Waiting for a bus every day for a year, I tried to make conversation; they turned away. And so I talked to myself out loud. And by the way, I find that audience very appreciative.

"So this one day I say, 'Labor Day coming up.' Silence. They turn away. I say, well, it's a challenge. The bus is late in coming. I say, 'Labor Day is the day we marched down Michigan Boulevard,' Chicago's main thoroughfare. 'Banners held high, steelworkers union, autoworkers, farm equipment workers packing house.'

"And he turns to me in the manner of Noel Coward and says, 'We loathe unions.' See, I got a pigeon here. No bus. No bus. Now I become the ancient mariner, fixing him with a glittering eye. And I say, 'How many hours a day do you work?' It's something of a *non sequitur* so he's caught unaware.

"So, he says, 'Eight.' This time I've got him pinned against the mailbox. And I say, 'How come you don't work 18 hours a day? Your great-grandparents worked 18 hours a day.' And he's looking out, and she is holding his hand, trembling, looking out as though for a passing patrol car. I still look, no bus. Now I've got it made.

"And I say, 'You know why you work eight and not 18? Because four guys got hanged 100 years ago. It's the Haymarket Affair in Chicago when guys got hanged fighting for the eight-hour day.' True. And I say, 'They were union guys.'

"By this time the couple are somewhat trembling. And the bus comes. And I never saw them again. (But, I'm convinced on the 35th floor of that upscale condominium, she's looking out the window every morning and says, 'Is that old nut still there?'"—Studs Terkel, author

## 82. Pile Example Upon Example to Hit Your Audience Hard.

"Last fall a man approached me in New Jersey. He said, 'Senator, I worked at this place, in one job, for 22 years. In that 22 years different companies owned the place. In not one of the three companies did I vest for a pension, because none of them owned the place long enough. So I am now retiring, after 22 years of working here, without a pension at all.'

"A woman came up to me on my annual walk along the Jersey Shore and said, 'Six months ago, my husband lost his job. Two months ago, I lost my job. We have three children and now we have no health insurance. I went to our pediatrician and he said if the kids get sick, he'll take care of them, but, Senator, this is America, and you shouldn't have to have a friendly pediatrician in order to get health care for your kids.'

"In California, a white-collar worker named Ron Smith who lost his job at McDonnell-Douglas two years ago told a journalist how his sense that he was 'starting to lose my grip' feeds into the divisiveness that is tearing our country apart: 'I get angry, and a lot of anger is coming out,' he said. 'I'm blaming everyone, minorities, aliens coming across the border. I don't know how much truth there is to it. I mean, I don't think there are any planners and engineers coming across the border. [But] it hurts when you go to an interview and you know damn well you can do the job, and you know they are looking at you and thinking, forget it.'"

—Senator Bill Bradley, New Jersey

## 83. Use a Laundry List of Items, Piled One Upon the Other, for Emphasis.

"Vast enterprises live on our attention and contrive to get it, often more by foul means than fair. Every day we are pushed to buy cars, cosmetics, health pills, pain killers, sleep remedies, invited to bank, to invest, to relieve our itching, to subscribe to publications, to join clubs, to take holidays abroad, to buy laptop computers."

—Saul Bellow, author

"Let every nation know, whether it wishes us well or ill, that we shall pay any price, bear any burden, meet any hardship, support any friend, oppose any foe to assure the survival and the success of liberty."—President John F. Kennedy

## 84. Point Out the Positives.

Often, we're required to speak about the bad news—a corporate crisis, an industry peril, a community battered by crime or poverty. But it may prove inspiring or at least offer hope to remember and point out the positive aspects of any situation. No one has ever expressed this outlook better than Lou Gehrig, beloved baseball player, in his moving farewell to baseball speech after debilitating illness forced him from the career he loved.

"Fans, for the past two weeks you have been reading about a bad break I got. Yet today I consider myself the luckiest man on the face of the earth. I have been in ballparks for 17 years and have never received anything but kindness and encouragement from you fans.

"Look at these grand men. Which of you wouldn't consider it the highlight of his career just to associate with them for even one day?

"Sure, I'm lucky. Who wouldn't consider it an honor to have known Jacob Ruppert; also the builder of baseball's greatest empire, Ed Barow; to have spent six years with that wonderful little fellow Miller Huggins; then to have spent the next nine years with that outstanding leader, that smart student of psychology—the best manager in baseball today—Joe McCarthy!

"Sure, I'm lucky. When the New York Giants, a team you would give your right arm to beat, and vice versa, sends you a gift, that's something! When everybody down to the groundskeepers and those boys in white coats remember you with trophies, that's something.

"When you have a wonderful mother-in-law who takes sides with you in squabbles against her own daughter, that's something. When you have a father and mother who work all their lives so that you can have an education and build your body, it's a blessing! When you have a wife who has been a tower of strength and shown more courage than you dreamed existed, that's the finest I know.

"So I close in saying that I might have had a tough break, but I have an awful lot to live for!"—Lou Gehrig, July 4, 1939

## 85. Use One Good Symbol to Put a Picture in Your Listener's Mind.

"From Stettin in the Baltic to Trieste in the Adriatic, an iron curtain has descended across the Continent."—Sir Winston Churchill

## 86. Coin a Term to Make Your Audience Remember Your Speech.

"We are kicking off the Clinton Administration's 'Mommagram' campaign. And that is a very carefully chosen phrase, because it really says what we want it to say. We are concerned about our mommas—whether we call them mothers, mommies, moms, whatever. We are concerned about all of the women in our country, and particularly older women. And we want this campaign to increase awareness of the importance of mammography among our nation's older women."
—First Lady Hillary Rodham Clinton

## 87. Use a Timeline to Illustrate the Speed of Progress.

"No man can fully grasp how far and how fast we have come. But condense, if you will, the 50,000 years of man's recorded history in a timespan of but half a century. Stated in these terms we know very little about the first 40 years, except at the end of them advanced man had learned to use the skins of animals to cover him. Then about 10 years ago under this standard man emerged from his cave to construct other kinds of shelter. Only 5 years ago man learned to write and use a cart with wheels.

"Christianity began less than 2 years ago. The printing press came this year and then less than 2 months ago, during this whole 50-year span of human history, the steam engine provided a new source of power. Newton explored the meaning of gravity.

"Last month, electric lights and telephones and automobiles and airplanes became available. Only last week did we develop penicillin and television and nuclear power."
—President John F. Kennedy

## 88. Use Positive Words.

This is the list of "positive, governing words" that GOP candidates were told to use when speaking about themselves or their policies:

| | | | |
|---|---|---|---|
| Active(ly) | Crusade | Light | Prosperity |
| Activist | Debate | Listen | Protect |
| Building | Dream | Mobilize | Proud/pride |
| Candid(ly) | Duty | Moral | Provide |
| Care(ing) | Empower(ment) | Movement | Reform |
| Challenge | Fair | Opportunity | Rights |
| Change | Family | Passionate | Share |
| Children | Freedom | Peace | Strength |
| Choice/choose | Hard work | Pioneer | Success |
| Citizen | Help | Precious | Tough |
| Commitment | Humane | Premise | Truth |
| Common sense | Incentive | Preserve | Unique |
| Compete | Initiative | Principle(d) | Vision |
| Confident | Lead | Pristine | We/us/our |
| Conflict | Learn | Pro-(issue—flag, | Workfare |
| Control | Legacy | children, | |
| Courage | Liberty | environment) | |

## 89. Use Negative Words.

They're great for convincing your audience your opponent's ideas are bad. This is the list of negative words and phrases that GOP candidates were told to use when speaking about their opponents:

| | | | |
|---|---|---|---|
| "Compassion" is | Decay | Incompetent | Shallow |
| not enough. | Deeper | Insecure | Sick |
| Anti-(issue) flag, | Destroy | Liberal | They/them |
| family, child, | Destructive | Lie | Threaten |
| jobs | Devour | Limit(s) | Traitors |
| Betray | Endanger | Pathetic | Unionized |
| Coercion | Failure | Permissive | bureaucracy |
| Collapse | Greed | attitude | Urgent |
| Consequences | Hypocrisy | Radical | Waste |
| Corruption | Ideological | Self-serving | |
| Crisis | Impose | Sensationalists | |

## 90. Get Some Good Books.

Trying to think of a clever, concise, and memorable way to make your point? Well, *why reinvent the wheel?* Chances are, someone somewhere has already said it. Get some reference materials: a book of quotations, a collection of proverbs, and a source for idioms. Here's an example of how the use of a proverb can strengthen the impact of a speech:

" 'It's what you learn after you know it all that counts,' goes a well-known proverb. And it inspires us, it is hoped, to continue learning all our lives—even after we are certain that we know it all."

## 91. Pile on the Guilt.

"You have a good job and make enough money to be comfortable. Does it bother you when you walk by a beggar on the street when you go to the bank to deposit that money?

"You sit down to a good meal every night. Perhaps *too* good, because you're always trying to lose a few pounds. Does it bother you that while you're complaining about the cost of your health club membership that mothers and children are scavenging dumpsters for food?"

## 92. Apply a Sports Story to Your Speech.

"It's really a dull story—probably one of the most boring records in sports. It's only a story about someone playing a game day in and day out, about not missing a single game for 13 years, about not making the headlines for anything other than sticking to playing the game. It may be a long story, and even a boring story—but it's certainly not ordinary.... In setting the record, Ripken put to work some basic values, like teamwork, integrity, and selflessness, as well as a commitment to play every game. With these values as his foundation, he took the everyday and made it into something great.

"Those of you celebrating a service anniversary here this evening may have missed a day here or there, but some of you started your annual streaks as long ago as in 1962....Like Cal Ripken, you bring a strong foundation of basic values to your job...."

—Phil Satre, president of Harrah's Entertainment

## 93. Introduce Your Speech With Examples Meant to Shock.

"We read of a New Orleans teacher who watched while two boys threw a smaller child off a second floor balcony, afraid to interfere because she thought the boys might then attack her. We read of high school students in Los Angeles who set fire to their teacher's hair because of low grades she had given them. We read of a school in Alexandria which was slashed, ripped, smashed, soaked, snipped, rammed, and detonated before it was burned to the ground..."

—Jeffrey R. Holand, president of Brigham Young University

## 94. Everybody Watches TV. Play Off a Popular TV Commercial.

"It keeps going and going. And I'm not talking about the Energizer Bunny. Instead I'm talking about the environmental revolution...."

## 95. Tell Them About Your Mother. This Makes You Seem More Human.

"I don't mean to get personal, but my mother has been my biggest fan over the years. She was proud of me when I graduated from college and got steady, indoor work without any heavy lifting. That was enough for her.

"But now that I'm chairman of a big company, and I make lots of money, and I get my name in the paper—well, she's really proud of her little boy.

"At least she was until recently. Now the poor lady is getting confused. That's because every time she opens a magazine or turns on the television, she's told that people like me are no good. She reads that people like me like to fire thousands of other people...that we like to close plants here in the United States, so we can give jobs to workers in China or Mexico.

"My poor mother! She used to tell her friends back in Kansas that I was a big shot. Now she just says that I have an office job!"—Robert Eaton, Chrysler CEO

## 96. Circle the Globe.

The earth is about 24,000 miles around. That's an important number to know, because it's always good to say how many times something will circle the earth. It's a good easy reference point.

"The paperwork that Americans send to the IRS each year, if laid end to end, would stretch 900,000 miles. That's enough paperwork to circle the Earth 36 times."

## 97. Use Quotes From Movies.

" 'If you build it, they will come.' Well, we're building a new service center for our customers and we hope they come and keep coming back."

## 98. Make Up a Funny Acronym.

"I'm going to keep this short before the MEGO factor kicks in. That stands for *My Eyes Glaze Over.*"

## 99. Offer Examples of Success.

Many of the world's biggest successes overcame repeated failures before they succeeded. Consider these examples to use in your inspiring speeches:

- R.H. Macy failed seven times before his store in New York caught on.
- Novelist John Creasey got 753 rejection slips before he published the first of his 564 books.

- Thomas Edison was thrown out of school in the early grades when the teachers decided he could not do the work.
- President Harry S Truman went broke in the men's clothing store he started.
- When Bob Dylan performed at a high school talent show, his classmates booed him off the stage.

## 100. The Seven Cardinal Rules for Conclusions.

1. Your conclusion should be worded strongly.

2. Your conclusion should never be ambiguous.

3. Your conclusion must be a logical extension of the body of your speech.

4. Your conclusion should cover all of the problems and assertions which your speech presents.

5. Your conclusion should be as concrete as possible.

6. Your audience must be able to relate to your conclusion.

7. Your conclusion should be practical.

**Part 3**

# 100 Fantastic
# Openings!

For many people, writing the beginning of their speech is the most difficult challenge of all. "Breaking the ice," or connecting with the crowd, getting its attention and then introducing the topic is often perceived as so daunting, the speechwriter can't get past this point to develop the rest of the speech.

In this chapter, I offer openings, more openings, and *ideas* for openings that you can use to launch your speech. There's something for everyone and every topic. But even if you don't use one of these openings verbatim, your imagination and creativity should be duly stimulated so that you'll come up with the perfect introduction to your talk.

## 1. A Glowing Recommendation

"We all hate that time of year when we get our annual job evaluations. Face it, even if we know we're doing a great job, we still get a bit nervous. Well, imagine how teachers felt when they read *these* evaluations from students:

- Help! I've fallen asleep and I can't wake up!
- Text makes a satisfying "thud" when dropped on the floor.
- This class was a religious experience for me—I had to take it all on faith.
- He is one of the best teachers I have had. He is well-organized, presents good lectures, and creates interest in the subject. I hope my comments don't hurt his chances of getting tenure.
- Teacher steadily improved throughout the course. I think he started drinking and it really loosened him up.
- Information was presented like a ruptured fire hose—spraying in all directions, no way to stop it.
- The course was very thorough. What wasn't covered in class was covered on the final exam.

"Well, I promise there will be no final exam after my speech—if you give me a better evaluation than those teachers got! Today, I'd like to chat about...."

## 2. Tee Off to a Great Start

"Englishman Dr. A.S. Lamb in the early 1900s wrote: 'Golf increases the blood pressure, ruins the disposition, spoils the digestion, induces neurasthenia, hurts the eyes, calluses the hands, ties kinks in the nervous system, debauches the morals, drives men to drink or homicide, breaks up the family, turns the ductless glands into internal warts, corrodes the pneumo-gastric nerve, breaks off the edges of the vertebrae, induces spinal meningitis and progressive mendacity, and starts angina pectoris.'

"I think he may have been against golf!

"Well, let me tell you what I'm against."

## 3. Education in Crisis

"Let's take a few minutes to consider how American students and workers stack up to their counterparts in Europe and Asia. As you know, the news is not good. The Help Wanted materials themselves document the problem quite well.

- Each year, 1 million American kids leave school before graduating.
- Hundreds of thousands more can barely read their diplomas.
- American students consistently rank at or near the bottom on international science and math tests—trailing not just the Japanese and Koreans, but the Hungarians and Finns as well.
- Outside school, the situation is not much better. An estimated 20 million adults are functionally illiterate, finding it hard not only to read an instruction manual on the job but to read the bus schedule to get to the job.
- Six in 10 major U.S. companies say they're having trouble finding people with the right skills. The problem is worse among small businesses.
- Once they're on the job, workers are unlikely to receive the training they'll need to succeed in the 21st-century workplace. Studies show that only about 10 percent of U.S. workers get any training at all—and most of that is spent on college-educated upper management, arguably those who need training the least."

## 4. An Average Day

"Tom Heymann, in his book, *On An Average Day,* points out that on an average day in the United States...

- 124 books are published.
- $1.6 billion is spent in shopping malls.
- Three government officials are indicted.

- Nine corporate mergers are consummated.
- 965,000 Cokes are consumed for breakfast.
- 101,369,863 hours are spent waiting in line.
- 1,658 people visit Graceland.
- Four people call Graceland asking to speak to Elvis.

"And one excellent speech is presented. Aren't you lucky to be here?"

## 5. The Wisdom of Yogi Berra

"The great Yankee catcher and manager Yogi Berra has imparted some dubious advice and observations to fans. Some of his famous quotes include:

- The other teams could make trouble for us if they win.
- I don't mind being surprised, so long as I know about it beforehand.
- Little League baseball is a very good thing because it keeps the parents off the streets.
- Mickey Mantle can hit just as good right-handed as he can left-handed. He's naturally amphibious.
- I really didn't say everything I said.
- Baseball is 99 percent mental. The other half is physical.
- I don't want to make the wrong mistake.

"Well, I hope my speech tonight makes more sense....

"In fact, after looking at those numbers, I'm very glad you all showed up tonight. I wasn't expecting anybody!"

## 6. Begin With Good News

"A report by Michael Cox and Richard Alm of the Federal Reserve Bank of Dallas puts some perspective on quality of life today compared to 20 years ago. Alm and Cox used quality of life measures to compare 1970 and 1990. They found some interesting things:

- The average size of a new home went from 1500 square feet to 2100 square feet.
- The number of people using computers rose from 100,000 to 76 million.
- The number of households with VCRs grew from zero to 67 million.
- Attendance at symphonies and concerts increased from 13 million to 44 million attendees.
- The amount of time worked to buy gas for a 100-mile trip, from 49 minutes to 31 minutes.
- The percentage of people finishing high school rose from 52 percent to 78 percent.

- People finishing college rose from 14% to 24%.
- And life expectanc rose from 71 to 75 years.

"These figures cast into doubt the idea that life has gotten worse for most Americans. Today, I'd like to share some more good news with you...."

## 7. And You Think *Your* Spouse Doesn't Communicate?

"In a survey recently conducted in Ireland, husbands were asked the question: 'Do you talk to your wife when you are making love?'

- 50 percent said they did not.
- 20 percent said yes.
- 25 percent said sometimes.
- 4 percent said they couldn't recall.
- 1 percent said only if there was a telephone handy.

"Well, I'm not quite sure if those types of surveys serve any purpose, but because I don't have a telephone handy, I'd like to talk to you directly."

## 8. Recycle *This* Lead

"Let me quickly share some recycling facts with you:

- Americans use enough corrugated cardboard in a year to make a bale the size of a football field and the height of the World Trade Center. About 40 percent of it is recycled.
- We create enough garbage every year to fill a convoy of 10-ton garbage trucks 145,000 miles long—more than halfway from here to the moon.
- About 70 million car batteries are recycled in the U.S. each year. The other 15 to 20 percent, with 165,000 tons of lead, go to landfills.
- Every year, Americans dispose of 1.6 billion pens, 2 billion razors and blades, and 18 billion diapers. They're all sitting in landfills somewhere.
- In 1988, about 9 million automobile bodies—more than American automobile plants produced that year—were recycled.

"Clearly, recycling our cars, milk cartons, tuna cans and diapers is a good thing. But recycling some worn-out ideas and obsolete philisophies can be bad for our business."

## 9. An Opening That Doesn't Suck!

"The three-letter airport identifier for Sioux City, Iowa, under attack by state officials, will be changed. The Federal Aviation Administration has agreed that SUX is an unacceptable abbreviation for the facility.

"Well, I hope that I don't give you a "Sioux City, Iowa" speech tonight!"

## 10. An Ambitious Start

"In a survey taken several years ago, all incoming freshman at MIT were asked if they expected to graduate in the top half of their class. Of those questioned, 97 percent responded that they did.

"But is there anything wrong with that? Remember that old saying: 'Aim for the stars, and if you don't succeed, you'll land pretty high anyway.'

"Well, I have high ambitions for our organization and I'd like to share them with you."

## 11. In Touch With the Dead

"The National Opinion Research Council (NORC) at the University of Chicago reports that in a recent 11-year period, the number of adults who say that have been in touch with the dead has risen from 27 percent to 42 percent. It is not true they had all listened to my speeches."

## 12. Know Your Audience

"When George Bush was running for president, he attempted to woo the support of the National Letter Carriers. He didn't get their support. Why? Campaign officials sent the message by Federal Express, whose deliveries the union refuses to accept.

"I hope I know my audience better than that. In fact, I *know* I do and let me share some information that I know you will be interested in...."

## 13. Common Sense?

"I'd like to share something with you from the Civil War. These were the articles of incorporation of the Springfield Militia:

• This Company shall be known as the Springfield Militia.

• In case of war, this company shall immediately disband.

"Now that makes sense to me! Once war comes along, that's serious business. In a way we, too, are in a war, a war against _____. But we can't disband. We must fight, because...."

## 14. A Serious Case of *Witzelsucht* (Vit'sel-Zoocht)

"I've been reading my medical dictionary lately. I do that frequently—just to scare myself about all the things that can kill me. I ran across a disease called *witzelsucht.*

"It's a 'a mental condition characteristic of frontal lobe lesions and marked by the making of poor jokes and puns and the telling of pointless stories, at which the patient himself is intensely amused.'

"Well, I promise I don't have *witzelsucht*, but let me tell you this story which cracks me up. Just teasing—today I would like to talk about...."

## 15. Heaven or Hell?

"According to a poll, 72 percent of Americans who believe in Heaven rate their chances of going there as good to excellent, but many say their friends' chances are considerably worse.

"Isn't it interesting how we perceive things? Well, today, I'd like to change your perceptions of...."

## 16. Just Call Me Cabbage Head

"When the Mattel Cabbage Patch Kid first appeared on toy store shelves, it was virtually inpossible to find one. In one particular city, the local radio station announced that Mattel was going to make Cabbage Patch Kids available to the townsfolk—but they had to go to the football field of the local university and wait. An airplane would fly overhead and the dolls would be dropped onto the field. People were supposed to hold their credit cards up so that a photographer with a telephoto lens in the airplane could get the numbers and charge the price of the dolls to the recipients' accounts.

"People actually showed up, waving American Express cards in the breeze.

"Well, I know you're not gullible, so today, I plan to tell you the truth about...."

## 17. Word-of-Mouth Advertising

"Bruce Barton, the famous advertising man, once pointed out that 'advertising is just one powerful form of education.' It can and often does speed progress. Elias Howe invented the sewing machine, but could get no one to buy it. A whole generation of women died without using this labor-saving device because there was no advertising to make them want it. Contrast that with the story of the automobile, the radio, or the refrigerator.

"The point is, if you want to sell someone something, you have to go out and tell them about it. That's why I'm here today, to tell you about ...."

## 18. Creativity: Seeing the Ordinary in a New Light

"It is generally acknowledged that bumper stickers were first introduced in the 1950s when a Kansas City printer, Forest P. Gill, saw some pressure-sensitive printing stock and was struck with the idea of a sticker as a substitute for the kind of tie-on or wire-on bumper signs being used at the time.

"Now, pressure-sensitive material had been around some time—and so had car bumpers. But Mr. Hill had the creative thought process of seeing two items and putting them together in a new way.

"And that is where many new ideas come from—seeing ordinary things in a new light. Tonight, I hope to shed some new light on....."

## 19. It All Depends on How You Introduce Yourself

"A man on drugs jumped over a cliff but did not quite succeed in killing himself. The rescue team tied his unconscious body into a litter and proceeded to evacuate by means of a 'fixed-flyaway.' This means that the litter is suspended a couple hundred feet below a helicopter, which then flies to a level place where they can set him down (carefully) and either load him into the aircraft or otherwise take further care of him. The patient is accompanied by one attendant tied into the litter.

"This patient began to regain consciousness during the flight. Remember, because he is flying across the sky and because he is marginally conscious he doesn't notice either the helicopter or the cable attaching him to it. The attendant, who happens to have a nice bushy beard, notices that the patient is starting to 'come around' and in an effort to keep him calm says in his most soothing voice: 'Don't worry, I'll take care of you. My name is Peter.'

"Well, you can imagine that the patient woke up really fast! And you can imagine that the attendant was careful how he introduced himself from then on. Well, I'd liked to introduce myself and the subject I'm speaking on tonight."

## 20. Starting With a Clean Slate

"Garth Peterson, a former janitor at Princeton University, once shared this information with *Omni* magazine: 'Most of the professors appreciated it when you washed off the blackboard but not Dr. [Albert] Einstein. Every morning he'd burst into tears. Way I see it, I had a job to do and I was bound and determined to do it right. He wasn't the only perfectionist in the university business.'

"Well, I know we have had our differences in the past, but today I would liko to start with a clean slate."

## 21. Here Be Dragons

"Browsing through marine book stores containing the lore of the sea, you can come across old ocean charts created centuries past. When the map makers of that day ran out of known world before they ran out of parchment, they printed the words, 'Here be dragons.'

"All of us have experienced that feeling at times when we face a difficult task containing many unknowns."

## 22. Made It!

"A woman friend once confessed to me that she had been doing 70 miles an hour on a highway with a 55-mile speed limit when she spotted a state trooper's car closing in behind her. The trooper hadn't turned on his siren yet so she stepped on the gas and zoomed up to 80 miles an hour toward a distant service station she knew was just down the road. Gunning the motor, she swooped into the station, jammed on her brakes, and ran into the ladies' room.

"After a while she came out to find the state trooper's car parked beside hers. He had his ticket book out. Walking up to the trooper with a big smile, she said, 'You didn't think I'd make it, did you?'

"Well, I'm sure many of you were surprised I made it today due to the bad weather (airline strike/playoffs, etc.)."

## 23. A Cronkite Opening

"Walter Cronkite signed off for many years with the famous line, 'That's the way it is.' Well, today I'd like to tell you the way it is—and, more importantly, how we must change it."

## 24. Foot-in-Mouth Disease

"An American businessman was attending an important banquet in Hong Kong and was seated next to an official of the Republic of China. The Chinese official said nothing and the businessman racked his brain on how to start a conversation. When the soup arrived, he said, 'Likeee soupee?' and the official nodded in affirmation. That was the entire extent of their conversation.

"After the coffee, the Chinese official was asked to say a few words, which he did in perfect English. At the end of the speech he sat down, turned to the diplomat and asked, 'Likee speechee?'

"Well, I hope I don't put my foot in my mouth today as I talk about...."

## 25. Those Wise Old Romans

"There's an old saying that many Roman orators used before making a speech. There is a time when nothing must be said and a time when something must be said—but never a time when everything must be said.'

"I promise not to pack 'everything' in my speech today. Instead, I will limit my remarks to three key areas."

## 26. About 20 Minutes

"The late Isaac Asimov, who was world-famous for his science writing, liked to tell this story about speaking at a college commencement. He was walking in the academic procession, which included, first the students, then the professors, and at the very end was the college president and Asimov.

"Our of sheer deviltry, Asimov muttered to the president, 'By the way, what shall I speak about?'

"The president whispered right back, 'About 20 minutes.'

"Well, today, I'll follow that advice and speak about 20 minutes on...."

## 27. The Proverbial Starting Off on the Right Foot

"The Portuguese have a saying: 'Visits always give pleasure—if not in the arrival, then in the departure.'

"I hope that one way or another I can give you a little pleasure today and that my speech will be so good, you hate to see me depart. Okay, that may be asking for too much. If you listen to my ideas with an open mind, I'll be happy."

## 28. Ecology and Free Lunch

"There are four laws of ecology:

• Everything is connected to everything else.

• Everything must go somewhere.

• Nature knows best.

• There is no such thing as a free lunch.

"Number four is very important to me because I just realized that to pay for my lunch, they expect me to speak here today!"

## 29. Cutting It Close

"I will make my remarks brief today and not make the mistake a long-winded preacher once made.

"The preacher was going on and on one Sunday when he saw one of his best parishioners get up and walk out of the church before the sermon was ended. The preacher was very annoyed, and when next he met the parishioner he asked him why he had walked out during his sermon.

" 'I went to get a haircut,' the parishioner replied.

" 'Well, in heaven's name,' protested the preacher, 'why didn't you get a haircut before you came to church?'

" 'Because, Reverend,' said the parishioner, 'when I came to church, I didn't need a haircut.' "

## 30. Lead With a Poem

"Let me start off with a fascinating poem written by William Butler Yeats about change:

Turning and turning in the widening gyre
The falcon cannot hear the falconer;
Things fall apart; the center cannot hold;
Mere anarchy is loosed upon the world,
The blood-dimmed tide is loosed, and everywhere
The ceremony of innocence is drowned;
The best lack all conviction, while the worst
are full of passionate intensity.

"Now, I didn't expect you to memorize that entire stanza, but there is one phrase in that poem that always gets my attention: Things fall apart; the center cannot hold.' And that is an apt description of the competitive world we face. Things are falling apart, it's not the same world we did business in a few years ago. The question is, what should we do about it?"

## 31. A 100-Mile Opening

"Do you know that sometimes when you sneeze, the air rushes out of your mouth at 100 miles per hour? That's as fast as the winds of a hurricane. Well, I hope I don't sneeze tonight and better yet, I promise not to be too windy. Instead I will get right to the point."

## 32. Ten Minutes of Attention

"A couple of months ago, I read a piece of research that said most people are able to listen to a speaker with undivided attention and remember everything he says for about 10 minutes.

"In the next 10 minutes, their minds begin to wander and daydream. And, after 20 minutes, the majority of people in any audience begin to have sexual fantasies.

"So, I know you will enjoy at least part of my talk today."

## 33. Rules for Office Workers in 1872

"I came across this list of rules for office workers in 1872. I'd like to share it with you today:

1. Office employees each day will fill lamps, clean chimneys, and trim wicks. Wash windows once a week.

2. Each clerk will bring in a bucket of water and a scuttle of coal for the day's business.

3. Make your pens carefully. You may whittle nibs to your individual taste.

4. Men employees will be given an evening off each week for courting purposes, or two evenings a week if they go regularly to church.

5. After 13 hours of labor in the office, the employee should spend remaining time reading the Bible and other good books.

6. Every employee should lay aside from each pay day a goodly sum of his earnings for his benefit during his declining years so that he will not become a burden on society.

7. Any employee who smokes Spanish cigars, uses liquor in any form, or frequents pool and public halls or gets shaved in a barber shop, will give good reason to suspect his worth, intentions, integrity, and honesty.

8. The employee who has performed his labor faithfully and without fault for five years, will be given an increase of five cents per day in his pay, providing profits from business permit it.

"Now the rules for our company are not as strict, and that shows how things have progressed in the last century. But one thing never changes in America. There will be always someone trying to steal your market."

## 34. Put Some "Think" Into Your Lead

"Someone once asked a little girl how she set about drawing a picture.

"She replied, 'First I have a think, and then I put a line around it.'

"Well, I had a 'think' and today, I'd like to put a speech around it."

## 35. Surviving a Tidal Wave

"When a tidal wave hits, there are basically three responses. First are the people who say, 'I've seen it all before.' They do nothing and are drowned. Second are those who say, 'I'm getting out of here,' and they hide and seldom have homes to come home to. Third are those who say, 'This is a tidal wave. I better learn to surf tidal waves.'

"Tonight, I'd like to talk about how our business needs to learn to surf tidal waves."

## 36. Success by Association

"I deeply appreciate this opportunity to be with you today. I feel like the man who entered his mule in the Kentucky Derby. His friends inquired whether he thought the animal really had a chance to win the race.

"The man replied, 'No, but I feel the association will do him good.'

"Just as I'm sure it will do me good to be associated with you today.

## 37. Advice From the Young

"My daughter called me with some words of advice for today's talk:

"She said, 'Don't tell them any funny stories about me when I was a child, or how you put yourself through college, or how you never had a VCR when you were a kid, or how it takes so much money just to survive...'

"And so, in conclusion...."

## 38. A Whopper of an Intro

"I promise not to make a Burger King Speech: One whopper after another."

## 39. The Long and Short of It

"Speaking of brevity, it is worth mentioning that the shortest inaugural address was George Washington's—just 135 words.

"The longest in our history was William Henry Harrison's in 1841. He delivered a two-hour, 9,000-word speech into the teeth of a freezing northwest wind. He came down with a cold the following day, and a month later he died of pneumonia.

"I think that I will keep my speech brief."

## 40. An Intro That Causes a Flush

"The visitor was about to address a large audience of Russians in Moscow and he hoped to impress them by starting off with, 'Ladies and Gentlemen' in their native language.

"He began his speech but could tell from the expression of the people in the front rows that he had said something terribly wrong. He learned that the signs on restroom doors, which he had used as a source, had been an unfortunate source. He had started his speech by saying, in Russian, 'Toilets and urinals.'

"I hope I have done a better job in preparing for tonight's speech...."

## 41. One Busy Person

"In the last 24 hours, you ate over three pounds of food. You drank nearly three quarts of water. You inhaled 438 cubic feet of air. You lost nearly a pound of waste. You spoke 25,000 words and moved 750 different muscles. You breathed more than 20,000 times. Your heart beat more than 100,000 beats. You exercised 7 million brain cells. Your blood traveled 168 million miles.

"With all that work you did, I hope you have enough energy to bear with me as I discuss...."

## 42. How to Keep Afloat

"During that flattering introduction, I could not help but think about the man who was killed in a recent flood. He made his way to Heaven and, as admission through the pearly gates, St. Peter asked him to tell the story of how he died in such a terrible flood.

"The man gave such a spellbinding account of how it all happened, he was asked to repeat it for all the other angels in Heaven.

"Sensing that such a repeat performance was a rare honor, the new arrival began thinking how he could make his watery demise even more exciting. However, he toned down his remarks considerably when one of the angels told him that Noah would be in the audience.

"I make this point here to emphasize that I am somewhat intimidated to be speaking about [subject] before an audience of such experts in the field, etc...."

## 43. Don't Speak Out of Tune

"I was flattered when I was asked to give the keynote speech. That is until my (wife/husband) pointed out that the keynote is the lowest note on the musical scale."

## 44. The Right Audience?

"The program chairman's introduction reassures me that I am speaking to the right audience.

"Bob Hope once accepted an invitation to address a convention of the American Bar Association. He began his talk by saying, 'My being here results from a slight misunderstanding. I thought I was to talk to the American Bra Association.' "

## 45. Short But Sweet from the Yankees

"As Yankee owner George Steinbrenner said to each of his managers, 'I won't keep you long....' "

## 46. A Lead With a Byte

"I am a bit intimidated today speaking before such a group of sophisticated New Yorkers (here, you can insert any other group description). It reminds me of the management consultant who died and was escorted through the pearly gates by St. Peter. Everything looked very modern and up-to-date except for one thing.

" 'Where are your computers?' asked the consultant.

" 'We don't need computers,' said St. Peter, 'If we don't know the answer to something, we just ask God.'

" 'And what if God doesn't know the answer?' replied the consultant.

" 'Well, then,' said St. Peter, 'We just ask a New Yorker (or the group or person you have selected).' "

## 47. A Mile-High Opening

"That was certainly a kind introduction and it reminds me of a story I once heard about Dizzy Dean, the legendary baseball pitcher. Dean, who was one of the most successful pitchers ever to play major league baseball, was equally proud of his ability as a hitter.

"Once, reacting to a called strike, Dean shouted at the umpire, 'You jerk, that ball was a mile high!'

"Whereupon the ump replied, calmly, 'Come off it, Dizzy, that ball was coming so fast you didn't even see it.'

" 'Well,' mumbled Dizzy, 'it sure sounded high.'

"As I said, Mr. Chairman, I liked your introduction, but it did sound a little high...."

## 48. A Jigsaw Puzzle

"Imagine a jigsaw puzzle that comes not in a box with a picture of the completed puzzle but in a brown paper bag with no picture of what the puzzle will look like after you've solved it. In other words, you would have all the pieces but no clues to aid you in completing the puzzle.

"That's what the future is like for our company. We have all the pieces but how are we going to put them together?"

## 49. Fashion Misstatement

"I'd like to start off by talking about fashion. I know I'm no fashion plate [pause to examine yourself], but sometimes it takes courage to set a trend. In fact a man called Jonas Hanway was jeered on the streets of London and almost arrested by the police for causing a commotion. His crime? He was carrying an umbrella. Umbrellas were only carried by women until that day.

"Now at our business, I think we're courageous and should set a few trends ourselves...."

## 50. The Competitive Edge

"You all might have heard of Ty Cobb, the famous baseball player. Sure, he was a great baseball player, but many thought he was mean, nasty, and just a little too competitive. In fact, when he got on first base, he had a nervous habit of kicking the bag.

"Guess what? When he retired from baseball, he confessed. By kicking the bag hard enough, Cobb could move it a full two inches closer to second base. That improved his chances for stealing and breaking up a double play by a slim margin.

"Like Ty Cobb, in this competitive world we all need an edge. And little things add up...."

## 51. Refute a Well-Known Assumption

"Good morning. It's always great to see so many familiar faces and old friends at this convention. Conventions are important in other ways, too. For example, I don't know how many of you know this, but Chicago didn't get the name 'windy city' because of the breeze blowing off Lake Michigan.

"That title came from the 1893 Chicago World Exposition. So many public speakers and politicians showed up to that convention, that an editor from *The New York Times* called Chicago 'the windy city'—referring not to the lake winds, but the bags of wind giving speeches.

"I guess Chicago as a convention town should have more appropriately been called 'The long-winded city.' But I promise not to add more wind tonight."

## 52. A Safe Opening

"Almost 90,000 Americans die in accidents every year. In 1992, 47 percent died in motor vehicle collisions, 15 percent fell to their deaths, 8 percent inadvertently poisoned themselves (typically with legal drugs), 5 percent perished in fires (mostly house fires), 4 percent suffocated or choked to death, another 4 percent drowned, and 3 percent died because of a medical mishap (usually during surgery).

"You will note that in that list no one has died of boredom listening to a speech. Today, I hope to keep that record intact."

## 53. Change

"Just for a moment, think about how quickly things change. Look at the way we communicate, for example. Forget overnight mail—we can fax to people in less than a minute. Forget about memos—get your message to anywhere in the world in seconds with e-mail. And believe me, you are truly outdated if you don't have your own Web site. Yes, everything, including the way we communicate, is changing at warp speed. But are we changing in our business? Are we looking for better, more efficient ways to get the job done for our customers?

"How can we make change happen in our business?"

## 54. Gearing Up for Change

"Let me share a quick story with you—about the implications of change. Did you know that, until 1965, the Swedes drove on the left-hand side of the road? The conversion to right-side driving was scheduled on a weekday at 5 p.m. All traffic stopped as drivers switched sides. This particular time was chosen specifically at a time when drivers would be most keyed up and alert—rather than first thing in the morning when they may have been too sleepy or too ingrained in routine to remember the changeover.

"Well, our company is not making a change *that* big, but I would like to discuss how we can make the transition as smooth as possible."

## 55. Copy This Intro

"A young executive was leaving the office at 6 p.m. when he found the CEO standing in front of a shredder with a piece of paper in his hand.

" 'Listen,' said the CEO, 'this is important, and my secretary has left. Can you make this thing work?'

" 'Certainly,' said the young executive. He turned the machine on, inserted the paper, and pressed the start button.

" 'Excellent, excellent!' said the CEO as his paper disappeared inside the machine. 'I just need one copy.'

"Well, I hope I'm a bit more competent and I hope that my comments do not lead you astray tonight."

## 56. Good Questions

"A father took his young son to the opera for the first time. The conductor started waving the baton, and the soprano began her aria. The boy watched everything intently and finally asked, 'Why is he hitting her with his stick?'

" 'He's not hitting her,' answered the father with a chuckle.

" 'Well then,' asked the boy, 'why is she screaming?'

"Well, those were good questions the son asked and I'd like to share some good questions with you today...."

## 57. It's All in the Translation

"My friend was visiting a small Southern town during the Christmas season where she found a nativity scene that showed great skill and talent. One small feature bothered her: The three wise men were wearing firemen's helmets.

"At a QuikStop on the edge of town, my friend asked the lady behind the counter about the helmets. She exploded into a rage, yelling at her, 'You darn Yankees never do read the Bible!' My friend assured her she did, but simply couldn't recall anything about firemen in the Bible.

"She jerked her Bible from behind the counter and ruffled through some pages, finally jabbed her finger at a passage. Sticking it in my friend's face she said 'See, it says right here, "The three wise man came from afar." '

"Well, I hope there is no misunderstanding tonight when I discuss...."

## 58. Country Song Titles

"I was going to come up with a great title for my speech, but I gave up because I knew I couldn't do as well as these titles from country songs:

- How Can I Miss You If You Won't Go Away?
- I Changed Her Oil, She Changed My Life.
- I Don't Know Whether to Kill Myself or Go Bowling.
- I Flushed You from the Toilets of My Heart.
- I Still Miss You, Baby, But My Aim's Gettin' Better.
- I Wanna Whip Your Cow.
- I'd Rather Have a Bottle In Front of Me Than a Frontal Lobotomy.
- I'm Gonna Hire a Wino to Decorate Our Home.
- I'm Just a Bug on the Windshield of Life.
- Please Bypass This Heart.
- They May Put Me in Prison, But They Can't Stop My Face From Breakin' Out.
- You're the Reason Our Kids Are So Ugly.

"Although I don't have a great title, let me share with you what I'd like to talk about tonight."

## 59. Famous Last Words

"Let me share some famous assumptions with you. I think many of you may recognize these words:

- Don't unplug it, it will just take a moment to fix.
- We won't need reservations.
- It's always sunny there this time of the year.
- They'd never be stupid enough to make him a manager.

"The point is, never assume anything! And today, let's not say 'We'll always make our sales quotas.' We will not make our quotas without a lot of hard work."

## 60. Job Interview Don'ts

"We are all nervous when we go on our first job interview. And we say and do some pretty strange things. Let me share with you some things that happened during actual job interviews:

- The job applicant challenged the interviewer to an arm wrestle.
- The candidate fell and broke his arm during the interview.
- The candidate said he never finished high school because he was kidnapped and kept in a closet in Mexico.
- A balding interviewer excused himself and returned to the office a few minutes later wearing a toupee.
- The applicant informed the interviewer that if he was hired he would demonstrate his loyalty by having the corporate logo tattooed on his forearm.
- The applicant interrupted the interview to phone her therapist for advice on how to answer specific interview questions.
- The candidate looked at the interviewer and said: "Why am I here?"

"Well, let me share with you why we are here today. It's to talk about...."

## 61. More Job Interview *Faux Pas*

"A lot of people get nervous during job interviews. And they say some strange things. In fact, let me share what some actual job candidates said during interviews:

- I have no difficulty in starting or holding my bowel movement.
- Once a week, I usually feel hot all over.
- I am fascinated by fire.
- I like tall women.
- I would have been more successful if nobody would have snitched on me.
- My legs are really hairy.

"Well, I promise to say nothing *that* strange tonight, as I talk about....."

## 62. That Bart!

"If you've ever watched the television show *The Simpsons,* you are familiar with young Bart Simpson's classroom misdeeds and subsequent punishments of writing on the blackboard 100 times, 'I will not...whatever.' Let me share some of those with you. By the way, if these sound like something your child would write, WORRY:

- Tar is not a plaything.
- I will not trade pants with others.

- I will not drive the principal's car.
- I will not pledge allegiance to Bart.
- I am not a dentist.
- Underwear should be worn on the inside.
- I will not conduct my own fire drills.
- My name is not Dr. Death.
- I will not bury the new kid.
- A burp is not an answer.
- The principal's toupee is not a Frisbee.
- And—this is one of my favorites—I will not sleep through my education.

"Think about that...I will not sleep through my education. What important things are we missing in life? That's what I would like to talk about today, the importance of _____ and how we may sleep through it if we don't start paying attention."

## 63. A "Stoned-Age" Opening

"There is nothing new about the drug culture in America.

- In 1865 opium was grown in the state of Virginia and a product was distilled from it that yielded 4 percent morphine.
- In 1867 it was grown in Tennessee; six years later it was cultivated in Kentucky. During these years opium, marijuana and cocaine could be purchased legally over the counter from any druggist.
- Both George Washington and Thomas Jefferson grew marijuana on their plantations.

"But the problem was never so intense, so destructive as it is today. What should we do about it? How can we keep our children out of harm's way? Let me share some ideas with you."

## 64. Famous Firsts

"It's always fun to talk about the first. Something about being first fascinates people. Let me quickly share some firsts you may not know about:

- Benjamin Franklin was the first head of the United States Post Office.
- The first telephone book ever issued contained only 50 names. It was published in New Haven, Connecticut, by the New Haven District Telephone Company in February, 1878.
- Wyoming was the first state to allow women to vote.

- The A & P was the first chain-store business to be established. It began in 1842.
- The Grand Canyon was first viewed by a white man on May 29, 1869—by geologist John Wesley Powell.

"Why am I interested in these bits of trivia concerning who was first? Well, I think our company should be first in _____."

## 65. Talk About the Weather

"Well, the weather outside is terrible and I am glad to see that so many of you could still make it. In special honor of this lousy weather, let me share some quick weather facts with you. Did you know that:

- Dirty snow melts faster than clean.
- In July 1801, 366 inches of rain fell on the town of Cherrapunji, India. That's more than 30 feet of water, deeper than many rivers and lakes.
- During the heating months of winter, the relative humidity of the average American home is 13 percent—nearly twice as dry as the Sahara Desert.
- It snows more in the Grand Canyon than it does in Minneapolis, Minnesota.

"Well, those facts prove that weather can be strange, but you being here today proves that you think this meeting is important. And we appreciate that. So let me move onto my main topic."

## 66. Look to the Classifieds!

"Let me quickly share some intriguing classified ads that have appeared in newspapers:

- Illiterate? Write today for free help.
- Dinner Special—Turkey $2.35; Chicken or Beef $2.25; Children $2.00.
- For sale: an antique desk suitable for lady with thick legs and large drawers.
- Four-poster bed, 101 years old. Perfect for antique lover.
- We do not tear your clothing with machinery. We do it carefully by hand.
- Tired of cleaning yourself? Let me do it.
- Man wanted to work in dynamite factory. Must be willing to travel.
- Auto Repair Service. Free pick-up and delivery. Try us once, you'll never go anywhere again.
- And finally, one of my favorites: Stock up and save. Limit one.

"That sums up pretty well what I want to talk about tonight. When is a great deal not a great deal?"

## 67. For the General Welfare

"Welfare reform has been a hot topic in the news lately. But, remember, the people on welfare have to deal with the government—that's not easy and can lead to a lot of confusion. Let me share with you some actual statements taken from welfare cards, letters, and forms:

- I am glad to report that my husband who was reported missing is dead.
- This is my eighth child. What are you going to do about it?
- I am very much annoyed to find you have branded my boy as illiterate. This is a dirty lie. I was married to his father a week before he was born.
- My husband got laid off from his job two weeks ago, and I haven't had any relief since.
- You have changed my little boy to a girl. Will this make any difference?

"Well, I'm hope that amused you. But to be honest, as you might have suspected, I am not here tonight to chat about welfare reform. I'd like to discuss another type of reform. I think we need to reform the way we approach customers (or organize our business)."

## 68. How to Make a Relationship Work

"I thought I would start off by answering the burning question of the day. What does it take to maintain a good relationship? Thankfully children have answered that question for us and here are some of their responses:

- 'Sensitivity don't hurt.'—Robbie, 8
- 'One of you should know how to write a check. Because, even if you have tons of love, there is still going to be a lot of bills.'—Ava, 8
- 'Tell them that you own a whole bunch of candy stores.'—Del, 6
- 'Spend most of your time loving instead of going to work.'—Dick, 7
- 'Don't forget your wife's name. That will mess up the love.'—Erin, 8
- 'Be a good kisser. It might make your wife forget that you never take out the trash.'—Dave, 8
- 'Don't say you love somebody and then change your mind. Love isn't like picking what movie you want to watch.'—Natalie, 8

"Well, now that children have answered that burning question, let's move onto another important issue. Today I'd like to answer the question...."

## 69. Avoiding the Truth

"It's funny to consider the creative ways that people avoid telling the truth. Let me share some great "truth-avoiding" quotes with you:

---

- 'I haven't committed a crime. What I did was fail to comply with the law.' —David Dinkins, New York City mayor, answering accusations that he failed to pay his taxes.

- 'They gave me a book of checks. They didn't ask for any deposits.' —Congressman Joe Early of Massachusetts, at a press conference to answer questions about the House Bank Scandal.

- 'Outside of the killings, Washington has one of the lowest crime rates in the country.'—Mayor Marion Barry, Washington, D.C.

- 'The streets are safe in Philadelphia. It's only the people who make them unsafe.'—Frank Rizzo, ex-police chief and mayor of Philadelphia.

"Well, today, I promise not to avoid the truth. In fact, let me share these very honest and blunt comments with you."

## 70. Lost in Translation

"Sometimes, things get lost in translation:

- In a Paris hotel elevator: 'Please leave your values at the front desk.'

- On a menu in a Swiss restaurant: 'Our wines leave you nothing to hope for.'

- In a Bangkok cleaners: 'Drop your trousers here for best results.'

- An ad by a Hong Kong dentist: 'Teeth extracted by the latest Methodists.'

- In a Rome laundry: 'Ladies, leave your clothes here and spend the afternoon having a good time.'

- In the window of a Swedish furrier: 'Fur coats made for the ladies from their own skin.'

- Detour sign in Kyushi, Japan: 'Stop—Drive sideways.'

- Norwegian cocktail lounge: 'Ladies are requested not to have children in the bar.'

- Copenhagen airline ticket office: 'We take your bags and send them in all directions.'

"Well, I hope that my speech today loses nothing in translation. I'd like to talk about...."

## 71. Weird Science

"What do Americans know about science? Sometimes what we know or *don't know* about science can be scary. Consider these observations:

- '$H_2O$ is hot water, and $CO_2$ is cold water.'

- 'Nitrogen is not found in Ireland because it is not found in a free state.'

- 'Water is composed of two gins, Oxygin and Hydrogin. Oxygin is pure gin. Hydrogin is gin and water.'
- 'Three kinds of blood vessels are arteries, vanes, and caterpillars.'
- 'The alimentary canal is located in the northern part of Indiana.'
- 'Germinate: To become a naturalized German.'
- 'Liter: A nest of young puppies.'
- 'Magnet: Something you find crawling all over a dead cat.'
- 'Vacuum: A large, empty space where the pope lives.'
- 'To keep milk from turning sour: Keep it in the cow.'

"Well, I promise to keep my facts straight today, as we talk about...."

## 72. Future Forecasts

"It's always fun to take a look at predictions for the future. Consider these forecasts, for example:

- In 2000 the Himalayas will be more than an inch higher than they were 50 years ago.
- In 2010, there will be 2.9 workers for every person receiving Social Security. In 1950, there were 16.6 workers for every person receiving Social Security.
- In 2010, a '1997' dollar will be worth about 63 cents.
- The annual number of births in America, which dipped below 4 million in 1994, is expected to climb again after 2000, breaking 4 million in 2008 and 4.5 million in 2018.
- Shortly after the year 2030, the number of Americans who have died since the founding of the nation will surpass the number of living Americans.
- In 2000, IBM predicts hard-disk drives (in PCs) will outsell television sets.
- Shortly after 2020, there will be more Americans over age 65 than under age 13.

"Well, I would also like to look into the future today. For our company to be successful in the near future, we must...."

## 73. On Second Thought...

"You invited me here today to give you a peek at the future of our organization (company, sales, etc.) I'm always cautious about making predictions. Consider these 'great' predictions that were just a little bit off:

- 'Airplanes are interesting toys but of no military value.'—Marshall Ferdinand Foch, French Military strategist and future World War I commander, 1911

- 'The horse is here to stay, but the automobile is only a novelty—a fad.'
—a president of the Michigan Saving Bank advising Horace Rackham (Henry Ford's lawyer) not to invest in the Ford Motor Company, 1903 (Rackham ignored the advice, bought $5,000 worth of stock and sold it several years later for $12.5 million.)

- 'Everything that can be invented has been invented.'
—Charles H. Duell, U.S. commissioner of patents, 1899

- 'Who the hell wants to hear actors talk?'
—Harry M. Warner, Warner Brothers, 1927

- 'There is no reason for any individual to have a computer in their home.'
—Kenneth Olsen, president and founder of Digital Equipment Corp., 1977

- 'What use could this company make of an electrical toy?'—Western Union president William Orton, rejecting Alexander Graham Bell's offer to sell his struggling telephone company to Western Union for $100,000

- 'Computers in the future may...perhaps only weigh 1.5 tons.'
—*Popular Mechanics* magazine, forecasting the development of computer technology, 1949

- 'We don't like their sound. Groups of guitars are on the way out.'
—Decca Records, rejecting the Beatles, 1962

- 'I have no political ambitions for myself or my children.'
—Joseph P. Kennedy, 1936

- 'Television won't be able to hold on to any market it captures after the first six months. People will soon get tired of staring at a plywood box every night.'—Darryl F. Zanuck, head of Twentieth Century Fox, 1946

"Well, I hope that the ideas I share with you here today are more on the mark. Today, I'd like to chat about...."

## 74. Start Their Day Off Right!

"I know that many of you start your day with a bowl of cereal. That single bowl in front of you every morning represents a very big business. Consider these facts:

- Americans buy 2.7 billion packages of breakfast cereal each year. If laid end to end, the empty cereal boxes from one year's consumption would stretch to the moon and back.

- The cereal with the highest amount of sugar per serving is Smacks, which is 53 percent sugar.

- Americans consume about 10 pounds or 160 bowls of cereal per person per year. But America ranks only fourth in per-capita cereal consumption. Ireland ranks first, England ranks second, and Australia ranks third.

- The cereal industry uses 816 million pounds of sugar per year, enough to coat each and every American with more than three pounds of sugar.

- 49 percent of Americans start each morning with a bowl of cereal, 30 percent eat toast, 28 percent eat eggs, 28 percent have coffee, 17 percent have hot cereal and fewer than 10 per cent have pancakes, sausage, bagels, or French toast.

- Breakfast cereals are the third most popular product sold at supermarkets in terms of dollar sales. The most popular products are, first, carbonated beverages, and, second, milk. Following breakfast cereal are cigarettes and bread.

- In 1993, more than 1.3 million advertisements for cereal aired on American television, or more than 25 hours of cereal advertising per day, at a cost of $762 million for the purchase of air time. Only auto manufacturers spend more money on television advertising.

"As you can see, even something as commonplace as breakfast cereal offers a fascinating story. That daily bowl of cereal has a lot of information packed around it. Let's consider the fascinating story and amazing facts and figures concerning our own product."

## 75. Oxymorons

"We're all familiar with oxymorons—phrases or descriptions comprised of two words that mean the opposite. Freezer burn is an example of an oxymoron. Another is jumbo shrimp. Plastic glasses. Civil war. Criminal law—although many claim the term criminal lawyer is actually a redundancy. Some critics of our armed forces would claim military intelligence is an oxymoron. While we often find amusement in such oxymorons, one description that we hope is *never* considered an oxymoron is customer service. We must always provide our customers with the best service. How do we do that?"

## 76. The Story of Kudzu

"In the 1930s, the federal government began planting kudzu, a fast-growing vine with deep roots, throughout the South to help stop erosion. Well, it stopped erosion, alright, but if you go down South today, you'll discover that kudzu has taken over. The vines have smothered other plants, climbed phone poles, taken over crops—kudzu keeps growing and nothing seems to stop it.

"My question to you today is this: Is our business suffering from corporate kudzu? Too many rules and regulations that keep growing and can't be stopped? I think we do. We have to find a more efficient way of getting the work done and a way to cut through the kudzu of rules and regulations that are strangling our efforts to provide better customer service and make a better product. Here's how we can do that...."

## 77. Humorous Bumper Stickers

"I always enjoy reading bumper stickers. Here are a few of my favorites:

- It's been lovely, but I have to scream now.
- I is a college student.
- Will Rogers never met a lawyer.
- It's lonely at the top, but you eat better.
- Cover me. I'm changing lanes.
- If it's too loud, you're too old.
- Want a taste of religion? Bite a minister.
- So many pedestrians, so little time.
- Just when you think you've won the rat race along come faster rats.
- It's as bad as you think and they are out to get you.

"In fact, I like to mention why that last bumper sticker is relevant to my speech today. Yes the competition is as bad as we think. It's tough out there and, yes, the competition is out to get us. What should we do about it?"

## 78. Questions With No Answers

"There are a lot of questions out there with no answers. Consider these hard-to-answer questions:

- Why do you need a driver's license to buy liquor when you can't drink and drive?
- Why are there flotation devices under plane seats instead of parachutes?
- How does the guy who drives the snowplow get to work in the mornings?
- If nothing ever sticks to teflon, how do they make teflon stick to the pan?
- Why is it that when you transport something by car, it's called a shipment, but when you transport something by ship, it's called cargo?
- Why is it that when you're driving and looking for an address, you turn down the volume on the radio?

"I don't have the answers to these questions. But I would like to supply answers to another question...."

## 79. The Shortest Sentence

" 'I am,' is the shortest complete sentence in the English language. 'I am finished,' is the phrase every audience loves to hear. So today, I promise I will keep my remarks brief."

## 80. Abused Advertising Slogans

"I'd like to start by looking at how well-known American advertising slogans have been translated, with dubious results, into other languages:

- When Braniff translated a slogan touting its upholstery, 'Fly in leather,' it translated to Spanish as 'Fly naked.'
- Coors beer put its slogan, 'Turn it loose,' into Spanish, where it was read as 'Suffer from diarrhea.'
- Chicken magnate Frank Perdue's line, 'It takes a tough man to make a tender chicken," sounds much more interesting in Spanish: 'It takes a sexually stimulated man to make a chicken affectionate.'
- Clairol introduced the 'Mist Stick,' a curling iron, into Germany only to find out that mist is slang for manure. Not too many people had use for the manure stick.

"Today, I hope my ideas don't get lost in translation, so I will make myself as clear as possible."

## 81. Murphy's Laws of Combat

"I ran across some very good rules for combat the other day:

1. If the enemy is in range, so are you.
2. Incoming fire has the right of way.
3. Don't look conspicuous; it draws fire.
4. The easy way is always mined.
5. Try to look unimportant; they may be low on ammo.
6. Professionals are predictable; it's the amateurs that are dangerous.
7. The enemy invariably attacks on two occasions:
   —when you're ready for them.
   —when you're not ready for them.
8. Teamwork is essential; it gives them someone else to shoot at.
9. The enemy diversion you have been ignoring will be the main attack.
10. A sucking chest wound is nature's way of telling you to slow down.
11. If your attack is going well, you have walked into an ambush.
12. Never draw fire; it irritates everyone around you.

"Now those rules are funny. Except that these same rules apply for many kids today—in our schools, our neighborhoods, and our playgrounds. Unfortunately, these institutions once considered safe havens for our children are now often combat zones of a different sort. How can we make a difference? Let me tell you about my organization."

## 82. Gaining Your Audience's Trust

"A recent Gallup Public Confidence poll revealed that only 29 percent of Americans express a great deal of confidence in newspapers. That's down from 51 percent from 1959. Television news fared just a little better with 35 percent.

"So who can you trust to give you the honest truth? How about me! Let me give you the truth today about...."

## 83. A Lead That Stays on Course

"Before I start, I'd like to ask for a show of hands. How many of you here today came by plane? Did you think much about how the pilot was going to get your plane across country and to your final destination?

"Your crew used the improved automatic pilot system called inertial guidance. It replaced the old line-of-sight computerized pilot.

"If you flew from Boston to Los Angeles, your destination was set on the inertial guidance system. It was constantly correcting. If the inertial guidance system hadn't changed directions by degrees every few minutes, you might be in the Pacific Ocean or Las Vegas. On a typical flight across country, the automatic pilot will make some 40 degrees of change in course.

"Why do I mention this? Because for us to be successful, we need to be like that high-tech guidance system. We always have to be making corrections to stay on course."

## 84. Jumping to Conclusions

"A man comes into a cafe and sits down in a corner. Seated at the bar is another man who is belting drinks down one after another.

"After the third drink, the drunk falls backward and ends up on the floor. The man rushes to him, picks him up, and puts him back on the seat. Two sips later, the man falls again and the Good Samaritan rushes to him again and puts him on the seat. Finally he says to the inebriated man, 'You should go home. Tell me where you live and I'll take you.'

The drunk mumbles an address, but it's obvious that he's in no condition to walk there. The good soul carries him out to the car, puts him in, and drives him to the house. He rings the bell. The wife opens the door, takes one look, and asks, 'Where's his wheelchair?'

"The point is, the man didn't look at all the facts before taking action. Well, today, before we make a decision, let's look at all the facts."

## 85. An Opening That Hits Its Mark

"French philosopher Jean-Paul Sartre once said, 'Words are loaded pistols.' I know that very well. The words you use can make a direct hit, or they can misfire. I have chosen my words very carefully today and would like to share them with you."

## 86. Working Together

"Have you ever watched a flock of geese flying in their traditional 'V' formation? Two engineers learned that each bird, by flapping its wings, creates an uplift for the bird that follows. Together, the whole flock gains something like 70 percent greater flying range than if they were journeying alone.

"Today, I'd like to talk about we all can improve our efficiency by working together."

## 87. A Bright Idea for a Lead

"Thomas Edison tried more than 2,000 experiments before he was able to get his light bulb to work. Upon being asked how he felt about failing so many times, he replied, 'I never failed once. I invented the light bulb. It just happened to be a 2,000-step process.'

"Well, today, I promise that I won't give you a complicated 2,000-step process. Instead, I'm going to give you three key steps to making our business more successful."

## 88. The Power of One

"Many people today are cynical and say, 'Why should I get involved?' The answer is because even one person *can* make a difference. Look at history. Did you know that:

- In 1645, one vote gave Oliver Cromwell control of England.
- In 1649, one vote caused Charles I of England to be executed.
- In 1845, one vote brought Texas into the Union.
- In 1868, one vote saved President Andrew Johnson from impeachment.
- In 1875, one vote changed France from a monarchy to a republic.
- In 1876, one vote gave Rutherford B. Hayes the presidency of the United States.
- In 1923, one vote gave Adolf Hitler leadership of the Nazi Party.
- In 1941, one vote saved Selective Service, just weeks before Pearl Harbor was attacked.
- In 1960, one vote change in each precinct in Illinois would have denied John F. Kennedy the presidency.

"So, today I'd like to talk about how you, as one person, can make a difference in helping us...."

## 89. Satisfying the Skeptics

"Before I begin, I'd like to address this story to the skeptics in the audience. In 1807, Robert Fulton attracted a large crowd to witness the first full-scale demonstration of the steamboat on the Hudson River. When he tried to get the engine started, the crowd shouted, 'It will never start! It will never start!'

"When the engine finally did start and the steamboat took off with a flurry of sparks and heavy smoke, the crowd was silent for a moment—but only for a moment. Then they began screaming, 'It will never stop! It will never stop!'

"Well, despite the skeptics, let me explain why we should back this new plan."

## 90. A Baseball Legend's Rules for a Long Life

"Satchel Paige, a famous baseball pitcher of indeterminate age, once offered his rules for a long life.

- Avoid fried meats, which angry up the blood.

- If your stomach disputes you, lie down and pacify it with cool thoughts.

- Keep the juices flowing by jangling around gently as you move.

- Go very light on the vices, such as carrying on in society. The social rumble ain't restful.

- Avoid running at all times.

- Don't look back. Something might be gaining on you.

"I'd like to add another rule onto that list. And that one is 'Avoid speaking to a group for more than 10 minutes. A long talk might anger up the audience's blood.' So today, let me—very briefly—talk about...."

## 91. A Self-Deprecating Opening

"In preparing these remarks, I asked my wife (husband, boss) about what kind of remarks might be appropriate for an audience as distinguished as this. 'Whatever you do,' she said, 'don't try to sound intellectual, sophisticated, or charming. Just be yourself.'"

## 92. In a Hurry

"A man ordered four expensive 30-year-old single malt scotches and had the bartender line them up in front of them. Without pausing, he downed each one.

" 'Wow,' the bartender commented. 'You seem to be in a hurry.'

"The man said, 'You would be, too, if you had what I have.'

" 'What do you have?' the bartender asked sympathetically.

" 'Fifty cents.'

"Well, I have more than fifty cents, but I know you have limited time, so let me keep my remarks short and to the point...."

## 93. Get Fired Up

"The phrase *get fired* can be good or bad. For example, no one wants to get fired from a job. Do you know how that saying came about? Clans of long ago ridded themselves of unproductive individuals by burning down their houses."

## 94. Books We'd Like to Read?

"I recently ran across a list of book titles that have been published recently:

• Reusing Old Graves.

• Highlights in the History of Cement.

• Virtual Reality—Exploring the Bra.

• Simply Bursting—A Guide to Bladder Control.

• Proceedings of the Second International Workshop on Nude Mice.

• And finally, a title which frankly scares me a bit—How to Avoid Huge Ships.

"Well, I'm not going to tell you how to avoid huge ships today, but I'd like to talk about avoiding some common mistakes in...."

or

"I know most of these titles sound irrelevant and I promise today to be on the mark and relevant. In fact the title of my speech, _____, sums up what I am concerned about and what we need to discuss here today."

## 95. "Excuse Me, Mr. Ranger..."

"Recently *Outside* magazine listed some questions that tourists have asked park rangers at the Grand Canyon:

• Was this man-made?

• Do you light it up at night?

• Is the mule train air-conditioned?

• What time does the two o'clock bus leave?

• And: Where are the faces of the presidents?

"We all get confused sometimes and I don't take anyone to task for asking dumb questions. In fact when I finish my short presentation, I would love to hear your questions...."

## 96. Take a Picture

Take a camera with you to the podium. Then say, "Normally if any picture is taken at a gathering like this, it's a photo of the speaker. But I think it should be the other way around. Without an audience, there would be no speaker. You are the important ones, here. So let me pause and take your picture for my scrapbook. It will remind me of this day."

Once you have snapped the picture, you can then launch into "the big picture," your topic of the day.

## 97. Dubious Achievements

"In England, a local newspaper, the *British Sunday Express*, gives awards for dubious achievements.

- For example, John Bloor received the 'Rubber Cushion' award when he mistook a tube of superglue for his hemorrhoid cream.
- The 'Crimewatch' award was given to Henry Smith who was arrested moments after returning home with a stolen stereo. His mistake was having tattooed on his forehead in large capital letters the words 'Henry Smith.' His lawyer told the court, 'My client is not a very bright young man.'
- And the 'Silver Bullet' award was given to a poacher who shot dead a stag standing above him on an overhanging rock and was killed instantly when it fell on him.

"Well, today, I am not here to hand out dubious awards, but rather I want to congratulate some people for some outstanding accomplishments...."

## 98. From the Mouths of Children

"Let me share some answers from children in response to questions about religion:

- Noah's wife was called Joan of Ark.
- The Fifth Commandment is: Humor thy father and mother.
- Christians can have only one wife. This is called monotony.
- The Pope lives in a vacuum.
- The patron saint of travelers is St. Francis of the Seasick.
- The natives of Macedonia did not believe, so Paul got stoned.
- The First Commandment: Eve told Adam to eat the apple.
- It is sometimes difficult to hear what is being said in church because the agnostics are so terrible.

"Well, I hope my answers today are more on the mark."

## 99. Teamwork Makes the Difference

"A father was watching his young son try to dislodge a heavy stone. The boy couldn't budge it. 'Are you sure you are using all your strength?' the father asked.

'Yes, I am,' said the exasperated boy. 'No, you are not,' the father replied. 'You haven't asked me to help you.'

"And I think we all need to combine our talents to make a difference. Today, I'd like to discuss how we can do that."

## 100. Bad Headlines

"Here are some headlines you may have missed:

- Police Begin Campaign to Run Down Jaywalkers.
- House Passes Gas Tax onto Senate.
- Safety Experts Say School Bus Passengers Should Be Belted.
- Iraqi Head Seeks Arms.
- Queen Mary Having Bottom Scraped.
- Panda Mating Fails—Veterinarian Takes Over.
- Eye Drops Off Shelf.
- Dealers Will Hear Car Talk at Noon.
- Lawmen from Mexico Barbecue Guests.
- Autos Killing 110 a Day, Let's Resolve to Do Better.
- War Dims Hopes for Peace.
- Smokers Are Productive, But Death Cuts Efficiency.
- Something Went Wrong in Jet Crash, Experts Say.

"Well, that last headline sure states the obvious. Today, I hope I don't state the obvious. In fact, I want to get you thinking about...."

**Part 4**

# More Great Stuff to Use in Your Speeches

I've been a writer for more than 20 years, a speechwriter for 15. During that time, I've collected a lot of "great stuff" you can use in your speeches. In this chapter are stories and anecdotes that you can weave into speeches to make them more entertaining and more informative.

I strongly suggest that you go through this section in detail with a highlighter (unless it's a library book, then I suggest you go and buy your own copy!). Then next time you have to give a speech, all you have to do is turn to this section, pick out the stories you highlighted and put them in your speech.

I did not put these stories into any specific category, because many can be used in many different formats. Again, the best way to approach this section is browse through it, pick out the material you like, and get ready to use it.

**Mickey Mantle, the great New York Yankee outfielder,** once said, "During my 18 years I came to bat almost 10,000 times. I struck out about 1,700 times and walked maybe 1,900 times. You figure a ballplayer will average about 500 at bats a season. That means I played seven years without ever hitting the ball."

This observation, coming from one of the great hitters of all time, should give us some perspective about the value of failures and mistakes.

**On Columbus's first voyage to the New World,** in 1492, the members of his crew were extremely uneasy about taking such a long journey through unknown waters—and for an unknown destination.

To reassure the sailors and to disguise the true length of the journey, Columbus kept two logs: One was a secret log in which he put the true distances they had sailed that day as best he could calculate them. The second log, which he shared with the crew, contained shorter distances so that the sailors would think they were closer to home than they actually were.

The irony is that the falsified figures turned out to be more accurate than those Columbus kept in his secret log.

# How to Give a Damn Good Speech

**The following is a list of surprising experiences** of noted inventors, athletes, actresses, leaders, and others whose names are known universally. Despite negative feedback and discouragement from others, they evidently believed in themselves enough to overcome all barriers and achieve fame.

- "That's an amazing invention, but who would ever want to use one of them?" President Rutherford Hayes remarked on Alexander Graham Bell's invention of the telephone in 1876.

- Chester Carlson, another young inventor, took his idea to 20 big corporations in the 1940s. After seven years of rejections, he was able to persuade Haloid, a small Rochester, New York, company, to purchase the rights to his electrostatic paper- copying process. Haloid has become Xerox Corporation.

- Franklin Delano Roosevelt, elected President of the United States for four terms, had been stricken with polio at the age of 39.

- Persistence paid off for General Douglas MacArthur. After applying for admission to West Point twice, he applied a third time and was accepted. The rest is history.

- In 1927 the head instructor of the John Murray Anderson Drama School instructed student Lucille Ball to "try any other profession. Any other."

- Buddy Holly was fired from the Decca record label in 1956 by Paul Cohen, who referred to Holly as "the biggest no-talent I ever worked with."

- Academy Award-winning writer, producer, and director Woody Allen failed motion picture production at New York University and City College of New York. He also flunked English at NYU.

- Wilma Rudolph was 20th in a family of 22 children. Born prematurely, her survival was doubtful. At 4 years of age she contracted scarlet fever and double pneumonia, leaving her with a paralyzed leg. By age 9, the metal leg brace, upon which she had become dependent, was removed and she began to walk without it. The doctors were amazed when, at age 13, she developed a rhythmic walk. Having been told she would never walk again, this little girl went on to win three Olympic gold medals.

**Once upon a time there was an enterprising businessman** who had a fantastic idea. He figured out a way to build the perfect automobile. He hired a team of young engineers and told them to buy one of every model car in the world and dismantle them.

He instructed them to pick out the best part from every car and to place it in a special room. Soon the room was filled with parts judged by the group to be the best engineered in the world—the best carburetor, the best set of brakes, the best steering wheel, the best transmission, and so on. It was an impressive collection—more than 5,000 parts in all.

Then he had all the parts assembled into one automobile—the pick of the world so to speak.

There was only one problem. The automobile refused to function—the parts would not work together.

**Luther Burbank, the famed horticulturist,** invited every guest who visited his home to sign the guest book. Each line in the book had a space for the guest's name, address, and special interests.

When inventor Thomas Edison visited Burbank, he signed the book and in the space for special interests, Edison wrote in the word, "Everything," followed by a large exclamation point.

That was almost an understatement. In his lifetime, Edison invented the incandescent light, the phonograph, the wax recording, and the hideaway bed. He also invented wax paper, a variety of cement, underground electrical wires, an electric railway car, an electric railroad signal, the light socket and light switch, a method for making synthetic rubber from goldenrod plants, the chemical phenol, and the motion picture camera.

**A millionaire developed a reputation for being a lavish tipper.** Ironically, this sometimes resulted in poorer service. Once, stopping at a New York hotel, he instructed his assistants to tip $1 for any service, no matter how trivial.

After a few weeks, he noticed that he must have been getting staggering amount of service, since the tips were running up to several hundred dollars a week. But his heavy mail, which sometimes contained 100 letters a day, was being brought up with less than absolute promptness. Finally, he put two and two together and investigated. Sure enough, he discovered that his mail was being delivered one letter at a time.

**The king was interviewing drivers for his coach and asked,** "How close would you come to the edge of the cliff?"

The first driver, wanting to brag about his skill, said, "Twelve inches, your majesty."

The second driver, not wanting to be outdone in the skills department, said, "Six inches, your majesty."

The third driver said, "I'd drive as far away from the cliff's edge as I could, your majesty."

Guess who got the job?

**When Steven Spielberg, the Oscar-winning film director,** was 13 years old, he was harassed by many of his bigger, tougher classmates. One bully gave him a hard time all year. During gym, the bully would knock Spielberg down, push his face in the dirt and give him a bloody nose.

Instead of trying to fight back, Spielberg devised a creative solution. One day he said to the bully, "Listen, I'm making an 8mm movie about fighting the Nazis, and I want you to play this war hero."

At first the bully laughed in Spielberg's face. Later, however, he said he was interested. He was a big 14-year-old, and Spielberg told him he looked like John Wayne. He outfitted the bully in a helmet, fatigues, and backpack and cast him as a heroic squad leader.

From then on, the "bully" became Spielberg's best friend.

**A University of Mississippi law student** came to a question on an exam that he couldn't answer. He gave as creative and lengthy an answer as he could, hoping to score points for cleverness. When he got the exam back, the student found that the professor had noted: "Though you missed most of the legal issues, you have a real talent for fiction."

The student was John Grisham, whose "talent for fiction" brought him seven best-selling novels.

**When the baseball strike of 1994 threatened trading-card manufacturer Pinnacle Brands** with hard times, the company didn't lay off employees. Instead, it challenged them to find creative ways to replace the $40 million in lost revenue. CEO Jerry Meyer told his workers, "I'm not going to save your jobs. You're going to save your jobs. You know what you can change and what you can do differently." Employees responded to the challenge: A custodian reported that the company spent $50,000 on sodas for conference rooms, and the expense was cut. A finance department worker created a database to streamline trademark searches, and saved the company $100,000. A public relations manager signed a deal to distribute pins at the Olympics, generating $20 million.

Pinnacle was the only one of the top five trading-card makers to avoid layoffs during the baseball strike.

**Procrustes was the villain in Greek mythology** who forced travelers to fit into his bed by stretching their bodies or cutting off their legs. The term procrustean is now used to characterize someone who has ruthless disregard for individual differences.

**When a Brooklyn business owner hired a consultant to help cut expenses and boost sales,** the consultant was made privy to all the owner's business records and transactions. The consultant uncovered some questionable transaction, which he reported to the authorities, who imposed a heavy fine, which the owner could not pay. Within a year, the owner had filed for bankruptcy, and the business was sold by a bankruptcy court. The purchaser who emerged as the new owner was the consultant.

**Baltimore Oriole shortstop Cal Ripken hasn't missed a game in more than 13 years,** breaking Lou Gehrig's record for most baseball games played consecutively. When asked if he ever went to the ballpark with a lot of aches and pains, Ripken replied, "Yeah, just about every day."

Although Ripken's casual reply makes it sound routine, overcoming everyday aches and pains without fail for 13 years is a remarkable achievement for an athlete. For anyone, for that matter. Throughout his long and distinguished career, Ripken has encountered the same daily challenges and setbacks as his fellow players and has risen above them all. His dedication, drive, and youthful energy have proven all but inexhaustible.

What's the secret behind Cal Ripken's incredible longevity and success in a career as demanding as professional baseball? One of the keys must surely be that he has conditioned himself to be comfortable being uncomfortable.

**During the First World War,** Nancy Astor immersed herself in hospital work at Cliveden, the Astor's English estate, which had been turned into a hospital for Canadian soldiers. More than 24,000 men were treated there and the Astors paid most of the medical bills.

Lady Astor had an unusual bedside manner. Hearing that two badly burned men had lost the will to live, she bent over them and said, "You're going to die, and I would, too, rather than go back to Canada." This roused them wonderfully, and Nancy went on to preach a lesson to the nurses on keeping patients interested in life.

**What makes people creative?** Sometimes it's having your life shaken up. For 19 years, George Valassis worked as an advertising executive for his father's brother. One day his uncle decided to retire, and his cousin took over the business. The cousin fired him.

Without warning, George lost a modest though comfortable job, and realized then and there that job security could vanish like a puff of smoke. So, he put his 19 years of experience to use in order to come up with an innovative idea.

He knew that advertisers like Procter & Gamble and General Foods were having a really tough time delivering coupons to customers quickly, so he came up with the idea of inserting books filled with coupons in newspapers. To this day, when you open the Sunday edition of your newspaper and see a book of coupons inside, you're looking at what the ad industry calls a "Valassis Insert."

George sold the company he built for big bucks. Yet if he hadn't gotten fired, would he have come up with this great idea? George doesn't think so. He says he just played the hand he was dealt.

**Gary Franks, a U.S. Congressman says,** "I remember taking copious notes and listening to everything the teacher had to say in preparation for my first test at Yale. I looked at the exam and saw it was everything I had studied. I wrote the answers to the three questions thinking, 'Boy, this is easy.'

# How to Give a Damn Good Speech

'As we waited to get our tests back, I was positive I'd get an A. Instead, my grade was a C. Under it, in big red letters, was written, 'I know what I said. What do you think?' "

**At the age of 5,** Glenn Cunningham suffered burns on his legs so severe that his doctors told him he had no chance of ever walking again. Cunningham, however, refused to listen. His mother watched as he painfully learned how to walk again, with one hand on each handle of an old plow for support. Day by day, Cunningham grew stronger. Eventually, he not only learned to walk again, but in 1934 set the world record for the mile.

**It all depends on your perspective.** And our perspective is colored by what we have embedded in our minds already. Consider the man who was bringing up his two daughters in a strictly secular manner—no religion. He reports that recently he was out driving with one daughter who, upon seeing a church with a large cross on the roof, asked, "Daddy, why does that building have a plus sign on it?"

**We all have expertise in different areas.** And we should not look down on those who don't have our expertise. They might know something we don't know. Consider the story of Lord Rutherford who once dismissed with contempt a newspaper reporter who sought his guidance to write a piece on his famous work, the atomic nucleus. The reporter did not fail to sense the scientist's arrogance. Resourceful as most hardboiled reporters are, he threw his shorthand notebook and challenged Rutherford to transcribe his shorthand. It was the shock of his life for the eminent scientist. But, he had the grace to apologize for the discourtesy.

**The congregation of a small stone church in England** decided that the stone, which formed the step up to the front door had become too worn by its years of use, and would have to be replaced. Unfortunately, there were hardly any funds available for the replacement. Then someone came up with the bright idea that the replacement could be postponed for many years by simply turning the block of stone over.

They discovered that their great-grandparents had beaten them to it.

**Bill Gates is at a party and it lasts until past 1 a.m.** Like all computer people who stay up late he gets hungry. He says, "Hey! How about us calling out for pizza?" His guests are taken aback—he has all these bucks, shouldn't he have some more class?—but agree. So he calls the take-out pizza place and comes back crestfallen. "They don't deliver after 1 a.m." he says. His friends say, "Bill, you forgot. You have all this *money*. How much is that pizza worth to you?" Bill stands there a minute then says, "I'll call again." He picks up the phone and gets them on the line and says, "This is Bill Gates and it's worth $252 for you to bring me pizza." He got his pizza *fast*.

**Grover Cleveland,** though constantly at loggerheads with the Senate, got on better with the House of Representatives. A popular story circulating during his presidency concerned the night he was roused by his wife crying, "Wake up! I think there are burglars in the house."

"No, no, my dear," said the president sleepily, "in the Senate maybe, but not in the House."

**A woman with a broken ankle was gingerly hobbling along on crutches** as she attempted to walk her dog. Because of her handicap, however, she was having a lot of trouble keeping the dog under control. Finally, the dog lunged forward, the leash slipped out of her hand, and the dog went running down the street. She called and called, but the dog wouldn't come back. Because she couldn't chase after it, she eventually gave up and went home.

A couple of hours later she heard something scratching at the door. When she went to the door she found her dog standing there with a dead rabbit in its mouth. Upon closer inspection, she realized it was the neighbors' pet rabbit. She knew she would never be able to tell them what happened, and since they were out of town for the weekend, she hit upon a plan.

She took the rabbit into the bathroom, washed it off, and blew its fur dry. Then she took the rabbit back to the neighbors' backyard and put the rabbit back in its cage. She thought the neighbors would discover the rabbit dead and think it died in the cage. They would never suspect what really happened.

On Monday, there was a knock at the door, and when she answered, her neighbor was standing there. He asked her if she had seen anyone in their backyard over the weekend. She said no. He said, "Did you see anything strange going on around our house or yard?" Again, she denied seeing anything suspicious. She said, "Why are you asking me these questions? What happened?" He said, "Well, something really strange is going on in my backyard. On Friday our rabbit died, so we buried it in the backyard. But when we came back from the weekend, it was back in the cage!"

**In World War II,** an English reporter who had heard so much about the bravery of the Gurkhas, citizens of Nepal serving as British soldiers, visited a camp just in front of the enemy lines. During the course of his reporting, he had occasion to observe a mission being conducted.

The mission was to airdrop a bunch of soldiers behind enemy lines to conduct some relatively light action. He watched the commander of the Gurkhas pitch the mission and then ask for volunteers. To his surprise, only about half the Gurkhas volunteered and were sent off.

Thoroughly disillusioned with the legends of Gurkha bravery, the reporter went back home. After the war, he happened to run into a Gurkha who had been there, and asked him why half the troops had failed to volunteer. It turned out that none of the squad, both those who volunteered and those who did not, were aware that they would get a parachute for the drop. Hence the low turnout.

# How to Give a Damn Good Speech

**A businessman related an incident from "some time back"** when IBM Canada Ltd. ordered some parts from a new supplier in Japan. The company noted in its order that acceptable quality allowed for 1.5 percent defects (a fairly high standard in North America at the time).

The Japanese sent the order, with a few parts packaged separately in plastic. The accompanying letter said: "We don't know why you want 1.5 per cent defective parts, but for your convenience, we've packed them separately."

**One day President and Mrs. Coolidge were visiting a government farm.** Soon after their arrival they were taken off on separate tours. When Mrs. Coolidge passed the chicken pens she paused to ask the man in charge if the rooster copulates more than once each day. "Dozens of times," was the reply. "Please tell that to the president," Mrs. Coolidge requested.

When the president passed the pens and was told about the roosters, he asked, "Same hen every time?" "Oh no, Mr. President, a different one each time." The president nodded slowly, then said, "Tell that to Mrs. Coolidge."

**True story.** A man in South Korea bought a sportshirt made by a Korean firm called Heet, with these instructions: For best results, wash in cold water separately, hang-dry and iron with warm iron. For not-so-good results, drag behind car through puddles, blow-dry on roof rack.

**On May 15, 1930,** the first airline stewardesses boarded planes with the following set of instructions:

- Keep the clock and altimeter wound up.
- Carry a railroad timetable in case the plane is grounded.
- Warn the passengers against throwing their cigars and cigarettes out the windows.
- Keep an eye on passengers when they go to the lavatory to be sure they don't mistakenly go out the emergency exit.

**A newspaper interviewer asked popular singer Tom Jones** whether he ever has problems with the husbands of the women who throw their underwear onto the stage during his performances.

"One night a woman came down to the stage to retrieve an undergarment and I gave her a big kiss. I asked her name, and if she was married. She said 'yes' and pointed out her husband at a nearby table. I explained to him that the kiss was all in fun and that I hoped he hadn't taken offense. He just smiled and said, 'Look, you pump up the tires, and I'll ride the bike.'"

**Ben McTaggart, a farmer in the Scottish Highlands,** was apprehended by the local constabulary after a routine inspection of his croft revealed a whisky still.

McTaggart appeared in court next day to face charges of evading payment of excise duties and the illegal manufacture of alcoholic spirits.

Reviewing the facts of the case before pronouncing verdict, the magistrate declared: "Mr. McTaggart, you have been found in possession of apparatus commonly used in the distillation of alcoholic liquors. Although this equipment was unused, and no trace of spirits could be found on your premises, the intent of the apparatus should be clear to all, and I am obliged to find you guilty of all charges brought against you in this court. Before I pronounce sentence, do you have anything to say in mitigation of your offence?"

McTaggart glowered at the magistrate and replied: "Your Honour, you can convict me of moonshining just because I have the equipment, but you'd better convict me of rape as well, because I have the equipment for that too!"

**Representative Tim Moore sponsored a resolution** in the Texas House of Representatives in Austin, Texas, calling on the House to commend Albert de Salve for his unselfish service to "his country, his state, and his community."

The resolution stated that "this compassionate gentleman's dedication and devotion to his work has enabled the weak and the lonely throughout the nation to achieve and maintain a new degree of concern for their future. He has been officially recognized by the state of Massachusetts for his noted activities and unconventional techniques involving population control and applied psychology."

The resolution was passed unanimously.

Representative Moore then revealed that he had only presented the motion to show how the legislature passes bills and resolutions often without reading them or understanding what they say. Albert de Salve was the Boston Strangler.

**When Japanese Prime Minister Nakasone visited President Reagan,** he asked for the auto import restrictions to be rescinded, saying "We've had a rougher time of it; consider Hiroshima."

The Gipper asked, "What has that got to do with it?"

"Well, we've never destroyed one of your cities," replied Nakasone.

Quickly Reagan cut in: "What about Detroit?"

**In the production of "The Diary of Anne Frank"** with Pia Zadora in the title role, when the Germans showed up, looking for hidden Jews, the audience started shouting "She's upstairs! She's upstairs!"

**Conservative Member of Parliament Geoffrey Dickens** tells of attending a fair in his constituency and being followed around by a sweet but exceptionally ugly woman whom he couldn't get rid of.

A few days later he got an admiring letter from her asking for his photograph, and signed, after her name, "(Horseface)."

Dickens was touched by her humorous modesty and sent off a picture autographed, "To Horseface, with best wishes, Geoffrey Dickens."

Some time later his secretary asked him, "Did you get that letter from the woman at the fair? I wrote 'Horseface' after her name so you'd know which one she was."

**She had a wedding to go to, and needed a wedding gift.** "Aha, thought she, I have that monogrammed silver tray from my wedding that I never use. I'll just take it to a silversmith and have him remove my monogram and put hers on it. Voilà, one cheap wedding present."

So she took it to the silversmith and asked him to remove her monogram and put the new one on. The silversmith took a look at the tray, shook his head, and said, "Lady, you can only do this so many times!"

**A carload of hunters, looking for a place to hunt, pulled into a farmer's yard.** The driver went up to the farmhouse to ask permission to hunt. The old farmer said, "Sure you can hunt, but would you do me a favor? That old mule standing over there is 20 years old and sick with cancer, but I don't have the heart to kill her. Would you do it for me?" The hunter said, "Sure," and headed for the car.

While walking back, however, he decided to pull a trick on his hunting buddies. He got into the car and when they asked if the farmer had said okay, he said, "No, we can't hunt here, but I'm going to teach that old cuss a lesson." With that, he rolled down his window, stuck his gun out and blasted the mule. As he exclaimed, "There, that will teach him!" a second shot rang out from the passenger side. And one of his hunting buddies shouted, "I got the cow!"

**Sometime in the early 1900s, P. T. Barnum,** the owner of the Barnum & Bailey circus and originator of the phrase "There's a sucker born every minute," offered $10,000 in cash to any person who could thoroughly dupe or sucker him.

Barnum was always looking for interesting new acts or novel creatures to exhibit, and one day he received a letter from a fellow in Maine who claimed to possess a cherry-colored cat and asked if Barnum were interested in such a thing for his circus.

Barnum contacted the man and said yes, if the cat were truly cherry-colored, he'd gladly put it on display. Well, a few days later a crate marked "live animal" arrived for him. When Barnum opened it, he found a somewhat frightened but otherwise perfectly ordinary-looking black housecat inside, along with a note which read:

"Maine cherries are black.

There's a sucker born every minute."

Thoroughly tickled, Barnum sent the man a check for $10,000.

**The choir director selected the 6-year-old boy with the sweetest face** for the opening scene of the play. "Now, all you have to do is, when I direct the choir to sing 'And the angel lit the candle,' you come onstage and light all the candles."

"I can do it! I can do it!" the little boy said, excited to be the one picked.

Rehearsals came and went, and finally the big night arrived. The choir was in grand voice, the stage was beautifully decorated with dozens of unlit candles all around, awaiting the moment when the cute littlest angel made his interest.

The director gave the downbeat, the orchestra began to play, and the choir swept into the introductory lines, ending with an expectant "And the angel lit the candle," and everyone looked stage right for the entrance.

No little boy. The director gave the downbeat again, and gestured for a louder line, to which the choir sang, "And the angel lit the candle," and again, all eyes looked stage right.

No little boy. The director, beginning to sweat, motioned with great, sweeping gestures, and the choir thundered into the line—the curtains belled slightly from the sound—"AND THE ANGEL LIT THE CANDLE!"

And into the silence, which followed came a clear, boy-soprano voice floating piercingly from stage right "And the cat peed on the matches!"

**There is a story about a monastery in Europe** perched high on a cliff several hundred feet in the air. The only way to reach the monastery was to be suspended in a basket, which was pulled to the top by several monks who pulled and tugged with all their strength. Obviously the ride up the steep cliff in that basket was terrifying.

One tourist got exceedingly nervous about halfway up as he noticed that the rope by which he was suspended was old and frayed. With a trembling voice he asked the monk who was riding with him in the basket how often they changed the rope. The monk thought for a moment and answered brusquely, "Whenever it breaks."

**Ronald Reagan was beyond the age at which most Americans retire** when he ran for the presidency in 1980. At age 69, he conducted a vigorous campaign, never passing up the chance to defuse the issue of his age with humor.

On one occasion, he remarked, "I want to say that I don't mind at all any of the jokes or remarks about my age. Thomas Jefferson made a comment about the Presidency and age. He said that one should not worry about one's exact chronological age in reference to his ability to perform one's task. And ever since he told me that, I stopped worrying."

Probably his best moment came during his second presidential election campaign, during his televised debate with Walter Mondale in 1984. A reporter asked Reagan if he was too old to serve another term. Reagan was more than ready for the question. He said, "I'm not going to inject the issue of age into this campaign," he began. "I am not going to exploit for political gain my opponent's youth and inexperience."

# How to Give a Damn Good Speech

**Walking down the street,** a man passes a house and notices a child trying to reach the doorbell. No matter how much the little guy stretches, he can't make it. The man calls out, "Let me get that for you," and he bounds onto the porch to ring the bell. "Thanks, mister," says the kid. "Now let's run."

**Tony attended the men's prayer breakfast** and heard a visiting psychologist speak on the importance of showing appreciation to the important people in one's life. Tony decided to start with his wife, so after work that night, he went to the shopping mall where he bought a dozen long-stemmed roses, a box of chocolates, and a pair of earrings. He chortled with self-satisfaction as he contemplated surprising his wife and showing her how much he appreciated her.

He stood at the front door with the roses in his right hand, the gaily wrapped box of candy under his arm, an open jewelry box displaying the earrings in his left hand. With an elbow he rang the doorbell. His wife came to the door, opened it, and stared at him for a long minute. Suddenly she burst into tears.

"Sweetheart, what's wrong?" asked the bewildered husband.

"It's been the worst day of my life," she answered. "First, Jimmy tried to flush his diaper down the toilet. Then Eric melted his plastic airplane in the oven. Then the dishwasher got clogged and overflowed all over the kitchen floor. Then Brittany came home from school with a note from the teacher saying that she beat up a boy in her class. And now you come home drunk!"

**A rabbi and a soap maker went for a walk together.** The soap maker said, "What good is religion? Look at all the trouble and misery of the world! Still there, even after years—thousands of years—of teaching about goodness and truth and peace. Still there, after all the prayers and sermons and teachings. If religion is good and true, why should this be?"

The rabbi said nothing. They continued walking until he noiced a child playing in the gutter. The rabbi said, "Look at that child. You say that soap makes people clean, but see the dirt on that youngster. Of what good is soap? With all the soap in the world, over all these years, the child is still filthy. I wonder how effective soap is, after all!"

The soap maker protested. "But, Rabbi, soap cannot do any good unless it is used!"

"Exactly," replied the rabbi. "Exactly."

**A famous author was autographing copies of his new novel** in a department store. One gentleman pleased him by bringing up not only his new book for signature, but two of his previous ones as well.

"My wife likes your stuff," he remarked apologetically, "so I thought I'd give her these signed copies for a birthday present."

"A surprise, eh?" hazarded the author.

"I'll say," agreed the customer. "She's expecting a Mercedes."

**The wit and charm of Adlai E. Stevenson II** made him a constant target for autograph-seekers. Once, as he left the United Nations Building in New York City and found himself surrounded by admirers, a small, elderly woman in the crowd finally succeeded approaching him.

"Please Mr. Ambassador," she said, holding out a piece of paper, "your autograph for a very, very old lady."

"Delighted!" Stevenson replied with a smile. "But where is she?"

**Golfer Tommy Bolt had a terrible temper.** Once, after missing six straight putts, generally leaving them teetering on the very edge of the cup, Bolt shook his fist at the heavens and shouted, "Why don't you come down and fight like a man!"

**There was a golf match** between a Supreme Court Justice and an equally distinguished Virginia bishop. The bishop missed four straight short putts without saying a single word. The Justice watched him with growing amusement and remarked, "Bishop, that is the most profane silence I ever heard."

**Former Undersecretary of the Interior John C. Whitaker** is reminded of how easy it is to get an out-of-perspective feeling about one's importance in government whenever he thinks of an 85-year-old woman who has lived her life in one spot in Nova Scotia. The population there swells to nine in summer and stays steady at two during the winter. Whitaker, who has been fishing there every year since he was 12, flew in one day. Miss Mildred welcomed him into her kitchen and said, "Johnny, I hate to admit I don't know, but where is Washington?"

When Whitaker realized that she wasn't kidding, he explained: "That's where the president is. That's like where you have the Prime Minister in Ottawa."

Then she asked how many people lived there, and Whitaker said there were about two million. She said, "Think of that, two million people living so far away from everything."

**"While I was playing with the Pirates,"** writes Joe Garagiola, "I gave a speech to the Pittsburgh Junior Chamber of Commerce. Trying to make the best of a terrible season, I said, 'We may not be high in the standings, and we don't win many ballgames, but you've got to admit we play some interesting baseball.' A voice from the back of the room yelled, "Why don't you play some dull games and win a few?"

**Says actor Tom Selleck,** "Whenever I get full of myself, I remember that nice couple who approached me with a camera on a street in Honolulu one day. When I struck a pose for them, the man said, 'No, no, we want you to take a picture of us.'"

**Billionaire J. P. Getty** was once asked the secret of his success. Said he, "Some people find oil. Others don't."

# How to Give a Damn Good Speech

**Shortly after John F. Kennedy blocked the hike in steel prices in 1961,** he was visited by a businessman who expressed wariness about the national economy. "Things look great," said JFK. "Why, if I wasn't president, I'd be buying stocks myself."

"If you weren't president," said the businessman, "so would I."

**Every writer has received rejection slips;** too many of them for most. One publication, the *Financial Times,* has quoted this one translated from a Chinese economic journal. It goes like this:

"We have read your manuscript with boundless delight. If we were to publish your paper, it would be impossible for us to publish any work of lower standard. And as it is unthinkable that in the next thousand years we shall see its equal, we are, to our regret, compelled to return your divine composition, and to beg you a thousand times to overlook our short sight and timidity."

**Even some of our greatest visionaries have exhibited occasional moments of shortsightedness.** Consider these surprising observations:

- "People have been talking about a 3,000-mile high-angle rocket shot from one continent to another, carrying an atomic bomb and so directed as to be a precise weapon... I think we can leave that out of our thinking."
—Dr. Vannevar Bush, the physicist who directed the effort to develop the atomic bomb, 1945
- "Nobody now fears that a Japanese fleet could deal an unexpected blow at our Pacific possessions....Radio makes surprise impossible."
—Josephus Daniels, Secretary of the U.S. Navy, 1922
- "Fooling around with alternating current is a waste of time. Nobody will use it, ever."—Thomas Edison
- "There is not the slightest indication that nuclear energy will be obtainable."—Albert Einstein, 1932
- "While theoretically and technically television may be feasible, commercially and financially I consider it an impossibility, a development of which we need waste little time dreaming."—Lee De Forest, inventor of the electron tube that made radio possible, 1926
- "It can be taken for granted that before 1980 ships, aircraft, locomotives and even automobiles will be atomically fueled."—David Sarnoff, 1955
- "As far as sinking a ship with a bomb is concerned, you just can't do it."
—Rear Admiral Clark Woodward, 1939

**In 1879, Procter & Gamble's best seller was candles.** But the company was in trouble. Thomas Edison had invented the light bulb, and it looked as if candles would become obsolete. However, at this time, it seemed that destiny played a

---

dramatic part in pulling the struggling company from the clutches of bankruptcy. A forgetful employee at a small factory in Cincinnati forgot to turn off his machine when he went to lunch. The result? A frothing mass of lather filled with air bubbles. He almost threw the stuff away but instead decided to make it into soap. The soap floated. Thus, Ivory soap was born and became the mainstay of Procter & Gamble.

Why was soap that floats such a hot item at that time? In Cincinnati, during that period, some people bathed in the Ohio River. Floating soap would never sink and consequently never got lost. So, Ivory soap became a best seller in Ohio and eventually across the country.

**Reuben Gonzales was in the final match** of a professional racquetball tournament. It was his first shot at a victory on the pro circuit, and he was playing the perennial champion. In the fourth and final game, at match point, Gonzales made a super "kill" shot into the front wall to win it all. The referee called it good. One of the two linesmen affirmed that the shot was in. But Gonzales, after a moment's hesitation, turned around, shook his opponent's hand, and declared that his shot had hit the floor first. As a result, he lost the match. He walked off the court. Everybody was stunned. Who could ever imagine it in any sport or endeavor? A player, with everything officially in his favor, with victory in his hand, disqualified himself at match point and lost!

When asked why he did it, Reuben said, "It was the only thing I could do to maintain my integrity." Reuben Gonzales realized that he could always win another match, but he could never regain his lost integrity.

**Have you ever heard the unusual account** of how the news of the battle of Waterloo reached England? The word was carried first by sailing ship to the southern coast. From there it was to be relayed by signal flags to London. When the report was received at Winchester, the flags on the cathedral began to spell it out: "Wellington defeated...."

Before the message could be completed, however, a heavy fog moved in. Gloom filled the hearts of the people as the fragmentary news spread throughout the surrounding countryside.

But when the mists began to lift, it became evident that the signals of Winchester Cathedral had really spelled out this triumphant message: "Wellington defeated the enemy!"

**Years ago a wealthy English family was entertaining friends at their home.** As the children swam in a pond, one ventured into the deep water and began to drown. A gardener who heard the screams jumped into the water and saved the child. The youngster's name was Winston Churchill. Deeply grateful to the gardener, the parents asked how they could ever repay him. He hesitated, but then said, "I wish my son could go to college someday to be a doctor."

"He will," said Churchill's parents. "We will pay his way."

# How to Give a Damn Good Speech

Years later when Sir Winston was Prime Minister, he became ill with pneumonia. The best physician the king could find was called to the bedside of the ailing leader. His name was Sir Alexander Fleming, the developer of penicillin and the son of that gardener who long ago saved his life. Churchill later said, "Rarely has a man owed his life twice to the same person."

**Years ago in Scotland, the Clark family had a dream.** Clark and his wife worked and saved, making plans for their nine children and themselves to travel to the United States. It had taken years, but they had finally saved enough money and had gotten passports and reservations for the whole family on a new liner to the United States.

The entire family was filled with anticipation and excitement about their new life. However, seven days before their departure, the youngest son was bitten by a dog. The doctor sewed up the boy but hung a yellow sheet on the Clarks' front door. Because of the possibility of rabies, they were being quarantined for 14 days.

The family's dreams were dashed. They would not be able to make the trip to America as they had planned. The father, filled with disappointment and anger, stomped to the dock to watch the ship leave. The father shed tears of disappointment and cursed both his son and God for their misfortune.

Five days later, the tragic news spread throughout Scotland—the mighty Titanic had sunk. The Clark family was to have been on that ship, but because the son had been bitten by a dog, they were left behind in Scotland.

When Mr. Clark heard the news, he hugged his son and thanked him for saving the family. He thanked God for saving their lives and turning what he had felt was a tragedy into a blessing.

**The Brooklyn Bridge,** which spans the East River and connects Manhattan Island to Brooklyn was inspired by a creative engineer named John Roebling. However, bridge-building experts throughout the world told him it could not be done. Roebling convinced his son, Washington, that the bridge could be built. The two of them planned how the obstacles could be overcome. With excitement, they hired their crew and began to build the bridge.

The project was only a few months under construction when a tragic accident on the site took the life of John Roebling and severely injured his son, Washington. Washington was left with permanent brain damage and was unable to talk or walk. Everyone felt that the project would have to be scrapped.

Even though Washington was unable to move or talk, his mind was as sharp as ever, and he still had a burning desire to complete the bridge. An idea hit him as he lay in his hospital bed, and he developed a code for communication. All he could move was one finger, so he touched the arm of his wife with that finger, tapping out the code to communicate to her what to tell the engineers who were building the bridge. For 13 years, Washington tapped out his instructions with his finger until the spectacular Brooklyn Bridge was finally completed.

**When young F. W. Woolworth was a store clerk,** he tried to convince his boss to have a ten-cent sale to reduce inventory. The boss agreed, and the idea was a resounding success. This inspired Woolworth to open his own store and price items at a nickel and a dime. He needed capital for such a venture, so he asked his boss to supply the capital for part interest in the store. His boss turned him down flat. "The idea is too risky," he told Woolworth. "There are not enough items to sell for five and ten cents." Woolworth went ahead without his boss's backing, and he not only was successful in his first store, but eventually he owned a chain of F. W. Woolworth stores across the nation.

**Years ago there was a group of brilliant young men** at the University of Wisconsin, who seemed to have amazing creative literary talent. They were would-be poets, novelists, and essayists. They were extraordinary in their ability to put the English language to its best use. These promising young men met regularly to read and critique each other's work. And critique it they did!

These men were merciless with one another. They dissected the most minute literary expression into a hundred pieces. They were heartless, tough, even mean in their criticism. The sessions became such arenas of literary criticism that the members of this exclusive club called themselves the "Stranglers."

Not to be outdone, the women of literary talent in the university were determined to start a club of their own, one comparable to the Stranglers. They called themselves the "Wranglers." They, too, read their works to one another. But there was one great difference. The criticism was much softer, more positive, more encouraging. Sometimes, there was almost no criticism at all. Every effort, even the most feeble one, was encouraged.

Twenty years later an alumnus of the university was doing an exhaustive study of his classmates' careers when he noticed a vast difference in the literary accomplishments of the Stranglers as opposed to the Wranglers. Of all the bright young men in the Stranglers, not one had made a significant literary accomplishment of any kind. From the Wranglers had come six or more successful writers, some of national renown such as Marjorie Kinnan Rawlings, who wrote *The Yearling*.

Talent between the two? Probably the same. Level of education? Not much difference. But the Stranglers strangled, while the Wranglers were determined to give each other a lift. The Stranglers promoted an atmosphere of contention and self-doubt. The Wranglers highlighted the best, not the worst.

**Flea trainers have observed a predictable and strange habit of fleas** while training them. Fleas are trained by putting them in a cardboard box with a top on it. The fleas will jump up and hit the top of the cardboard box over and over and over again. As you watch them jump and hit the lid, something becomes obvious. The fleas continue to jump, but they are no longer jumping high enough to hit the top. Apparently, Excedrin headache 1,738 forces them to limit the height of their jump.

# How to Give a Damn Good Speech

When you take off the lid, the fleas continue to jump, but they will not jump out of the box. They won't jump out because they can't jump out. Why? They have conditioned themselves to jump just so high. Once they have conditioned themselves to jump just so high, that's all they can do!

Many times, people do the same thing. They restrict themselves and never reach their potential. Just like the fleas, they fail to jump higher, thinking they are doing all they can do.

**Once, while traveling in Virginia,** Thomas Jefferson stopped at a country inn and got into conversation with a stranger. The stranger mentioned some mechanical operations he had seen recently, and Jefferson's knowledge of the subject convinced him that Jefferson was an engineer. Then they got to talking about agriculture, and the stranger decided that Jefferson was a farmer. More talk led the stranger to believe Jefferson was a lawyer; then a physician. Finally the topic of religion was broached, and the stranger concluded that Jefferson was a clergyman, though he wasn't sure of what denomination.

The following day he asked the landlord the name of the tall man he had engaged in conversation the night before. "What," said the landlord, "don't you know the Squire? That was Mr. Jefferson." "Not President Jefferson?" exclaimed the stranger. "Yes," nodded the landlord, "President Jefferson!"

**Charlie Chaplin competitions were quite popular** throughout the United States in the early part of the century. The best imitator of the great actor was awarded a special prize. One such competition was secretly attended by Charlie Chaplin himself, who took part in the competition. Great was his surprise when the committee only awarded him the third prize.

**The Pope had just finished a tour of the Napa Valley** and was taking a limousine to San Francisco. Having never driven a limo, he asked the chauffeur if he could drive for a while. The chauffeur climbed in the back of the limo and the Pope took the wheel. The Pope proceeded to Silverado, and started accelerating to see what the limo could do. He got to about 90 mph, and suddenly he saw the red and blue lights of the California Highway Patrol in his mirror. He pulled over and the trooper came to his window. The trooper, recognizing who it was, called in to report to his chief.

"It's not Ted Kennedy again, is it?" asked the chief.

"No, Sir!" replied the trooper, "This guy's more important."

"Is it the Governor?" asked the chief.

"No! Even more important!" replied the trooper.

"Is it the President???" asked the chief.

"No! Even more important!" said the trooper.

"Well, who the heck is it?" screamed the chief.

"I don't know, Sir," said the trooper, "but he's got the Pope as his chauffeur."

**Fire authorities in California** found a corpse in a burnt-out section of forest while assessing the damage of a forest fire. The deceased male was dressed in a full wetsuit, complete with a dive tank, flippers, and face mask. A post-mortem examination revealed that the person died not from burns but from massive internal injuries. Dental records provided a positive identification. Investigators then set about determining how a fully clad diver ended up in the middle of a forest fire.

It was revealed that, on the day of the fire, the person went for a diving trip off the coast—some 20 miles from the forest. The firefighters, seeking to control the fire as quickly as possible, called in a fleet of helicopters with very large buckets. The buckets were dropped into the ocean for rapid filling, then flown to the forest fire and emptied.

You guessed it. The unfortunate diver was hauled out of the Pacific by one of these giant buckets and dumped onto the forest fire.

**A Mexican newspaper reported that** bored Royal Air Force pilots stationed on the Falkland Islands devised what they consider a marvelous game. Noting that the local penguins are fascinated by airplanes, the pilots searched out a beach where the birds are gathered and fly slowly along it at the water's edge. Perhaps 10,000 penguins turn their heads in unison watching the planes go by, and when the pilots turn around and fly back, the birds turn their heads in the opposite direction, like spectators at a slow-motion tennis match. The paper reported, "The pilots fly out to sea and directly to the penguin colony and overfly it. Heads go up, up, up, and 10,000 penguins fall over gently onto their backs."

**Accuracy is important to everyone,** and most of us feel pretty good about attaining a 99.9-percent level. But let's look at what would happen at 99.9 percent accuracy in these situations:

- 2 million documents would be lost by the IRS each year.
- 811,000 faulty rolls of 35mm film would be loaded each year.
- 22,000 checks would be deducted from the wrong bank accounts each hour.
- 1,314 phone calls would be misplaced by telecommunication services every minute.
- 12 babies would be given to the wrong parents each day.
- 268,500 defective tires would be shipped each year.
- 14,208 defective personal computers would be shipped each year.
- 2,488,200 books would be printed with the wrong cover each year.
- 5,517,200 cases of soft drinks would be flat.
- Two plane landings daily at O'Hare International Airport in Chicago would be unsafe.

# How to Give a Damn Good Speech

**A young couple who had just witnessed a Bill Cosby performance** went backstage hoping to get the comedian's autograph in their newly born son's baby book. An aide took the book to Cosby, and when it was returned the couple excitedly looked for his signature. They couldn't find it, and they left the theater disappointed.

Days later, however, the mother found it on one of the inside pages. Under "Baby's first sentence" was written "I like Bill Cosby."

**One of the golfers on the pro tour some years ago** was a pompous egomaniac with the emotional maturity of a 6-year-old. He could do nothing wrong and always had a quick excuse for any loss: it was a lousy course, the other golfers were cheating, the weather was terrible, etc.

As if these faults were not enough, he was also not above hustling a few extra dollars playing amateurs in cities on the tour for $50 a hole. One day he was approached by a man wearing dark glasses and carrying a white cane who offered to play him for $100 a hole.

"Why, I can't play you," the professional protested. "You're blind, aren't you?"

"Yes, I am," replied the man. "But that's all right. I was a state champion before I went blind. I think I can beat you."

Now the conceited one had not been doing well lately—he needed the money. Anyway, blind or not, if the guy was crazy enough to challenge him, why not? "You did say $100 a hole?"

The blind man nodded.

"Well, all right. It's a deal. But don't say I didn't warn you—you'll lose your money. When would you like to play?"

"Any night at all," replied the blind man. "Any night at all."

**Babe Ruth had hit 714 home runs during his baseball career** and was playing one of his last full major league games. It was the Braves versus the Reds in Cincinnati. But the great Ruth was no longer as agile as he had once been. He fumbled the ball and threw badly, and in one inning alone his errors were responsible for most of the five runs scored by Cincinnati.

As the Babe walked off the field after the third out and headed toward the dugout, a crescendo of yelling and booing reached his ears. Just then a boy jumped over the railing onto the playing field. With tears streaming down his face, he threw his arms around the legs of his hero.

Ruth didn't hesitate for one second. He picked up the boy, hugged him, and set him down on his feet, patting his head gently. The noise from the stands came to an abrupt halt.

Suddenly there was no more booing. In fact, a hush fell over the entire park. In those brief moments, the fans saw two heroes: Ruth, who in spite of his dismal day on the field could still care about a little boy; and the small lad, who cared about the feelings of another human being. Both had melted the hearts of the crowd.

---

**Admiral Heihachio Togo,** whose brilliant tactics had destroyed the Russian fleet at the Battle of the Sea of Japan in 1905, visited the United States shortly after the Russo-Japanese War. At a state dinner in Admiral Togo's honor, statesman William Jennings Bryan was asked to propose a toast. Because Bryan was well-known as a strict teetotaler, it was feared that an embarrassing breakdown of protocol was about to occur. But as Bryan stood to propose his toast, he held up his glass and said, "Admiral Togo has won a great victory on water, and I will therefore toast him with water. When Admiral Togo wins a victory on champagne I will toast him in champagne."

**Some years ago, Art Fry, a scientist in the commercial office of 3M,** came up with an idea for one of the company's best-selling products. It seems that Art Fry dealt with a small irritation every Sunday as he sang in the church choir. After marking his pages in the hymnal with small bits of paper, the small pieces would invariably fall out all over the floor.

Suddenly, an idea struck Fry. He remembered an adhesive developed by a colleague that everyone thought was a failure because it did not stick very well. "I coated the adhesive on a paper sample," Fry recalls, "and I found that it was not only a good bookmark, but it was great for writing notes. It will stay in place as long as you want it to, and then you can remove it without damage."

Yes, Art Fry hit the jackpot. The resulting product was called Post-it! and has become one of 3M's most successful office products.

**Most of us experience some degree of anxiety.** But it's surprising how much we expend on things we can do nothing about. Here is how the anxiety of the average person is divided up:

40 percent—things that will never happen.
30 percent—things about the past that can't be changed.
12 percent—criticism from others, mostly untrue.
10 percent—health, which gets worse with stress.
 8 percent—real problems that will be faced.

**The following is an actual radio conversation** released by the Chief of Naval Operations, on October 10, 1995:

Hail: Please divert your course 15 degrees to the North to avoid a collision.

Reply: Recommend you divert YOUR course 15 degrees to South to avoid a collision.

Hail: This is the Captain of a U.S. Navy ship. I say again, divert YOUR course.

Reply: No. I say again, you divert YOUR course.

Hail: THIS IS THE AIRCRAFT CARRIER ENTERPRISE, WE ARE A LARGE WARSHIP OF THE US NAVY. DIVERT YOUR COURSE NOW!

Reply: This is a lighthouse.... Your call.

# How to Give a Damn Good Speech

**A basketball coach told some friends about a dream he had.** "I was walking down the street," he said, "when this Rolls Royce pulled up beside me. Inside, there was a beautiful young woman—blonde, maybe 24 or 25 years old. She asked me to get in. She took me to a fantastic restaurant where we ate and drank and she paid the bill. Then she asked me if I wanted to go home with her. And I said yes. And we did."

"Then what happened?" a listener urged.

"The best part of all!" the coach drooled. "She introduced me to her two brothers, and both of them were over 7 feet tall!"

**Tip O'Neill,** U.S. Congressman and former speaker of the House of Representatives, enjoyed telling the story of the only election he ever lost. As a very young man, he ran for the city council in his hometown of Cambridge, Massachusetts. After his defeat, the elderly lady who lived next door said she had voted for him even though he had never bothered to ask for her vote. O'Neill was surprised. He pointed out that he had shoveled her snow every winter. Cut her grass every summer. Couldn't he just assume that he had her vote? But the woman just looked at him and said: "Tip, people like to be asked."

**The first management conference we know of was called in 1882** by the German Post Office. The topic—and only chief executive officers were invited—was how not to be afraid of the telephone. Nobody showed up. The invitees were insulted. The idea that they should use the telephone was unthinkable. The telephone was for underlings.

**I was thinking, "What a crummy picture I've got here."** At that time, I had closed the balcony, just so I didn't have to put ushers upstairs, and kept expenses down. I thought, "If I had another crummy picture upstairs, I could double the gross. I don't need another manager or anything."—The chairman and CEO of AMC Entertainment explaining how he got the idea for the multiplex film theater in the mid 1950s.

**Steve Ross, who put together the Time Warner merger,** was a self-made man who left an estate worth millions. He liked to tell a story that played a central role in his life. Ross, as a teenager, was summoned to his father's deathbed to receive this advice: There are those who work all day, those who dream all day, and those who spend an hour dreaming before setting to work to fulfill those dreams. "Go into the third category," his father said, "because there's virtually no competition."

**At the turn of the century,** the name William Sidis was synonymous in the United States with "child prodigy." His father, a Harvard professor of abnormal psychology, contended that geniuses were made, not born. At 2, the boy could type in

English and French; at 5, he wrote a treatise on anatomy; at 11, he was admitted to Harvard and delivered a lecture on the fourth dimension that was too sophisticated for most of his audience; at 12, he withdrew from college and spent most of the rest of his life working in menial jobs and making a special study of streetcar transfers.

**When Stewart Udall suggested that America's most popular poet** read at John F. Kennedy's inauguration, the president-elect's first reaction was: "Oh, no. You know that Robert Frost always steals any show he is part of." Kennedy's fear proved well-founded. As 60 million people watched on TV, the 86-year-old Frost, his papers and white hair fluttering in the bitter wind, fumbled. Unable to read his commissioned poem because of the glaring sun, he finally gave up and recited, from memory, "The Gift Outright." It was a triumph, a recovery so brilliant that some thought he'd staged it.

**When Andre-Francois Rafray agreed to buy** Jean Calment's four-room apartment in Arles, France, in 1965, he thought he was getting a good deal. Under the French *viager*, or "for life" system, Rafray, a notary public, would pay Calment the equivalent of $500 a month, and allow her to live in the flat until her death. In return he would own the apartment when she died. At that time, Calment was 90 and would obviously not live much longer. Rafray died of cancer at his home on Christmas day, 1995, aged 77. Calment, meanwhile, is still alive, at 122, the oldest living person on earth.

**Henry Ford hired an efficiency expert to go through his plant.** He said, "Find the nonproductive people. Tell me who they are, and I will fire them!"

The expert made the rounds with his clipboard in hand and finally returned to Henry Ford's office with his report. "I've found a problem with one of your administrators," he said. "Every time I walked by, he was sitting with his feet propped up on the desk. The man never does a thing. I definitely think you should consider getting rid of him!" When Henry Ford learned the name of the man the expert was referring to, Ford shook his head and said, "I can't fire him. I pay that man to do nothing but think—and that's what he's doing."

**The song, "Who's Afraid of the Big Bad Wolf?"** became enormously popular with Americans fighting the Great Depression in the 1930s. But how it became a hit surprised even its creators.

The song was in Walt Disney's animated cartoon, "Three Little Pigs," which opened at New York's Radio City Music Hall in May 1933. Disney expected a good response but, to his disappointment, critics and audiences were ho-hum about it.

Then the lightning struck. After the movie was shown in other theaters, it suddenly caught on. Radio stations and band leaders were asking Disney for permission to play one of the songs featured in the film: "Who's Afraid of the Big Bad Wolf?"

Disney hadn't even arranged to publish the music, and to meet demands for sheet music, he had to send musicians with flashlights into darkened theaters to copy down words and music from the screen.

The song soon swept the country as a plucky response to the grinding economic times. Even President Roosevelt said the movie was one of his favorites.

**Don Keough was president and chief operating officer of the Coca-Cola Company.** The following are what he calls "Keough's Commandments for Losing."

1. Quit taking risks.
2. Be content.
3. Before you make any move, always ask yourself, "What will the investors think?"
4. Avoid change.
5. Be totally inflexible—stay on the course, no matter what.
6. Rely totally on research and experts to make decisions for you.
7. Be more concerned with status than service.
8. Concentrate on your competitor instead of your customers.
9. Put yourself first in everything you do, ahead of your customers and suppliers.
10. Memorize the formula "TGE...That's Good Enough" to set a ceiling on quality.
11. Then add a bonus rule:
12. Find a way to rationalize the slowing of growth.

**The following are Wal-Mart founder Sam Walton's rules for success:**

1. Commit with a passion to your business.
2. Share profits with your employees. If you treat them as partners, they will treat you as a partner, and together you will perform beyond your wildest dreams.
3. Motivate your partners. Money and ownership are not enough. Set high goals, encourage competition, and then keep score.
4. Communicate everything you can to your employees. The more they know, the more they will understand. Information is power, and the gain you get from empowering your associates more than offsets any risk of informing your competitors.
5. Show appreciation for a job well done.
6. Celebrate success, and in those inevitable failures, find some humor. Don't take it so seriously.

7. Listen to everyone in your company, especially the ones who actually talk to customers. They really know what's going on out there.

8. Exceed your customers' expectations and they'll always come back.

9. Control your expenses better than your competition.

10. Swim upstream. If everyone else is going it one way, there is a good chance you can find your niche by going in the opposite direction.

**Seymour Cray, the founder of Cray Research and legendary free spirit in the management community,** was once asked—according to a story in *The Wall Street Journal*—to produce a one-year and a five-year plan. The next day, he produced two three-ring binders, each containing a single sheet of paper. In the first binder, Cray had written,"Five-Year Plan: To produce the world's fastest computers."

The sheet in the second binder read, "One-Year Plan: To complete one-fifth of the Five-Year Plan."

**When looking at products,** it's important to realize that the dynamics of change can make a product obsolete, almost overnight. Just think about a few examples:

• Vacuum tubes were replaced by semiconductors.

• Propeller planes by jets.

• Cloth diapers by paper diapers.

• Vinyl records by cassette tapes and now compact discs.

• Wood tennis rackets by carbide.

• And digital watches by quartz.

**Where do we get the word "chairman"?** It comes from the custom during the Middle Ages when the master of the house and his lady were the only ones who owned and sat on chairs. The rest of the household, although it shared a communal dining table, sat on stools or cushions at a lower level. Guests of great importance was honored by being invited to "take the chair."

**"None of us should have been surprised** by the recent census figures that show that government—local, state, and federal—now employs more people than all manufacturing concerns in America combined. Or that the Justice Department has more lawyers than the 10 largest law firms in America combined. Or that the Commerce Department has more people than Microsoft, Apple Computer, and Compaq Computer combined.

"During the last 50 years, when the number of American farmers declined by nearly two-thirds, the number of Department of Agriculture employees increased by one-third."

—Norman R. Augustine, CEO of Martin Marietta Corporation

---

# How to Give a Damn Good Speech

**Louis Armstrong's reply** to a question about the definition of jazz: "Man, if you gotta ask, you'll never know."

**The trouble presidents encounter in consensus-building** reminds me of the dilemma Abraham Lincoln faced when he presided over a nation that was split down the middle on the issue of slavery. In 1863 Lincoln, perplexed and worried about the future of a nation breaking apart at the seams, wrote one of the most profound statements about human rights of all time, the Emancipation Proclamation.

He took these ideas to his cabinet, which numbered only six then, and he asked for consensus. He asked for their support.

The vote was two "ayes," five "nays."

Lincoln announced the vote as recorded, two "ayes," five "nays." And he, said, "the 'ayes' have it."

**Once when Muhammad Ali was flying,** the stewardess came over and asked him to fasten his seatbelt. Ali told the stewardess, "Superman don't need no seatbelt."

The stewardess replied, "Champ, Superman don't need no plane."

**During Christmas break from college,** the kid wanted to borrow his father's car to drive to a New Year's Eve party at his fraternity house. He lived in Massachusetts and the fraternity house was in Vermont. The father needed the car New Year's Day, and was concerned about the son hitting one of the roadblocks that police set up over the holiday.

The agreement that was reached was that the son would be allowed to use the car, but he would not drink at all.

So he drove to Vermont, got completely trashed, and attempted to drive home. Just before he reached Massachusetts, he hit a roadblock. There were a few other cars stopped already, so he was told to get out of the car and stand in a line of people that were being administered the infamous sobriety test. Somehow the policeman skipped him, and he was left standing off to the side while the people behind him were showing the police officer how well they could touch their finger to their nose, walk a straight line, etc.

At 7 a.m., his father got up to answer the doorbell. There were two state troopers there; one from Vermont and one from Massachusetts. They immediately asked him if he was the owner of a Ford Taurus. He replied, "Yes, I am." One of the policeman asked him if he was driving the car the previous evening, and he said that his son had been the driver. The police officer asked to speak to his son.

When the kid found himself in front of the two state troopers, he knew he was in some sort of trouble. But he also realized that his blood alcohol level had come down considerably, and that he would pass any test they might give him. So upon questioning, he admitted that he was driving the car, that he had been in Vermont, but when asked if he had been drinking he said, "No!" When the policemen asked if they could see his car, the kid was unable to remember the drive, and was worried that he may have hit something or someone. He said that the car was out back under the car port.

And when the four of them walked out to look at the car, instead of looking at the car he had driven the night before, there was a Vermont State Police cruiser parked there.

**Nearly everyone knows that Judith Martin,** better known as the syndicated columnist Miss Manners, is exceedingly correct. She saw an advertisement in the newspaper that a Maryland jewelry store was having a sale in her silver pattern. Upon arriving at the store, she told the jeweler she was looking for additional dessert spoons in her pattern and had been making do with the larger soup spoons.

"That's not much of a hardship," the employee said. "It is for me," Martin responded. Caught up in the moment, the saleswoman joked, "Who do you think you are, Miss Manners?"

The easily recognizable Miss Manners looked at the woman, unable to respond. And then it registered. "Oh my God!" the saleswoman said.

**Recently, in an archeological excavation in the Middle East,** a large stone tablet was unearthed. Scholars determined that it was an ancient audit report, complaining about the use of papyrus scrolls by the scribes. It was clear that such scrolls lacked the integrity of stone and clay tablets.

**Back when Hubert Humphrey was active in politics,** he and his campaign manager took a few days for a fishing trip in Northern Minnesota. While they were in a small town, a busload of tourists pulled in. Humphrey's campaign manager suggested that this was a good opportunity to impress a few voters and that he go on the bus and "pump them up" a bit—then Humphrey could go shake everybody's hand.

The manager got on the bus. However, instead of introducing his candidate he pretended to be the mayor welcoming everybody to town. Then looking toward Humphrey he said, "I guess I should mention that we have a guy here who thinks he's Hubert Humphrey, and he does look and talk an awful lot like Hubert Humphrey. But he's a harmless fellow and we kind of like him, so we'd appreciate it if you would just kind of be nice to him."

After Humphrey shook their hands he commented on how strangely they acted.

**A volunteer fire brigade team was trying to get down a cat** that was high up in a tree. After the work of several hours they managed to get the animal down. The owner of the cat—an older lady—was happy and promised to serve the brave men a cup of coffee. The chief said, "Thanks but we'll have to go back to the station." They got up in their fire engines and drove away, running over the cat.

---

# How to Give a Damn Good Speech

**One Sunday late in Lent,** a Sunday School teacher decided to ask her class what they remembered about Easter. The first little fellow suggested that Easter was when all the family comes to the house and they eat a big turkey and watch football. The teacher suggested that perhaps he was thinking of Thanksgiving, not Easter, so she let a pretty young girl answer. She said Easter was the day when as you come down the stairs in the morning you see all the beautiful presents under the tree. At this point, the teacher was really feeling discouraged. But after explaining that the girl was probably thinking about Christmas, she called on a lad with his hand tentatively raised in the air. Her spirits immediately perk up as the boy says that Easter is the time when Jesus was crucified and buried. She felt she had gotten through to at least one child until he added, "And then He comes out of the grave and if He sees His shadow we have six more weeks of winter."

**During the early 1990s,** an economist was asked to talk to a group of business people about the recession. She tacked up a big sheet of white paper. Then she made a black spot on the paper with her pencil and asked a man in the front row what he saw. The man replied promptly, "A black spot." The speaker asked every person the same question, and each replied, "A black spot." With calm and deliberate emphasis the speaker said: "Yes, there is a little black spot, but none of you mentioned the big sheet of white paper. And that's my speech."

**Thanks to the poet Henry Wadsworth Longfelow,** everyone has heard of the "midnight ride of Paul Revere." But few have heard of Israel Bissel, a humble post rider on the Boston-New York route.

After the Battle of Lexington and Concord on April 19, 1775, Bissel was ordered to raise the alarm in New Haven, Connecticut. He reached Worchester, Massachusetts, normally a day's ride, in two hours. There, according to tradition, his horse promptly dropped dead. Pausing only to get another mount, Bissel pressed on and by April 22 was in New Haven—but he didn't stop there! He rode on to New York, arriving April 24, and then stayed in the saddle until he reached Philadelphia the next day. Bissel's 126-hour, 345-mile ride signaled American militia units throughout the Northeast to mobilize for war.

**During the Revolutionary War,** a loyalist spy appeared at the headquarters of Hessian commander Colonel Johann Rall, carrying an urgent message. General George Washington and his Continental army had secretly crossed the Delaware River that morning and were advancing on Trenton, New Jersey, where the Hessians were encamped.

The spy was denied an audience with the commander and instead wrote his message on a piece of paper. A porter took the note to the Hessian colonel, but because Rall was involved in a poker game he stuffed the unread note into his pocket. When the guards at the Hessian camp began firing their muskets in a futile attempt to stop Washington's army, Rall was still playing cards.

---

Without time to organize, the Hessian army was captured. The battle occurred the day after Christmas, 1776, giving the colonists a late present—their first major victory of the war.

**David Erikson of Chatham, Massachusetts,** an editor with the Adams-Laux Publishing Company, walked into the office one day to find himself the only man employed with the business. The next day, a sign on the men's room door was covered with a new, hand-made sign that read, "Dave's Room."

**You never know where inspiration may come from.** L. Frank Baum, author of *The Wizard of Oz*, had finished the outline to the story, but hadn't come up with the name of the enchanted land where Dorothy, the Tin Man, Scarecrow, and the Cowardly Lion sought the help of the Wizard. As he gathered up his files, Baum's eyes fell upon a drawer in his filing cabinet marked, "O-Z."

# Part 5

# 250 Great Quotations

You've found throughout this book some fantastic quotations to use for openers, and to reinforce other components of your speech. In this chapter, I've collected an additional 250 great quotes for your consideration.

Of course, voluminous collections of great quotations are available in the book stores and libraries, and I recommend you have a good one on hand. But I think you'll find this chapter a handy source for powerful sayings that will add impact to your speeches. Many are from more obscure sources who might not be listed in other references.

Read through this chapter and highlight the quotes you like. Then next time you need to give a speech, the quotes you need will be there, simply waiting to be used at the right moment in the right speech.

1. The Wright brothers flew right through the smoke screen of impossibility.
   *Charles F. Kettering, American electrical engineer and inventor*

2. Remember, no one can make you feel inferior without your consent.
   *Eleanor Roosevelt*

3. Never doubt that a small group of thoughtful, committed citizens can change the world. Indeed, it is the only thing that ever has.
   *Margaret Mead, anthropologist*

4. Don't compromise yourself. You are all you've got.
   *Janis Joplin, singer*

5. In passing, also, I would like to say that the first time Adam had a chance he laid the blame on a woman.
   *Nancy Astor, British politician, first woman to sit in the House of Commons*

6. It's so clear that you have to cherish everyone. I think that's what I get from these older black women, that every soul is to be cherished, that every flower is to bloom.
   *Alice Walker, writer*

7. Few things are harder to put up with than the annoyance of a good example.
   *Mark Twain*

8. Many persons have a wrong idea of what constitutes true happiness. It is not attained through self-gratification but through fidelity to a worthy purpose.
   *Helen Keller*

9. I was gratified to be able to answer promptly, and I did. I said I didn't know.
   *Mark Twain*

10. Let thy speech be better than silence, or be silent.
    *Dionesius The Elder*

11. When in doubt tell the truth.
    *Mark Twain*

12. Greater than the threat of mighty armies is an idea whose time has come.
    *Victor Hugo, French novelist*

13. Everyone is ignorant, only on different subjects.
    *Will Rogers*

14. Every man has a sane spot somewhere.
    *Robert Louis Stevenson*

15. Failure, rejection and mistakes are the perfect stepping stones to success.
    *Dr. Alan Goldberg, sports psychologist*

16. A manager who spends the day talking about strategy is a person who has found a way to get paid for doing almost nothing.
    *Scott Adams, cartoonist*

17. You either have to be first, best, or different.
    *Loretta Lynn, country music singer*

18. The telephone is a good way to talk to people without having to offer them a drink.
    *Fran Lebowitz, humorist*

19. The secret of getting ahead is to get started. The secret of getting started is breaking your complex, overwhelming tasks into small manageable tasks, and then starting on the first one.
    *Mark Twain*

20. Some are born great, some achieve greatness, and some hire public-relations writers.
    *Daniel Boorstin, historian*

21. No competition, no progress.
    *Bela Karolyi, gymnastics coach*

22. Life's most persistent and urgent question is: What are you doing for others?
    *Martin Luther King, Jr.*

23. I think that maybe if women and children were in charge we would get somewhere.
    *James Thurber, humorist*

24. Self-education is, I firmly believe, the only kind of education there is.
    *Isaac Asimov, writer*

25. I do not know anyone who has got to the top without hard work. That is the recipe. It will not always get you to the top, but should get you pretty near.
    *Margaret Thatcher, British politician*

26. The dog in the kennel barks at his fleas; the dog that hunts does not feel them.
    *Chinese proverb*

27. Intuition is the source of scientific knowledge.
    *Aristotle*

28. Most time is wasted, not in hours, but in minutes. A bucket with a small hole in the bottom gets just as empty as a bucket that is deliberately kicked over.
    *Paul J. Meyer, writer*

29. We thought that because we had power, we had wisdom.
    *Steven Vincent Benet, poet*

30. We don't know half of one millionth of 1 percent about anything.
    *Thomas Alva Edison*

31. I don't give a damn for a man that can spell a word only one way.
    *Mark Twain*

32. Perhaps I know best why it is man alone who laughs: He alone suffers so deeply that he had to invent laughter.
    *Friedrich Wilhelm Nietzsche, German philosopher*

33. Everything that is done in the world is done by hope.
    *Martin Luther*

34. Experience is not what happens to you; it is what you do with what happens to you.
    *Aldous Huxley, writer*

35. It's all right letting yourself go, as long as you can get yourself back.
    *Mick Jagger, rock star*

36. Conscience is a mother-in-law whose visit never ends.
    *H. L. Mencken, American writer, editor, and critic*

37. Common sense is what tells us the earth is flat and the sun goes around it.
    *Anonymous*

38. People who claw their way to the top are not likely to find very much wrong with the system that enabled them to rise.
*Arthur Schlesinger, Jr., adviser to President John F. Kennedy*

39. Bureaucracy is a giant mechanism operated by pygmies.
*Honore De Balzac, French writer*

40. A scientist recently revealed that it took millions of years to carve out the Grand Canyon. A government job, no doubt.
*Anonymous*

41. The longer the title, the less important the job.
*George McGovern, politician*

42. I have everything now I had 20 years ago except now it's all lower.
*Gypsy Rose Lee, dancer*

43. Glory is fleeting, but obscurity is forever.
*Napoleon Bonaparte*

44. Victory goes to the player who makes the next-to-last mistake.
*Savielly Grigorievitch Tartakower, 20th-century chess master*

45. Don't be so humble—you are not that great.
*Golda Meir, Israeli prime minister to a visiting diplomat*

46. Not everything that can be counted counts, and not everything that counts can be counted.
*Albert Einstein*

47. I do not feel obliged to believe that the same God who has endowed us with sense, reason, and intellect has intended us to forego their use.
*Galileo Galilei*

48. I'm living so far beyond my income that we may almost be said to be living apart.
*e e cummings, poet*

49. I'll moider da bum.
*Heavyweight boxer Tony Galento, when asked what he thought of William Shakespeare*

50. I find that the harder I work, the more luck I seem to have.
*Thomas Jefferson*

51. Whether you think that you can, or that you can't, you are usually right.
*Henry Ford*

52. The only way to get rid of a temptation is to yield to it.
*Oscar Wilde*

53. The secret of success is to know something nobody else knows.
    *Aristotle Onassis*

54. I would have made a good Pope.
    *Richard M. Nixon*

55. The mistakes are all waiting to be made.
    *Savielly Grigorievitch Tartakower, chess master, on the game's opening position*

56. Reality is merely an illusion, albeit a very persistent one.
    *Albert Einstein*

57. One of the symptoms of an approaching nervous breakdown is the belief that one's work is terribly important.
    *Bertrand Russell, 20th-century philosopher and mathematician*

58. If you haven't got anything nice to say about anybody, come sit next to me.
    *Alice Roosevelt Longworth*

59. In the end, everything is a gag.
    *Charlie Chaplin*

60. You got to be careful if you don't know where you're going, because you might not get there.
    *Yogi Berra*

61. He who hesitates is a damned fool.
    *Mae West*

62. The graveyards are full of indispensable men.
    *Charles de Gaulle*

63. I am not young enough to know everything.
    *Oscar Wilde*

64. Everywhere I go I'm asked if I think the university stifles writers. My opinion is that they don't stifle enough of them.
    *Flannery O'Connor, writer*

65. Anything that is too stupid to be spoken is sung.
    *Voltaire*

66. I don't know anything about music. In my line you don't have to.
    *Elvis Presley*

67. Vote early and vote often.
    *Al Capone*

68. If I were two-faced, would I be wearing this one?
    *Abraham Lincoln*

# How to Give a Damn Good Speech

69. Iron rusts from disuse; water loses its purity from stagnation and in cold weather becomes frozen; even so does inaction sap the mind.
*Leonardo da Vinci*

70. Distrust any enterprise that requires new clothes.
*Henry David Thoreau*

71. Every day I get up and look through the Forbes list of the richest people in America. If I'm not there, I go to work.
*Robert Orben, writer*

72. Nothing is wrong with California that a rise in the ocean level wouldn't cure.
*Ross MacDonald, writer*

73. Do what you can, with what you have, where you are.
*Theodore Roosevelt*

74. Always do right—this will gratify some and astonish the rest.
*Mark Twain*

75. America, anybody can be president. That's one of the risks you take.
*Adlai Stevenson*

76. No man has a good enough memory to make a successful liar.
*Abraham Lincoln*

77. Never mistake motion for action.
*Ernest Hemingway*

78. A pessimist sees the difficulty in every opportunity; an optimist sees the opportunity in every difficulty.
*Sir Winston Churchill*

79. I think it would be a good idea.
*Mahatma Gandhi, when asked what he thought about Western civilization*

80. The only thing necessary for the triumph of evil is for good men to do nothing.
*Edmund Burke, 18th-century Irish political leader and author*

81. I'm not a member of any organized political party—I'm a Democrat!
*Will Rogers*

82. The mystery of government is not how Washington works but how to make it stop.
*P. J. O'Rourke, writer*

83. Denial ain't just a river in Egypt.
*Mark Twain*

84. A pint of sweat saves a gallon of blood.
*General George S. Patton*

85. He can compress the most words into the smallest idea of any man I know.
    *Abraham Lincoln*

86. The difference between fiction and reality? Fiction has to make sense.
    *Tom Clancy, writer*

87. When I was kidnapped, my parents snapped into action. They rented out my room.
    *Woody Allen*

88. It is better to be feared than loved, if you cannot be both.
    *Machiavelli*

89. There's many a best-seller that could have been prevented by a good teacher.
    *Flannery O'Connor*

90. The average person puts only 25 percent of his energy and ability into his work. The world takes off its hat to those who put in more than 50 percent of their capacity, and stands on its head for those few and far between souls who devote 100 percent.
    *Andrew Carnegie*

91. It is all one to me if a man comes from Sing Sing or Harvard. We hire a man, not his history.
    *Henry Ford*

92. Ability is the art of getting credit for all the home runs somebody else hits.
    *Casey Stengel, baseball manager*

93. Men have become the tools of their tools.
    *Henry David Thoreau*

94. One never repents on having spoken too little, but often of having spoken too much.
    *Philippe De Commynes*

95. Tact is the ability to describe others as they see themselves.
    *Abraham Lincoln*

96. You have to have something to make you want to get out of bed in the morning. Look at it this way, when you wake up in the morning, get up. And when you get up, do something. The most important thing is to have a point, a direction you're headed. If kids had that, it would help them over any rough spots in life. If you can get a kid to fall in love with something, his lifestyle will go in that direction. It doesn't have to be anything fancy, just something.
    *George Burns*

97. It's not the size of the dog in the fight, it's the size of the fight in the dog.
    *Mark Twain*

98. In Germany they came first for the Communists, and I didn't speak up because I wasn't a Communist. Then they came for the Jews, and I didn't speak up because I wasn't a Jew. Then they came for the trade unionists, and I didn't speak up because I wasn't a trade unionist. Then they came for the Catholics, and I didn't speak up because I was a Protestant. Then they came for me, and by that time no one was left to speak up.
*Martin Niemoeller, German Lutheran pastor*

99. Even if you're on the right track, you'll get run over if you just sit there.
*Will Rogers*

100. The time for action is past! Now is the time for senseless bickering!
*Ashleigh Brilliant, writer*

101. For every action there is an equal and opposite government program.
*Bob Wells, comedian*

102. You can get more with a kind word and a gun than you can with a kind word alone.
*Al Capone*

103. Obstacles are those frightful things you see when you take your eyes off your goal.
*Henry Ford*

104. Some men are born mediocre, some men achieve mediocrity, and some men have mediocrity thrust upon them.
*Joseph Heller, writer*

105. There is more to life than increasing its speed.
*Mohandas K. Gandhi*

106. Never eat anything at one sitting that you can't lift.
*Miss Piggy*

107. Never play cards with a man called Doc. Never eat in a place called Mom's. Never sleep with a woman whose troubles are worse than your own.
*Nelsen Algren, writer*

108. A word to the wise ain't necessary, it is the stupid ones who need all the advice.
*Bill Cosby, entertainer*

109. I have found the best way to give advice to your children is to find out what they want and advise them to do it.
*Harry S Truman*

110. Never advise anyone to go to war or to get married.
*Anonymous*

111. I love being married. It's so great to find that one special person you want to annoy for the rest of your life.
*Rita Rudner, comedian*

112. Argument is the worst sort of conversation.
*Jonathan Swift, author*

113. The foolish and the dead alone never change their opinion.
*James Russell Lowell, editor and diplomat*

114. Every child is an artist. The problem is how to remain an artist once he grows up.
*Pablo Picasso*

115. Trying to understand modern art is like trying to follow the plot in a bowl of alphabet soup.
*Anonymous*

116. A bank is a place that will lend you money if you can prove that you don't need it.
*Bob Hope*

117. This will never be a civilized country until we expend more money for books than we do for chewing gum.
*Elbert Hubbard, philosopher and writer*

118. This is not a novel to be tossed aside lightly. It should be thrown with great force.
*Dorothy Parker, American author and wit*

119. Be careful about reading health books. You may die of a misprint.
*Mark Twain*

120. The longer I live the more beautiful life becomes.
*Frank Lloyd Wright*

121. The cynics are right nine times out of ten.
*H.L. Mencken, writer*

122. I don't know the key to success, but the key to failure is trying to please everybody.
*Bill Cosby, entertainer*

123. There's no business like show business, but there are several businesses like accounting.
*David Letterman*

124. I find it rather easy to portray a businessman. Being bland, rather cruel and incompetent comes naturally to me.
*John Cleese, comedian and actor*

125. There is a certain relief in change, even though it be from bad to worse; as I have found in traveling a stagecoach, that it is often a comfort to shift one's position and be bruised in a new place.
*Washington Irving, author*

126. Today, loving change, tumult, even chaos is a prerequisite for survival, let alone success.
*Tom Peters, author and management guru*

127. The unexamined life is not worth living.
*Socrates*

128. If the facts don't fit the theory, change the facts.
*Albert Einstein*

129. The trouble with our times is that the future is not what it used to be.
*Paul Valery*

130. Progress is a nice word. But change is its motivator and change has its enemies.
*Robert F. Kennedy*

131. There is nothing more difficult to take in hand, more perilous to conduct, or more uncertain in its success, than to take the lead in the introduction of a new order of things, because the innovator has for enemies all those who have done well under the old conditions and lukewarm defenders in those who may do well under the new.
*Machiavelli*

132. The thing that impresses me the most about America is the way parents obey their children.
*King Edward VIII*

133. Grown-ups never understand anything for themselves, and it is tiresome for children to be always and forever explaining things to them.
*Antoine de Saint-Exupery, author of* The Little Prince

134. Take away love and our earth is a tomb.
*Robert Browning*

135. Never raise your hand to your children; it leaves your midsection unprotected.
*Robert Orben, humorist*

136. Human beings are the only creatures that allow their children to come back home.
*Bill Cosby*

137. Even when freshly washed and relieved of all obvious confections, children tend to be sticky.
*Fran Lebowitz, writer*

138. More than any other time in history, mankind faces a crossroads. One path leads to despair and utter hopelessness. The other, to total extinction. Let us pray we have the wisdom to choose correctly.
*Woody Allen*

139. If computers get too powerful, we can organize them into a committee—that will do them in.
*Anonymous*

140. A committee is a cul-de-sac down which ideas are lured and then quietly strangled.
*Anonymous*

141. A camel is a horse invented by a committee.
*Anonymous*

142. There is no monument dedicated to the memory of a committee.
*Anonymous*

143. Common sense is the collection of prejudices acquired by age 18.
*Albert Einstein*

144. Everybody gets so much information all day long that they lose their common sense.
*Gertrude Stein*

145. Death is life's way of telling you you've been fired.
*Anonymous*

146. It's not that I'm afraid to die; I just don't want to be there when it happens.
*Woody Allen*

147. Democracy means that anyone can grow up to be president, and anyone who doesn't grow up can be vice president.
*Johnny Carson*

148. When you get to the end of your rope, tie a knot and hang on.
*Franklin D. Roosevelt*

149. Diplomacy is the art of saying "Nice doggie" until you can find a rock.
*Will Rogers*

150. Dreams have but one owner at a time. That is why dreamers are lonely.
*Erma Bombeck*

151. When I read about the evils of drinking, I gave up reading.
*Henny Youngman, comedian*

152. Economics is extremely useful as a form of employment for economists.
*John Kenneth Galbraith, economist and author*

153. Education's purpose is to replace an empty mind with an open one.
     *Malcolm S. Forbes, former publisher* Forbes *magazine*

154. Education is the ability to listen to almost anything without losing your temper.
     *Robert Frost, poet*

155. Try this sometime. Get a group of children in a room with a light fixture hanging just out of their grasp. Then watch what happens: One child will jump to touch it, and before you know it, every kid in the room will be leaping like Michael Jordan. They're testing their skill, stimulated by the challenge of reaching something beyond their normal grasp. Put the same children in a room where everything is easily in reach, and there will be no jumping, no competition, no challenges. The problem with American education is a low ceiling of expectations. We have built schools that demand and teach too little, and the children have stopped jumping.
     *Carroll Campbell, educator*

156. It is only when we forget our learning, do we begin to know.
     *Henry David Thoreau*

157. It is a miracle that curiosity survives formal education.
     *Anonymous*

158. There is no easy method of learning difficult things. The method is to close the door, give out that you are not at home, and work.
     *Albert Einstein*

159. Man is the only animal that blushes. Or needs to.
     *Mark Twain*

160. Whenever I'm caught between two evils, I take the one I've never tried.
     *Mae West*

161. I have discovered that all human evil comes from this—man's being unable to sit still in a room.
     *Blaise Pascal, scientist and philosopher*

162. Example is not the main thing in influencing others. It is the only thing.
     *Albert Schweitzer*

163. If you can't imitate him, don't copy him.
     *Yogi Berra*

164. Experience is that marvelous thing that enables you to recognize a mistake when you make it again.
     *Anonymous*

165. Faith isn't faith until it's all you're holding on to.
     *Anonymous*

166. I am convinced that it is not fear of death, of our lives ending, that haunts our sleep so much as the fear that our lives will not have mattered, that as far as the world is concerned, we might as well never have lived. What we miss in our lives, no matter how much we have, is that sense of meaning.
*Harold Kushner, author and rabbi*

167. Always do what you are afraid to do.
*Ralph Waldo Emerson*

168. Be strong and of good courage, do not fear or be in dread of them: for it is the Lord your God who goes with you; he will not fail you or forsake you.
*Deuteronomy 31:6*

169. Puritanism: The haunting fear that someone, somewhere, may be happy.
*H. L. Mencken*

170. A free society is a place where it's safe to be unpopular.
*Adlai Stevenson*

171. Well, if crime fighters fight crime and fire fighters fight fire, what do freedom fighters fight? They never mention that part to us, do they?
*George Carlin*

172. Friend: Someone who overlooks your failures and tolerates your successes.
*Anonymous*

173. To find out a girl's faults, praise her to her girl friends.
*Benjamin Franklin*

174. A mirror reflects a man's face, but what he is really like is shown by the kind of friends he chooses.
*Proverbs 27:19*

175. Friends help you move. Real friends help you move dead bodies.
*Anonymous*

176. Only a life lived for others is worth living.
*Albert Einstein*

177. Too many people are ready to carry the stool when the piano needs to be moved.
*Anonymous*

178. It is more blessed to give than to receive.
*Acts 20:35*

179. Parents were invented to make children happy by giving them something to ignore.
*Ogden Nash, poet*

180. There's no trick to being a humorist when you have the whole government working for you.
*Will Rogers*

181. I always wanted to be somebody, but I should have been more specific.
*Lily Tomlin*

182. Men can only be happy when they do not assume that the object of life is happiness.
*George Orwell*

183. Until further notice, celebrate everything.
*Anonymous*

184. People are just about as happy as they make up their minds to be.
*Abraham Lincoln*

185. Reality's the only obstacle to happiness.
*Anonymous*

186. Health is merely the slowest possible rate at which one can die.
*Anonymous*

187. Early to rise and early to bed makes a male healthy and wealthy and dead.
*James Thurber*

188. Health nuts are going to feel stupid someday, lying in hospitals dying of nothing.
*Redd Foxx, comedian*

189. Start every day off with a smile—and get it over with.
*W.C. Fields*

190. Put all your eggs in one basket, and watch the basket.
*Mark Twain*

191. The best measure of a man's honesty isn't his income tax return. It's the zero adjust on his bathroom scale.
*Anonymous*

192. Honesty is the best image.
*Ziggy, cartoon character*

193. There are three kinds of lies: lies, damned lies, and statistics.
*Benjamin Disraeli, 19th-century British prime minister*

194. The human race has one really effective weapon, and that is laughter.
*Mark Twain*

195. The human race is faced with a cruel choice: work or daytime television.
*Anonymous*

196. Nobody knows the age of the human race, but everybody agrees that it is old enough to know better.
*Anonymous*

197. When pride comes, then comes disgrace, but with humility comes wisdom.
*Proverbs 11:2*

198. Some grow with responsibility, others just swell.
*Anonymous*

199. Everything is funny as long as it is happening to Somebody Else.
*Will Rogers*

200. We will be known forever by the tracks we leave.
*Dakota Indian proverb*

201. I don't care to belong to any organization that accepts me as a member.
*Groucho Marx*

202. To be nobody but yourself in a world which is doing its best, night and day, to make you like everybody else, means to fight the hardest battle which any human being can fight; and never stop fighting.
*e e cummings*

203. If you can't be funny, be interesting.
*Harold Ross*, New Yorker *editor*

204. Some men see things as they are and ask why. Others dream things that never were and ask why not.
*George Bernard Shaw*

205. The test of a first-rate intelligence is the ability to hold two opposed ideas in the mind at the same time, and still retain the ability to function.
*F. Scott Fitzgerald*

206. Everyone is entitled to be stupid, but some abuse the privilege.
*Anonymous*

207. Don't you wish there were a knob on the TV to turn up the intelligence? There's one marked "Brightness," but it doesn't work.
*Gallagher, comedian*

208. The mass of men lead lives of quite desperation.
*Henry David Thoreau*

209. Only the shallow know themselves.
*Oscar Wilde*

210. If stupidity got us into this mess, then why can't it get us out?
*Will Rogers*

211. With the exception of man, no being wonders at his own existence.
*Arthur Schopenhauer, philosopher*

212. Too many people are thinking of security instead of opportunity. They seem more afraid of life than death.
*James F. Byrnes, business guru*

213. Keep true, never be ashamed of doing right; decide on what you think is right, and stick to it.
*George Eliot, novelist*

214. You take all the experience and judgment of men over 50 out of the world and there wouldn't be enough left over to run it.
*Henry Ford*

215. Never ask the barber if you need a haircut.
*Philip Theibert, writer*

216. The world of the '90s and beyond will not belong to managers or those who make the numbers dance, as we used to say, or those who are conversant with all the business and jargon we use to sound smart. The world will belong to passionate, driven leaders—people who not only have an enormous amount of energy but who can energize those whom they lead.
*Jack Welch, CEO of General Electric*

217. I'll tell you what makes a great manager: A great manager has a knack for making ballplayers think they are better than they are. He forces you to have a good opinion of yourself. He lets you know he belives in you. He makes you get more out of yourself. And once you learn how good you really are, you never settle for playing anything less than your best.
*Reggie Jackson, baseball star*

218. Good listeners generally make more sales than good talkers.
*Anonymous*

219. The reason why worry kills more people than work is that more people worry than work.
*Robert Frost*

220. Women like quiet men because they think they are listening.
*Anonymous*

221. Life is something that happens when you can't get to sleep.
*Fran Lebowitz, writer*

222. I love deadlines. I like the whooshing sound they make as they fly by.
*Douglas Adams, science-fiction writer*

223. The man is a success who has lived well, laughed often and loved much; who has gained the respect of intelligent men and the love of children; who has filled his niche and accomplished his task; who leaves the world better than he found it, whether by an improved poppy, a perfect poem or a rescued soul; who never lacked appreciation of earth's beauty or failed to express it; who looked for the best in others and gave the best he had.
*Robert Louis Stevenson*

224. My doctor told me to stop having intimate dinners for four. Unless there are three other people.
*Orson Welles*

225. I told the doctor I broke my leg in two places. He told me to quit going to those places.
*Henny Youngman, comedian*

226. You're never too old to grow younger.
*Mae West*

227. An invasion of armies can be resisted; an invasion of ideas cannot be resisted.
*Victor Hugo, author*

228. The mind is like a parachute. It doesn't work if it is not open.
*Anonymous*

229. Boys will be boys, and so will a lot of middle-aged men.
*Anonymous*

230. Being a woman is a terribly difficult trade, since it consists pricipally of dealing with men.
*Joseph Conrad, writer*

231. A billion here, a billion there, pretty soon it adds up to real money.
*Senator Everett Dirksen*

232. A man who stands for nothing will fall for anything.
*Malcolm X*

233. There's an old saying, "Never send a boy to do a man's job, send a lady."
*John F. Kennedy*

234. There is no deodorant like success.
*Elizabeth Taylor*

235. Definition of Insanity: Doing the same thing over and over, and expecting a different result.
*Anonymous*

236. The trouble with the future is that they keep moving it closer.
*Anonymous*

237. Having served on various committees, I have drawn up a list of rules. Never arrive on time; this stamps you as a beginner. Don't say anything until the meeting is half over; this stamps you as being wise. Be as vague as possible; this avoids irritating the others. When in doubt, suggest that a subcommittee be appointed. Be the first to move for adjournment; this will make you popular; it's what everyone is waiting for.
*Anonymous*

238. "The Man Who Thinks He Can"

If you think you are beaten, you are;
If you think you dare not, you don't.
If you like to win, but think you can't,
It's almost a cinch you won't.
If you think you'll lose, you're lost,
For out in the world we find
Success begins with a fellow's will;
It's all in the state of mind.

If you think you're outclassed, you are;
You've got to be sure of yourself before
You can ever win a prize.
Life's battles don't always go
To the stronger or faster man;
But soon or late the man who wins
Is the man who thinks he can.

*Walter D. Wintle, American poet*

239. In the end, all business operations can be reduced to three words: people, product, and profits. People come first.
*Lee Iacocca, American business legend*

240. It's a healthy thing now and then to hang a question mark on the things you have long taken for granted.
*Bertrand Russell, philosopher and mathematician*

241. Speech is civilization itself. The word, even the most contradictious word, preserves contact—it is silence which isolates.
*Thomas Mann, author*

242. How often we are listening to yesterday when today stands ready to speak.
*Joan Walsh Anglund, writer and illustrator*

243. The average sale is made after the prospect has said "no" six times.
*Jeffrey P. Davidson, marketing consultant*

244. The person who says it cannot be done should not interrupt the person doing it.
*Chinese proverb*

245. Nothing will ever be attempted, if all possible objections must be first overcome.
*Samuel Johnson*

246. There can be no fairer ambition than to excel in talk; to be affable, gay, ready, clear, and welcome.
*Robert Louis Stevenson*

247. If in the last few years you haven't discarded a major opinion or acquired a new one, check your pulse. You may be dead.
*Frank Gelett Burgess, American designer and author*

248. To get money you must spend it.
*Titus Maccius Plautus (254-184 B.C.), Roman playwright*

249. Good ideas and innovations must be driven into existence by courageous patience.
*Hyman G. Rickover, American admiral*

250. Make no little plans, they have no magic to stir men's blood and probably themselves will not be realized. Make big plans; aim high in hope and work, remembering that a noble, logical diagram once recorded will never die, but long after we are gone will be a living thing, asserting itself with ever-growing insistency. Remember that our sons and grandsons are going to do things that would stagger us. Let your watchword be order and your beacon beauty.
*Daniel H. Burnham, architect and city planner; built Chicago's first skyscraper*

# Part Six

# Almanac

...................................................................................................................................

The information in this section can be very useful when you are putting together a speech. When you know what date you're giving the speech on, go to this almanac and find out what happened on that date. Chances are you'll find something useful to weave into your speech. Here are a few examples:

- Today is February 21 and an invention was installed for the first time on this date. This invention proves that society has always worried about the problem of crime. The invention? The first electric burglar alarm was installed Boston on this date.

- I am not up here to tell you stories. You see today, February 24 is the birthday of Wilhelm Karl Grimm...the famous fairy tale teller. I don't think I can beat him at telling stories, so today, I'll tell you the plain truth.

- Today, March 30, is a day it became easier to correct our mistakes. You see, on this date, 1858, Hyman L. Lipman of Philadelphia patented a pencil with an attached eraser. We all make mistakes ....

- On this date, April 10, 1849, the safety pin was patented by Walter Hunt of New York City. He immediately sold the patent rights for $100. I think there is a lesson there. Don't always jump at the first offer.

## January 1

### Birthdays

1735 Paul Revere, U.S. patriot and part-time jockey

1752 Elizabeth (Betsy) Ross, flagmaker

1895 J. Edgar Hoover, former FBI director

1909 Barry Goldwater, senator

1909 John Glenn, astronaut and Ohio senator

1919 J.D. Salinger, author (*Catcher in the Rye*)

1922 Rocky Graziano, boxer

### Events

1673 Regular mail delivery began between New York City and Boston.

1772 First traveler's checks were issued in London.

1892 Ellis Island became the reception center for new immigrants.

1954 The Rose and Cotton Bowl were the first sport colorcasts.

1971 Cigarette advertisements were banned on TV.

# January 2

## Birthdays

1920 Isaac Asimov, scientist, writer

1936 Roger Miller, singer, songwriter

1939 Jim Bakker, televangelist

## Events

1890 Alice Sanger became first the female White House staffer.

1965 Joe Namath signed a contract with the New York Jets for $427,000.

1971 No fault divorce was instituted in California.

# January 3

## Birthdays

1892 J.R.R. Tolkien, linguist, author (*The Hobbit, Lord of the Rings*)

1909 Victor Borge, pianist, comedian

1956 Mel Gibson, actor

## Events

1870 Work on the Brooklyn Bridge begun (completed on May 24, 1883).

1888 First drinking straw was patented by M.C. Stone, Washington, D.C.

1938 First March of Dimes was organized.

# January 4

## Birthdays

1643 Sir Issac Newton, scientist

1785 Jacob Grimm, storyteller

1809 Louis Braille

1813 Sir Issac Pitman, shorthand inventor

## Events

1790 President Washington delivered the first State of the Union address.

1863 Four-wheeled roller skates were patented by James Plimpton of New York.

1885 First U.S. appendectomy was performed in Davenport, Iowa, by Dr. William Grant.

# January 5

## Birthdays

1779 Zebulon Montgomery Pike (discoverer of Pikes Peak, Colorado)

1855 King Camp Gillette, inventor of the safety razor

1918 Jeanne Dixon, astrologer

## Events

1914 Henry Ford announced a minimum wage of $5 for an eight-hour day.

1959 Bozo the Clown begins TV show.

1987 For the first time, the U.S. budget exceeded $1 trillion.

# January 6

## Birthdays

1412 Joan of Arc, French soldier and martyr

1878 Carl Sandburg, poet

1914 Danny Thomas, entertainer

## Events

1838 Samuel Morse made the first public demonstration of telegraph.

1930 First diesel engine automobile trip was completed.

1942 First around-the-world flight was completed by the Pan Am "Pacific Clipper."

# January 7

## Birthdays

1800 Millard Fillmore, 13th President

1948 Kenny Loggins, singer

## Events

1714 The typewriter was patented (it was built years later).

1789 First national presidental election was held in the United States.

# January 8

## Birthdays

1862 Frank Nelson Doubleday, publisher and founder of Doubleday and Co.

1935 Elvis Presley, singer

## Events

1815 Battle of New Orleans made a hero out of Andrew Jackson (the War of 1812 had ended on Dec. 24, 1814, but nobody knew).

# January 9

## Birthdays

1901 Chic Young, creator of the "Blondie" comic strip

1913 Richard M. Nixon, 37th President

1941 Joan Baez, folk singer

## Events

1799 First income tax was imposed in England.

1945 General Douglas MacArthur returned to the Philippines.

# January 10

## Birthdays

1738 Ethan Allen, Revolutionary War fighter

1887 Robinson Jeffers, poet

1904 Ray Bolger, Oz's Tin Man

## Events

1776 *Common Sense* by Thomas Paine published.

1863 First underground railway opened in London.

# January 11

## Birthdays

1755 Alexander Hamilton, first Secretary of the U.S. Treasury

1807 Ezra Cornell, founded Western Union Telegraph and Cornell University

## Events

1915 Jacob Ruppert and Huston purchase New York Yankees for $460,000.

1935 Amelia Earhart flew from Hawaii to California.

# January 12

## Birthdays

1737 John Hancock, signer of the Declaration of Independence

1876 Jack London, writer

1906 Henny Youngman, comedian

## Events

1922 Mrs. Hattie Caraway became the first woman elected to U.S. Senate.

1969 The New York Jets beat Baltimore Colts in Super Bowl III.

1971 Television show *All in the Family* premieres.

# January 13

## Birthdays

1834 Horatio Alger, Jr., author

1925 Gwen Verdon, actress

1931 Charles Nelson Reilly, actor

## Events

1854 Anthony Foss obtained a patent for the accordion.

1906 First "radio set" was advertised in *Scientific American*. It claimed to receive signals up to *one mile* away. Price: $7.50.

1920 An editorial in *The New York Times* claimed rockets would never fly.

# January 14

## Birthdays

1741 Benedict Arnold, revolutionary general

1875 Albert Schweitzer, doctor, humanitarian

1920 Andy Rooney, humorist

## Events

1690 Clarinet invented in Nuremberg, Germany.

1784 The Revolutionary War formally ended.

1914 Henry Ford introduced the assembly line for his cars.

1952 *Today* show premieres on NBC.

# January 15

## Birthdays

1906 Aristotle Onassis, industrialist and shipping magnate

1908 Edward Teller, fathered the H-bomb

1929 Martin Luther King, Jr., social leader and dreamer

## Events

1861 Steam elevator was patented by Elisha Otis, forming base for his elevator company.

1870 Donkey was first used as a symbol of the Democratic Party in *Harper's Weekly*.

1948 The Pentagon Building in Washington, D.C., was completed.

1967 CBS and NBC both broadcast Super Bowl I.

# January 16

## Birthdays

1909 Ethel Merman, singer, actress

1911 Dizzy Dean, baseball player

1935 A. J. Foyt, auto racer

## Events

1920 18th Amendment, prohibition, went into effect.

1956 Egyptian President Gamel Abdel Nasser pledges to reconquer Palestine.

1991 Allied forces under U.S. command attacked Iraq.

# January 17

## Birthdays

1706 Benjamin Franklin

1942 Muhammad Ali, boxer

1944 Joe Frazier, boxer

## Events

1861 Flush toilet was patented by Mr. Thomas Crapper.

1929 Popeye made his first appearance in comic strip, *Thimble Theatre*.

1950 Great Brink's robbery was staged in Boston, at a loss of $28 million to the company.

# January 18

## Birthdays

1779 Peter Roget, English physician, wrote a thesaurus, invented the slide rule.

1782 Daniel Webster, early American orator and politician

1813 Joseph Farwell Glidden, invented first commercially usable barbed wire

1882 A.A. Milne, "father" of *Winnie the Pooh*

1892 Oliver Hardy, of the comedy team Laurel and Hardy

1904 Cary Grant, actor

1913 Danny Kaye, actor, comedian

## Events

1644 First UFO sighting America by Pilgrims in Boston.

1911 First shipboard landing of a plane (from Tanforan Park to the USS Pennsylvania).

1913 Captain Robert Falcon Scott reached the South Pole.

1919 Versailles Peace Conference.

# January 19

## Birthdays

1736 James Watt, made the steam engine workable

1807 General Robert E. Lee

1809 Edgar Allen Poe, writer

1839 Paul Cezanne, painter

1946 Dolly Parton, singer, actress

## Events

1861 Georgia became the fifth state to secede.

1886 The Aurora Ski Club, the first in the United States, was founded in Minnesota.

1903 First regular transatlantic radio broadcast between the U.S. and England.

# January 20

## Birthdays

1894 Harold L. Gray, creator of "Little Orphan Annie"

1896 Nathan Birnbaum (better known as George Burns), comedian

1937 Joan Rivers, comedian, talk show hostess

## Events

1892 First basketball game was played.

1953 First live televised coast-to-coast inauguration address.

# January 21

## Birthdays

1813 John C. Fremont, mapmaker and explorer of Western United States

1824 Lt. Gen. Thomas Jonathan "Stonewall" Jackson

1940 Jack Nicklaus, golfer

1941 Placido Domingo, tenor

## Events

1908 New York City regulation prohibited women from smoking in public.

1954 USS Nautilus, first atomic powered submarine, launched at Groton, CT.

# January 22

## Birthdays

1561 Sir Francis Bacon, philosopher, essayist

1788 Lord Byron, poet

1937 Joseph Wambaugh, police writer

## Events

1901 Britain's Queen Victoria died at 82.

1943 The Battle of Anzio.

1947 KTLA, the first commercial TV station west of the Mississippi, signed on the air in Hollywood.

1973 Supreme Court approved abortion (*Roe v. Wade*).

# January 23

## Birthdays

1756 Mozart, musical prodigy, composer

1832 Edouard Manet, French painter

1899 Humphrey Bogart, actor

## Events

1849 Mrs. Elizabeth Blackwell became the first woman physician in the U.S.

1909 First radio-assisted rescue at sea.

1964 24th Amendment ratified; barred poll tax in federal elections.

# January 24

## Birthdays

1862 Edith Wharton, novelist

1917 Ernest Borgnine, actor

1941 Neil Diamond, singer

## Events

1899 The rubber heel was patented by Humphrey O'Sullivan.

1922 Eskimo Pie was invented in Iowa by Christian K. Nelson.

1935 First cans of beer went on sale in Richmond, Virginia.

# January 25

## Birthdays

1759 Robert Burns, poet

1882 Virginia Woolf, author

1919 Edwin Newman, newscaster

## Events

1915 Alexander Bell called Thomas Watson in San Francisco from New York.

1949 First Emmy Awards were given out.

1949 First Israeli election.

1959 First transcontinental commercial jet flight (Los Angeles to New York City for $301).

1961 First live, nationally televised, presidential news conference.

# January 26

## Birthdays

1880 General Douglas MacArthur

1925 Paul Newman, actor

1961 Wayne Gretzky, hockey player

## Events

1926 Television is first demonstrated by J. L. Baird in London.

1954 Groundbreaking for Disneyland, the Magic Kingdom, in Anaheim.

1961 First woman personal physician to the President, J. G. Travell.

# January 27

## Birthdays

1832 Charles Lutwidge Dodgson (Lewis Carroll), author

1850 Samuel Gompers, first president of the American Federation of Labor

1900 Hyman G. Rickover, U.S. admiral, father of the modern nuclear navy

1948 Mikhail Baryshnikov, dancer, actor

## Events

1870 First sorority, Kappa Alpha Theta, founded at DePauw University in Greencastle, IN.

1880 Thomas Edison was granted a patent for an electric incandescent lamp.

1888 National Geographic Society was founded in Washington, D.C.

1948 First tape recorder was sold.

1973 United States and North Vietnam signed a cease-fire agreement.

# January 28

## Birthdays

1887 Arthur Rubinstein, pianist

1933 Susan Sontag, writer

1936 Alan Alda, actor

## Events

1878 George W. Coy hired as the first full-time telephone operator.

1878 First telephone exchange was established at New Haven, CT.

1915 U.S. Coast Guard was established.

1932 First state unemployment insurance act was enacted in Wisconsin.

1956 Elvis Presley's first TV appearance (*Dorsey Brothers Stage Show*).

1986 Challenger 10 exploded on takeoff. All seven crew members, including schoolteacher Christa McAuliffe, were killed.

# January 29

## Birthdays

1737 Thomas Paine, political essayist

1843 William McKinley, 25th President

1850 Lawrence Hargrave, inventor of the box kite

1860 Anton Chekhov, Russian writer

1874 John D. Rockefeller Jr., financier, founded University of Chicago

1880 Claude William Dukenfield (better known as W.C. Fields), comedian

## Events

1845 Edgar Allen Poe's *The Raven* was first published.

1861 Kansas became the 34th state.

1904 First athletic letters were given to the University of Chicago football team.

# January 30

## Birthdays

1882 Franklin D. Roosevelt, 32nd President

1930 Gene Hackman, actor

1937 Vanessa Redgrave, actress

## Events

1917 First jazz record in U.S. cut.

1933 Adolf Hitler was named German chancellor.

1941 Franklin D. Roosevelt makes his "Four Freedoms" speech.

# January 31

## Birthdays

1797 Franz Schubert, composer

1872 Zane Grey, novelist

1919 Jackie Robinson, first black Major League baseball player

## Events

1928 Scotch tape first marketed by 3M.

1950 President Truman authorized production of the H-Bomb.

1961 Ham the chimp is first animal sent into space by the United States.

# February 1

## Birthdays

1901 Clark Gable, actor

1904 S. J. Perelman, humorist

## Events

1790 U.S. Supreme Court convened for the first time, in New York City.

1920 The first armored car is introduced.

# February 2

## Birthdays

1882 James Joyce, writer

1938 Tom Smothers, comedian

1947 Farrah Fawcett, actress

## Events

1876 National Baseball League formed with eight teams.

1935 Lie detector first used in court at Portage, WI.

1981 *Late Night with David Letterman* premieres.

# February 3

## Birthdays

1811 Horace Greeley, editor (told young men to go west)

1907 James Michener, writer

1918 Joey Bishop, comedian

## Events

1815 World's first commercial cheese factory is established in Switzerland.

1966 Luna 9, first lunar landing.

# February 4

## Birthdays

1902 Charles A. Lindbergh, "Lucky Lindy"

1921 Betty Friedan, activist, writer

1947 Dan Quayle, U.S. vice-president

## Events

1824 J.W. Goodrich introduces rubber galoshes to the public.

1847 First U.S. telegraph company established, in Maryland.

1957 First electric portable typewriter placed on sale at Syracuse, NY.

# February 5

## Birthdays

1840 John Boyd Dunlop, developed the pneumatic rubber tire

1878 Andre-Gustave Citroen, French automaker

1900 Adlai E. Stevenson, statesman

1919 Red Buttons, comedian, actor

## Events

1825 Hannah Lord Montague of New York grabs her scissors and creates the first detachable collar on one of her husband's shirts, in order to reduce her laundry load.

1921 New York Yankees purchase 20 acres in the Bronx for Yankee Stadium.

# February 6

## Birthdays

1895 George Herman "Babe" Ruth

1911 Ronald Reagan, 40th President

1919 Zsa Zsa Gabor, actress

## Events

1952 Elizabeth II becomes queen of Great Britain.

1968 Former President Dwight Eisenhower shot a hole-in-one.

# February 7

## Birthdays

1804 John Deere, pioneer manufacturer of agricultural implements

1812 Charles Dickens, author

1885 Sinclair Lewis, writer

1962 Garth Brooks, musician

## Events

1827 Ballet introduced to the U.S. at Bowery Theatre, New York City.

1882 Last bare-knuckle champion John L. Sullivan KOs Paddy Ryan in Mississippi.

# February 8

## Birthdays

1820 William Tecumseh Sherman, Civil War general

1828 Jules Verne, author who pioneered science fiction

1906 Chester F. Carlson, invented xerography

1931 James Dean, actor (*Rebel Without a Cause*)

## Events

1861 Confederate States of America formed.

1883 Louis Waterman begins experiments that lead to invention of the fountain pen.

1908 Boy Scouts of America founded.

1957 NY Public Library's bookmobile starts in front of City Hall.

# February 9

## Birthdays

1773 William Henry Harrison, 9th President

1914 Carmen Miranda, singer, actress

1941 Carole King, singer

## Events

1877 U.S. Weather Service is founded.

1895 Volleyball is invented by W.G. Morgan in Massachusetts.

1964 First appearance of the Beatles on the *Ed Sullivan Show*.

# February 10

## Birthdays

1893 Jimmy Durante, comedian

1950 Mark Spitz, swimmer

1955 Greg Norman, golfer

## Events

1763 Treaty of Paris ends the French and Indian War.

1870 YWCA is founded in New York City.

1942 Glenn Miller's "Chattanooga Choo Choo" goes gold.

# February 11

## Birthdays

1847 Thomas Alva Edison, inventor

1925 Virginia Johnson, doctor

1936 Burt Reynolds, actor

## Events

1958 First flight with black stewardess, R. C. Taylor, Ithaca, NY.

1968 Madison Square Garden III closes. M.S.G. IV opens.

# February 12

## Birthdays

1802 Abraham Lincoln, 16th President

1809 Charles Darwin, evolutionist

1880 John L. Lewis, labor leader

## Events

1908 Anna Jeanes bequests $1,000,000 to all-girl Swarthmore College

1908 First New York to Paris auto race (via Alaska and Siberia) begins. George Schuster wins after 88 days.

# February 13

## Birthdays

1885 Bess Truman, wife of President Harry S Truman

1892 Grant Wood, painter of *American Gothic*

## Events

1937 *Prince Valiant* comic strip appears; known for historical detail and fine detail drawing.

1955 Israel acquires four of the seven Dead Sea Scrolls.

# February 14

## Birthdays

1894 Benjamin Kubelski (a.k.a. Jack Benny), actor, comedian

1913 Mel Allen, sportscaster

1913 Jimmy Hoffa, missing labor leader

## Events

1876 Bell files an application for a patent for the telephone.

1929 St. Valentine's Day Massacre in Chicago—seven gangsters killed by rivals disguised as cops.

# February 15

## Birthdays

1564 Galileo Galilei, astronomer

1797 Henry Engelhard Steinway, piano maker

1809 Cyrus Hall McCormick, inventor

1820 Susan B. Anthony, women's suffragette

## Events

1898 USS Maine sinks in Havana harbor, cause unknown.

1903 First Teddy Bear introduced in America.

# February 16

## Birthdays

1903 Edgar Bergen, ventriloquist

1959 John McEnroe, tennis player

## Events

1937 Nylon patented by W. H. Carothers.

1946 First commercially designed helicopter tested at Bridgeport, CT.

# February 17

## Birthdays

1766 Thomas Malthus, economist

1844 A. Montgomery Ward, mail-order guru

1908 Walter Lanier "Red" Barber, sports announcer

1963 Michael Jordan, basketball star

## Events

1864 CSS "HL Hunley" becomes first submarine to sink an enemy ship.

1876 Sardines were first canned, Eastport, ME.

# February 18

## Birthdays

1745 Count Alessandro Giuseppe Antonio Anastasio Volta, invented the electric battery

1848 Louis Comfort Tiffany, glassmaker

1957 Vanna White, game show hostess

## Events

1930 A cow is flown (and milked in flight) for first time. Her milk was sealed in paper containers and dropped by parachute over St. Louis, MO.

1953 Premiere of first 3-D feature film, *Bwana Devil*, at New York City.

# February 19

## Birthdays

1916 Eddie Arcaro, jockey

1924 Lee Marvin, actor

1960 Prince Andrew, royalty

## Events

1864 The Knights of Pythias' first lodge was formed in Washington D.C.

1878 Thomas Alva Edison patents the phonograph.

1945 Marines land on Iwo Jima.

# February 20

## Birthdays

1898 Enzo Ferrari, car designer and manufacturer

1902 Ansel Adams, photographer

1927 Sidney Poitier, actor

1934 Bobby Unser, auto racer

## Events

1673 First recorded wine auction held in London.

1937 First automobile/airplane combination tested, Santa Monica, CA.

1962 John Glenn, aboard Friendship 7, is first American to orbit the Earth.

# February 21

## Birthdays

1927 Erma Bombeck, humorist

1931 Larry Hagman, actor

## Events

1804 First self-propelled locomotive on rails demonstrated, Wales.

1858 First electric burglar alarm is installed in Boston, MA.

1878 First telephone book is issued, New Haven, CT.

# February 22

## Birthdays

1732 George Washington, 1st President

1810 Frederic Chopin, composer

## Events

1630 Popcorn is introduced by an Indian, Quadequina, to English colonists at their first Thanksgiving dinner.

1879 First 5-and-10 cent store opened by F.W. Woolworth, Utica, NY.

# February 23

## Birthdays

1685 George Frideric Handel, composer

1940 Peter Fonda, actor, son of Henry

**Events**

1836 Alamo is besieged by Santa Anna, entire garrison eventually killed.

1905 Rotary Club is founded by four men in Chicago.

1945 U.S. Marines raise flag on Iwo Jima, famous photo and statue.

# February 24

**Birthdays**

1786 Wilhelm Karl Grimm, story teller

1836 Winslow Homer, painter

1885 Admiral Chester Nimitz, in charge of Pacific Fleet during WWII

1955 Steven Jobs, co-founder of Apple Computer

**Events**

1949 First rocket to reach outer space launched at White Sands, NM.

1964 Cassius Clay beats Sonny Liston for the heavyweight championship.

1989 Funeral for Japan's Emperor Hirohito costs $80 billion dollars; attracts all major world leaders.

# February 25

**Birthdays**

1841 Auguste Renoir, painter

1873 Enrico Caruso, singer

1943 George Harrison, musician (Beatles)

**Events**

1838 A London pedestrian walks 20 miles backward and 20 miles forward in eight hours.

1913 16th Amendment ratified, authorizing income tax.

1919 Oregon is first state to tax gasoline (1 cent per gallon).

# February 26

**Birthdays**

1846 William "Buffalo Bill" Cody, frontiersman

1852 John Harvey Kellogg, physician, inspired the flaked cereal industry

**Events**

1870 First New York City subway line was opened to the public.

1919 Congress established Grand Canyon National Park, AZ.

1951 22nd Amendment ratified, limiting President to two terms.

# February 27

**Birthdays**

1807 Henry Wadsworth Longfellow, poet

1902 John Steinbeck, writer

1932 Elizabeth Taylor, actor

**Events**

1922 Supreme Court unanimously upheld the 19th Amendment (woman's right to vote).

1939 Supreme Court outlawed sit-down strikes.

1982 Wayne Williams found guilty of murdering two of 28 blacks in Atlanta.

# February 28

**Birthdays**

1915 Zero Mostel, actor (*Fiddler on the Roof*)

1930 Gavin MacLeod, actor (*Love Boat, Mary Tyler Moore Show*)

1948 Bernadette Peters, actress, Tony winner

## Events

1854 Republican Party formed at Ripon, WI.

1940 First televised basketball game, New York City.

1983 The final episode of *M*A*S*H*.

# February 29

## Birthdays

1860 Herman Hollerith, invented first electric tabulating machine

1904 Jimmy Dorsey, bandleader

## Events

A Leap Year!

# March 1

## Birthdays

1917 Dinah Shore, actress, talk show host

1927 Harry Belafonte, entertainer

1954 Ron Howard, actor

## Events

1781 The Articles of Confederation adopted by Continental Congress.

1790 First U.S. census began.

1937 First permanent automobile license plates issued, Connecticut.

1981 MTV goes on the air, broadcasting "Video Killed The Radio Star" by the Buggles.

# March 2

## Birthdays

1793 Sam Houston, statesman, general

1904 Theodore Geisel (a.k.a. Dr. Seuss), author

1917 Desi Arnaz, famous Cuban bandleader

## Events

1836 Texas declares its independence from Mexico.

1923 *Time* magazine first published.

1949 First street light on automatic system, New Milford, CT.

# March 3

## Birthdays

1831 George M. Pullman, inventor-financier (Pullman Car)

1847 Alexander Graham Bell, inventor of the telephone

## Events

1791 Congress passed a resolution ordering U.S. Mint be established.

1812 Congress passes first foreign aid bill.

1931 "Star Spangled Banner" officially became U.S. national anthem.

# March 4

## Birthdays

1394 Prince Henry the Navigator, sponsored Portuguese voyages of discovery

1888 Knute Rockne, football player, coach

## Events

1793 George Washington's second inauguration, shortest speech (133 words.)

1841 Longest inauguration speech (8,443 words), William Henry Harrison.

1902 American Automobile Association opens.

# March 5

## Birthdays

1583 Gerhardus Mercator, cartographer

1908 Rex Harrison, actor (*The Ghost and Mrs. Muir*, *My Fair Lady*)

## Events

1770 Boston Massacre—five people killed.

1946 "Iron Curtain" speech by Winston Churchill

# March 6

## Birthdays

1831 General Philip H. Sheridan, military leader

1923 Ed McMahon, master of ceremonies

## Events

1836 The Alamo falls.

1857 Dred Scott decision.

1930 Brooklyn's Clarence Birdseye puts the first individually packaged frozen foods on sale, Springfield, MA.

# March 7

## Birthdays

1934 Willard Scott, weatherman, original Ronald McDonald

1938 Janet Guthrie, race car driver

## Events

1926 Transatlantic phone service begins between New York and London.

1933 The game "Monopoly" is invented.

1981 Walter Cronkite's final appearance as CBS anchor.

# March 8

## Birthdays

1841 Oliver Wendell Holmes, Supreme Court justice

1859 Kenneth Grahame, author (*The Wind in the Willows*)

## Events

1910 Baroness de Laroche of Paris becomes first licensed female pilot.

1946 First helicopter licensed for commercial use, New York City.

1950 First woman medical officer assigned to naval vessel, B. R. Walters.

# March 9

## Birthdays

1454 Amerigo Vespucci, explorer

1918 Mickey Spillane, mystery writer

1943 Bobby Fischer, chess player

## Events

1822 Charles Graham of New York was granted a patent for artificial teeth.

1860 First Japanese ambassador to the U.S.

1996 Nathan Birnbaum (a.k.a. George Burns), entertainer, actor, dies at 100 years old.

# March 10

## Birthdays

1964 Prince Edward of England

## Events

1876 The first telephone call made by Alexander Graham Bell.

1888 The Salvation Army of England sends group to U.S. to begin welfare and religious activity here.

# March 11

## Birthdays

1903 Lawrence Welk, bandleader

1916 Harold Wilson, former British Prime Minister

1926 Ralph D. Abernathy, civil rights leader

## Events

1302 According to Shakespeare, this is Romeo and Juliet's wedding day.

1847 John Chapman, "Johnny Appleseed," died, Allen County, IN.

1888 Blizzard struck the northeastern United States; 400 people died.

# March 12

## Birthdays

1831 Clement Studebaker, automobile pioneer

1928 Edward Albee, playwright

1946 Liza Minnelli, singer, actress

## Events

1939 Pope Pius XII was crowned ceremonies at the Vatican.

1959 House joined the Senate approving statehood for Hawaii.

# March 13

## Birthdays

1914 Sammy Kaye, bandleader

1939 Neil Sedaka, singer-songwriter

## Events

1639 Harvard University was named for clergyman John Harvard.

1852 The *New York Lantern* publishes the first cartoon showing the character "Uncle Sam," based on a real U.S. officer who served in the War of 1812, Samuel Wilson.

# March 14

## Birthdays

1864 Casey Jones, locomotive engineer

1879 Albert Einstein, scientist

1920 Hank Ketcham, cartoonist (*Dennis the Menace*)

## Events

1743 First town meeting in America was held at Boston's Faneuil Hall.

1794 Eli Whitney received patent for cotton gin.

# March 15

## Birthdays

1767 Andrew Jackson, 7th President

1916 Harry James, bandleader

1926 Jerry Lewis, humanitarian, comedian

## Events

1913 Woodrow Wilson holds first presidential press conference.

1937 First blood bank established, Chicago, IL.

1937 First state contraceptive clinic opened, Raleigh, NC.

# March 16

## Birthdays

1751 James Madison, 4th President

1906 Henny Youngman, comedian

**Events**

1802 Law signed to establish U.S. Military Academy at West Point, NY.

1945 U.S. forces defeat Japanese at Iwo Jima.

# March 17

**Birthdays**

1804 James Bridger, scout, fur trader, mountain man par excellance

1834 Gottlieb Daimler, automobile pioneer

1919 Nat King Cole, entertainer

**Events**

1753 First official St. Patrick's Day.

1906 President Theodore Roosevelt coined the term "muckrake."

1941 National Gallery of Art opened in Washington, D.C.

# March 18

**Birthdays**

1837 Grover Cleveland, 22nd and 24th President

1858 Rudolf Diesel, invented an engine

1963 Vanessa Williams, first black Miss America

**Events**

1850 American Express founded.

1881 Barnum and Bailey's Greatest Show on Earth in New York City.

1931 First electric razor marketed by Schick, Inc.

# March 19

**Birthdays**

1860 William Jennings Bryan, "The Great Commoner," orator, statesman

1891 Earl Warren, Supreme Court chief justice

1947 Glenn Close, actress

1955 Bruce Willis, actor

**Events**

1918 Congress approved daylight saving time.

1931 Nevada legalized gambling.

1953 Academy Awards ceremony telecast for the first time.

# March 20

**Birthdays**

1828 Henrik Ibsen, author

1904 B.F. Skinner, psychologist, pioneer of behaviorism

1928 Fred Rogers, a lovely day in the neighborhood!

**Events**

1852 Harriet Beecher Stowe's *Uncle Tom's Cabin* published.

1899 Martha Place of Brooklyn, became first woman to die by electrocution.

# March 21

**Birthdays**

1685 Johann Sebastian Bach, composer

1813 James Jesse Strang, America's only crowned king (king of the Mormons)

1869 Florenz Ziegfeld, of Follies fame

**Events**

1918 During World War I, Germany launched the Somme Offensive.

1963 Alcatraz federal penitentiary, San Francisco Bay, was closed.

1965 Martin Luther King, Jr. begins march from Selma to Montgomery, AL.

# March 22

## Birthdays

1923 Marcel Marceau, mime

1930 Stephen Sondheim, composer, lyricist (*West Side Story, A Little Night Music*)

1931 William Shatner, actor (*Star Trek, T.J. Hooker*), author (*Tek War*)

1948 Andrew Lloyd Webber, composer (*Evita, Cats, Jesus Christ Superstar*)

## Events

1733 Joseph Priestley (father of soda pop), invented carbonated water.

1882 Congress outlawed polygamy.

1972 Congress approves the Equal Rights Amendment; states never ratify.

# March 23

## Birthdays

1904 Joan Crawford, actress

1922 Marty Allen, comedian

## Events

1775 Patrick Henry reputed to have said, "Give me liberty or give me death!"

1806 Lewis and Clark reach the Pacific Coast.

1929 First telephone installed in the White House.

1983 First artificial heart recipient Dr. Barney Clark died after 112 days.

# March 24

## Birthdays

1855 Andrew W. Mellon, financier

1902 Thomas E. Dewey, Ohio politician, tried to beat Truman

1930 Steve McQueen, actor

## Events

1972 Great Britain imposed direct rule over Northern Ireland.

1989 Oil tanker Exxon Valdez runs aground on Alaska's Prince William Sound—causes world's worst oil spill.

# March 25

## Birthdays

1920 Howard Cosell, sports commentator

1934 Gloria Steinem, feminist, former Playboy bunny

1940 Anita Bryant, former Miss America

1942 Aretha Franklin, singer

## Events

1954 RCA manufactures the first color television set.

1960 The first guided missile launched from a nuclear powered submarine is launched from the USS Halibut.

# March 26

## Birthdays

1875 Robert Frost, poet

1911 Tennessee Williams, playwright

1930 Sandra Day O'Connor, first woman U.S. Supreme Court justice

## Events

1885 The Eastman Film Company manufactured the first commercial motion picture film.

1937 Spinach growers of Crystal City, TX, erect a statue of Popeye.

1953 Dr. Jonas Salk announced a new vaccine against polio.

# March 27

## Birthdays

1813 Nathaniel Currier, lithographer (Currier and Ives)

1863 Sir Henry Royce, one of the founders of Rolls-Royce

## Events

1794 President Washington and Congress authorized creation of U.S. Navy.

1860 M. L. Byrn of New York patented corkscrew.

# March 28

## Birthdays

1914 Edmund Muskie, former U.S. Secretary of State

1928 Zbigniew Brzezinski, former National Security Adviser

1955 Reba McEntire, singer

## Events

1794 Nathan Briggs, New Hampshire, gets patent for the washing machine.

1930 Cities of Constantinople and Angora changed to Istanbul and Ankara.

1979 Nuclear accident at Three Mile Island near Middletown, PA.

# March 29

## Birthdays

1790 John Tyler, 10th President

1867 Cy Young, winningest baseball pitcher ever (509 wins)

1918 Pearl Bailey, singer, actress

## Events

1848 Niagara Falls stops flowing—for one day—because of an ice jam.

1886 Coca-Cola is created (it had cocaine at the time).

1973 Last U.S. troops leave Vietnam, nine years after the Tonkin Resolution.

# March 30

## Birthdays

1853 Vincent Van Gogh, artist

1930 Peter Marshall, game show host (Hollywood Squares)

1937 Warren Beatty, actor

## Events

1858 Hyman L. Lipman of Philadelphia patented a pencil with an attached eraser.

1867 Secretary of State William Henry Seward purchase Alaska from Russia for $7.2 million.

1870 15th Amendment passes, guarantees right to vote regardless of race.

1932 Amelia Earhart is first woman to make solo crossing of the Atlantic.

# March 31

## Birthdays

1596 Rene Descartes, philosopher

1732 Franz Josef Haydn, composer

1915 Henry Morgan, actor, first to take off shirt on TV

1927 Cesar Chavez, labor leader

## Events

1870 Thomas P. Mundy became the first black to vote in U.S. (Perth Amboy, NJ).

1880 Wabash became first town completely illuminated with electric light.

1889 The Eiffel Tower in Paris was completed and officially opened to the public.

1923 First dance marathon, New York City; Alma Cummings setting record of 27 hours.

1932 Ford Motor Company publicly unveiled its V-8 engine.

# April 1

## Birthdays

1815 Otto von Bismarck, statesman

1883 Lon Chaney, actor

1922 William Manchester, author (*Death of a President*)

1932 Debbie Reynolds, actress, dancer

## Events

1778 Oliver Pollock, a New Orleans businessman, creates the "$" symbol.

1853 Cincinnati became first U.S. city to pay firefighters a regular salary.

1863 First wartime conscription law in U.S. went into effect.

1889 The first dishwashing machine is marketed, Chicago.

# April 2

## Birthdays

1805 Hans Christian Andersen, storyteller

1834 Frederic A. Bartholdi, sculptor who created the Statue of Liberty

1875 Walter Chrysler, auto pioneer

1924 Doris Day, actress, girl next door

## Events

1513 Ponce de Leon landed near what is now St Augustine, FL.

1877 The first Easter Egg Roll is held on the White House lawn—Rutherford B. Hayes is president.

1935 Sir Watson-Watt is granted a patent for radar.

# April 3

## Birthdays

1783 Washington Irving, writer ("Rip Van Winkle," "Legend of Sleepy Hollow")

1924 Marlon Brando, actor

1942 Wayne Newton, singer

## Events

1860 Pony Express began between St. Joseph, MO, and Sacramento, CA. The riders simultaneously left both cities.

1882 Jesse James shot dead in St. Joseph, MO, by Robert Ford.

1910 Highest mountain in North America, Alaska's Mt McKinley, was climbed.

# April 4

## Birthdays

1895 Arthur Murray, dance instructor

1928 Maya Angelou, author, poet

1938 A. Bartlett Giamatti, former baseball commissioner

## Events

1818 Congress decided U.S. flag is 13 red and white stripes and 20 stars.

1841 William Henry Harrison dies of pneumonia and becomes the first U.S. president to die in office.

1968 Dr. Martin Luther King, Jr. shot to death, Memphis, TN.

# April 5

## Birthdays

1649 Elihu Yale, philanthropist who founded Yale University

1856 Booker T. Washington, pioneering educator

1916 Gregory Peck, actor

## Events

1614 Indian princess Pocahontas marries English colonist John Rolfe.

1792 George Washington casts first presidential veto ever.

1887 Anne Sullivan teaches "water" to Helen Keller.

# April 6

## Birthdays

1874 Erich Weiss (a.k.a. Harry Houdini), escapist

1892 Donald Wills Douglas, founded an aircraft company

## Events

1896 Modern Olympics Anniversary (First modern Olympiad).

1906 First animated cartoon is copyrighted.

1917 U.S. declares war on Germany (WWI).

# April 7

## Birthdays

1506 St. Francis Xavier, missionary

1770 William Wordsworth, poet

1928 James Garner, actor (*Maverick* movies and series, etc.)

1939 Francis Ford Coppola, director

## Events

0030 Scholars calculate this as the date that Jesus of Nazareth was crucified by Roman troops, Jerusalem.

1927 Using phone lines, TV was sent from Washington, D.C. to New York City.

1953 First jet transatlantic non-stop flight (west to east).

# April 8

## Birthdays

1893 Mary Pickford, America's sweetheart

1912 Sonja Henie, ice skater

1918 Betty Ford, former First Lady

## Events

1730 First Jewish congregation in United States consecrates synagogue.

1766 The first patent is granted for a fire escape—a wicker basket on a pulley and a chain, designed by a London watchmaker.

# April 9

## Birthdays

1905 J. William Fulbright, U.S. Senator

1919 John Presper Eckert, co-inventor of first electronic computer (ENIAC)

1926 Hugh Hefner, publisher

## Events

1833 First tax-supported public library, at Peterborough, NH.

1953 *TV Guide* publishes their first issue.

1959 NASA announces first seven astronauts.

# April 10

## Birthdays

1829 William Booth, founder of the Salvation Army

1847 Joseph Pulitzer, awarded newspaper prizes

1880 Frances Perkins, first woman in a Cabinet-level position

## Events

1849 Safety pin patented by Walter Hunt of New York City. He immediately sells the patent rights for $100.

1866 American Society for the Prevention of Cruelty to Animals organized.

1912 RMS Titanic sets sail.

1916 First professional golf tournament held.

1960 Senate passed the landmark Civil Rights Bill.

# April 11

## Birthdays

1862 Charles Evans Hughes, Chief Justice

1893 Dean Acheson, statesman

1928 Ethel Kennedy, wife of Robert

## Events

1876 Benevolent and Protective Order of Elks organized.

1921 Iowa imposed first state cigarette tax.

1951 President Truman fires General Douglas McArthur.

# April 12

## Birthdays

1777 Henry Clay, "The Great Compromiser"

1930 Tiny Tim, singer

## Events

1861 Fort Sumter, SC, shelled by Confederate troops under General Beauregard. The Civil War begins.

1938 First U.S. law requiring medical tests for marriage licenses, New York

1945 Franklin Delano Roosevelt dies of a cerebral hemorrhage, Warm Springs, GA.

# April 13

## Birthdays

1721 John Hanson, first U.S. President under the Articles of Confederation

1743 Thomas Jefferson, 3rd President

1899 Alfred Butts, inventor of the game "Scrabble"

## Events

1796 First elephant brought to America.

1902 J. C. Penney opened his first store, in Kemmerer, WY.

1964 Sidney Poitier became first black man to win an Oscar for best actor.

# April 14

## Birthdays

1904 Sir John Gielgud, actor, singer

1925 Rod Steiger, actor

1935 Loretta Lynn, Ms. Country Music, coal miner's daughter

## Events

1828 First edition of Noah Webster's dictionary is published.

1865 President Abraham Lincoln shot in Ford's Theatre by J.W. Booth.

1956 Ampex Corporation demonstrates first commercial videotape recorder.

# April 15

## Birthdays

1452 Leonardo da Vinci, painter and visionary

1933 Roy Clark, country singer

1933 Elizabeth Montgomery, actress (*Bewitched*)

## Events

1865 President Lincoln dies, 7:22 a.m.

1912 "Unsinkable" RMS Titanic sinks at 2:20 a.m.

1923 Insulin becomes generally available for diabetics.

1941 First helicopter flight of one-hour duration, Stratford, CT.

1955 Ray Kroc starts the McDonald's chain of fast food restaurants.

## April 16

### Birthdays

1867 Wilbur Wright, inventor

1889 Charlie Chaplin, actor, comedian, movie director

### Events

1926 The Book-of-the-Month Club opens for business.

1929 New York Yankees become first team to use numbers on uniforms.

## April 17

### Birthdays

1837 John Pierpont Morgan, bailed out the U.S.

1897 Thornton Wilder, American novelist

1923 Harry Reasoner, CBS News correspondent

### Events

1492 Christopher Columbus signs contract with Spain to find the Indies.

1524 New York Harbor discovered by Giovanni Verrazano.

1961 U.S.-backed Bay of Pigs invasion in Cuba.

## April 18

### Birthdays

1857 Clarence Darrow, lawyer

1922 Barbara Hale, actress (Perry Mason)

1946 Hayley Mills, actress

### Events

1775 Paul Revere makes his famous ride.

1934 First "Washateria" (laundromat) is opened, Fort Worth, TX.

1956 Don Larsen became first pitcher to pitch perfect World Series game.

## April 19

### Birthdays

1877 Ole Evinrude, invented the outboard marine engine

1932 Jayne Mansfield, actress

1935 Dudley Moore, comedian, actor, pianist

### Events

1775 American Revolution begins at Lexington Common with the firing of "the shot heard 'round the world."

1933 U.S. leaves the gold standard.

1982 Sally Ride announced as first woman astronaut.

1993 Branch Davidian compound, Waco, TX, burned, killing dozens

1995 The Murrah Federal Building in Oklahoma City, OK, bombed, killing many children and adults.

## April 20

### Birthdays

1889 Adolf Hitler, dictator of Nazi Germany

1893 Harold Lloyd, comedian, actor

1941 Ryan O'Neal, actor

## Events

1902 Marie and Pierre Curie isolated the radioactive element radium.

1962 New Orleans Citizens' Council offers free one-way ride to blacks to move North.

1971 U.S. Supreme Court upheld use of busing to achieve racial desegregation.

# April 21

## Birthdays

1816 Charlotte Bronte, author of *Jane Eyre*

1838 John Muir, naturalist

1926 Queen Elizabeth II, monarch of the United Kingdom

## Events

753 B.C. City of Rome founded

1649 Maryland Toleration Act passed, allowing all freedom of worship.

1898 Spanish American war begins.

1918 The "Red Baron," Manfred von Richtofen, is shot down and killed in World War I air battle.

# April 22

## Birthdays

1904 J. Robert Oppenheimer, Manhattan Project physicist

1937 Jack Nicholson, actor (*One Flew Over the Cuckoo's Nest, The Shining*)

## Events

1864 U.S. Congress authorized "In God We Trust" on coinage.

1889 Oklahoma land rush officially started.

1915 First use of poison gas (chlorine, by Germany) World War I.

1970 First Earth Day.

# April 23

## Birthdays

1564 William Shakespeare, playwright, poet

1791 James Buchanan, 15th President

1928 Shirley Temple Black, child actress, U.S. ambassador

1932 Halston, fashion designer

## Events

1954 Hammerin' Hank Aaron hits the first of his 755 homers.

1969 Sirhan Sirhan sentenced to death for killing Bobby Kennedy.

1985 New Coke debuts.

# April 24

## Birthdays

1620 John Graunt, statistician, founded the science of demography

1815 Anthony Trollope, poet

1942 Barbra Streisand, singer, actor

## Events

1800 Library of Congress founded with $5,000 allocation.

1833 A patent is granted for the first soda fountain.

1897 First reporter, William Price, assigned to White House.

1961 JFK accepts "sole responsibility" following the Bay of Pigs.

1981 IBM-PC anniversary.

# April 25

## Birthdays

1874 Guglielmo Marconi, radio pioneer

1918 Ella Fitzgerald, singer

## Events

1792 Highwayman Nicolas J. Pelletier first person executed by guillotine.

1901 New York becomes first state requiring license plates for cars. The fee was $1.

1945 Delegates from 45 countries met in San Francisco, organizing the U.N. The United Nations Conference starts.

1961 Robert Noyce granted a patent for the integrated circuit.

# April 26

## Birthdays

1785 John James Audubon, ornithologist

1900 Charles Richter, famed for earthquake measurement

1906 Gracie Allen, comedian, actress

## Events

1607 First British to establish an American colony land at Cape Henry, VA.

1986 The Chernobyl incident—world's worst nuclear power plant disaster.

1989 Comedienne Lucille Ball dies in Los Angeles, several days after suffering a heart attack.

# April 27

## Birthdays

1791 Samuel F. B. Morse, invented Morse code

1822 Ulysses S. Grant, 18th President

1900 Walter Lantz, Woody Woodpecker's creator

## Events

1937 U.S. Social Security system makes its first benefit payment.

1946 First radar installation aboard a commercial ship installed.

1965 R. C. Duncan patents the "Pampers" brand disposable diaper.

# April 28

## Birthdays

1758 James Monroe, 5th President

1878 Lionel Barrymore, actor, the first of the Barrymore clan

1930 James Baker III, Treasury secretary during Reagan Administration

## Events

1754 Mutiny on the *HMS Bounty* occurs.

1914 W. H. Carrier patents the design of his air conditioner.

1919 First successful parachute jump is made.

1952 World War II Pacific peace treaty takes effect.

1961 Warren Spahn pitches a no-hitter at age 41.

# April 29

## Birthdays

1863 William Randolph Hearst, newspaper publisher (*San Francisco Examiner*)

1899 Duke Ellington, musician, composer

1901 Hirohito, former Japanese emperor

## Events

1429 Joan of Arc leads Orleans, France, to victory over the English.

1553 A Flemish woman introduces the practice of starching linen into England.

1913 Gideon Sundback of Hoboken, NJ, patented the zipper.

# April 30

### Birthdays

1912 Eve Arden, actress (*Our Miss Brooks*)

1925 Cloris Leachman, actress

1933 Willie Nelson, singer, actor

### Events

1789 George Washington inaugurated as first president of the U.S.

1803 U.S. more than doubles its size through the Louisiana Purchase.

1808 The first practical typewriter is finished by Italian Pellegrini Turri. He built it for a blind friend.

# May 1

### Birthdays

1769 Duke of Wellington

1909 Kate Smith, singer ("God Bless America")

### Events

1841 First wagon train leaves Independence, MO, for California.

1860 First school for the deaf founded.

1873 First U.S. postal card issued.

# May 2

### Birthdays

1837 Henry Martyn Robert, author of *Robert's Rules of Order*

1903 Benjamin Spock, pediatrician, activist

1904 Bing Crosby, crooner

### Events

1670 Hudson Bay Company founded.

1885 *Good Housekeeping* magazine is first published.

1945 Russia takes Berlin.

# May 3

### Birthdays

1874 Francois Coty, perfume maker

1898 Golda Meir, Israeli leader

1919 Pete Seeger, folk singer

### Events

1765 First U.S. medical school opened.

1919 America's first passenger flight (New York to Atlantic City).

1971 National noncommercial network radio begins programming.

# May 4

### Birthdays

1796 Horace Mann, educator

1929 Audrey Hepburn, actress

1959 Randy Travis, singer

### Events

1626 Indians "sell" Manhattan Island for $24 cloth and buttons.

1878 Phonograph shown for first time at the Grand Opera House.

1970 Four students killed by National Guard at Kent State University (61 seconds, 22 rounds, nine wounded, four dead)

# May 5

### Birthdays

1867 Nellie Bly, name became a synonym for female star reporter

1976 Sage Stallone, son of Sly

## Events

1891 Carnegie Hall opens in New York City.

1948 First air squadron of jets aboard a carrier.

## May 6

### Birthdays

1818 Karl Marx, author of the *Communist Manifesto*

1856 Sigmund Freud, psychologist

1856 Robert Peary, Arctic explorer

1915 Orson Welles, actor, director (*Citizen Kane*)

1931 Willie Mays, baseball player, the "Say Hey Kid"

### Events

1851 Patent granted to Dr. John Farrie for a "refrigeration machine."

1954 Roger Bannister breaks the four-minute mile in 3:59:4.

## May 7

### Birthdays

1812 Robert Browning, poet

1833 Johannes Brahms, composer

1840 Peter Ilich Tchaikovsky, composer

1901 Gary Cooper, actor (*High Noon, The Plainsman*)

1909 Edwin Land, founded instant photography (Polaroid)

### Events

1824 Beethoven's Ninth Symphony presented for first time.

1915 British ship *Lusitania* sunk by German submarine, 128 Americans die.

1945 World War II ends in Europe. Nazis surrender to General Eisenhower at Reims, France.

## May 8

### Birthdays

1828 Henri Dunant, founded Red Cross, YMCA

1884 Harry S Truman, 32nd President

1926 Don Rickles, comedian, actor

### Events

1541 Spanish explorer Hernando de Soto discovers Mississippi River.

1951 Dacron men's suits introduced.

1971 Joe Frazier beats Muhammad Ali at Madison Square Garden.

## May 9

### Birthdays

1800 John Brown, abolitionist

1860 James M. Barrie, author (*Peter Pan*)

1918 Mike Wallace, CBS News correspondent

1946 Candice Bergen, actress

1949 Billy Joel, singer, piano man

### Events

1754 First newspaper cartoon in America. Divided snake—"join or die."

1926 Americans Byrd and Bennett make first airplane flight over North Pole.

1961 Chairman of FCC Newton N. Minow criticizes TV as a "vast wasteland."

## May 10

### Birthdays

1899 Fred Astaire, dancer, actor (*Showboat, The Towering Inferno*)

1902 David O. Selznick, film producer.

## Events

1869 With the driving of the Golden Spike at Promontory Point, Utah, the Transcontinential Railroad is completed.

1930 First planetarium to open to the public—Adler Planetarium, Chicago.

1960 The *USS Nautilus* completes the first circumnavigation of the globe underwater.

# May 11

## Birthdays

1888 Irving Berlin, composer

1904 Salvador Dali, surrealist artist

1912 Phil Silvers, comedian, actor (*Sgt. Bilko, McHale's Navy*)

## Events

1752 First U.S. fire insurance policy is issued, Philadelphia.

1812 The waltz is introduced into English ballrooms. Most observers consider it disgusting and immoral.

1929 First regularly scheduled TV broadcasts (three nights per week).

1947 B.F. Goodrich manufactures the first tubeless tire, Akron, OH.

# May 12

## Birthdays

1812 Edward Lear, poet

1820 Florence Nightingale, nurse

1925 Yogi Berra, New York Yankees catcher and manager

## Events

1926 Airship Norge is first vessel over the North Pole.

1940 Nazi blitzkrieg conquest of France began by crossing the Muese River.

# May 13

## Birthdays

1842 Sir Arthur Sullivan, of Gilbert and Sullivan fame

1914 Joe Louis, heavyweight

1950 Stevie Wonder, musician

## Events

1607 English land to found Jamestown (first permanent settlement).

1804 Lewis and Clark begin expedition of Louisiana Purchase with Sacajawea.

1950 The Diner's Club issues its first credit cards.

# May 14

## Birthdays

1919 Heloise and her helpful hints

1944 George Lucas, producer, director

1946 Robert Jarvik, inventor of the Jarvik 7 artificial heart

## Events

1853 Gail Borden applies for patent for making condensed milk.

1942 U.S. Women's Army Auxiliary Corps (WAAC) founded.

1948 Prime Minster David Ben-Gurion establishes the State of Israel.

# May 15

## Birthdays

1859 Pierre Curie, physicist

1918 Eddy Arnold, singer

1919 Wladziu Valentino Liberace, pianist

## Events

1602 Cape Cod was discovered by the English navigator Bartholomew Gosnold.

1918 U.S. air mail begins between Washington, D.C., Philadelphia, and New York.

1930 A United Air Lines flight from Oakland, CA, to Cheyenne, WY, carried the first airline "air hostess" (stewardess)— Ellen Church.

1934 Department of Justice offers $25,000 reward for John Dillinger, dead or alive.

1940 Nylon stockings on sale for the first time in the United States.

# May 16

## Birthdays

1801 William H. Seward, who bought Alaska at two cents an acre

1905 Henry Fonda, actor

1913 Woody Herman, bandleader

1952 Pierce Brosnan, actor

## Events

1866 Congress authorizes nickel five-cent piece (the silver half-dime was used up to this point).

1868 Senate fails by one vote to impeach President Andrew Johnson.

1929 First Academy Awards were given out. *Wings* won best picture; best actor went to Emil Jennings; best actress, Janet Gaynor.

1971 First class mail now costs eight cents (was six cents).

# May 17

## Birthdays

1936 Dennis Hopper, actor, easy rider

1956 "Sugar" Ray Leonard, middleweight boxer

## Events

1620 First merry-go-round seen at a fair in Philippapolis, Turkey.

1792 Twenty-four merchants form the New York Stock Exchange at 70 Wall Street.

1875 First Kentucky Derby run at Churchill Downs. Winner was Aristides.

1939 First sports telecast—Columbia vs Princeton, college baseball.

# May 18

## Birthdays

1872 Bertrand Russell, philosopher, mathematician

1898 Frank Capra, director (*It's a Wonderful Life*)

1902 Meredith Willson, musician-composer (*The Music Man*)

1913 Perry Como, singer

## Events

1804 Napoleon became Emperor of France.

1830 Edwin Budding of England signs an agreement for manufacture of his invention, the lawn mower.

1917 U.S. passes Selective Service act.

1951 United Nations moved into its New York City headquarters.

1980 Mount St. Helens blew up in Washington State.

# May 19

## Birthdays

1795 John Hopkins, philanthropist

1890 Ho Chi Minh, Vietnamese communist
leader

## Events

1862 The Homestead Act becomes law.

1928 Fifty-one frogs entered in first annual
"Frog Jumping Jubilee" at Angel's
Camp in Calaveras County, California.

# May 20

## Birthdays

1818 William George Fargo, helped to found
Wells, Fargo and Company

1908 James Stewart, actor

1913 William Hewlett, co-founder of
Hewlett-Packard Company

1946 Cher, singer, actress

## Events

1506 Christopher Columbus died in poverty
in Spain.

1874 Levi Strauss markets his blue jeans
with copper rivets, priced at $13.50 *a
dozen*.

1926 Thomas Edison said Americans
preferred silent movies over talkies.

1927 At 7:40 a.m., Charles Lindbergh takes
off from New York to cross Atlantic.

# May 21

## Birthdays

1878 Glenn Curtis, aircraft pioneer

1917 Raymond Burr, actor (*Perry Mason,
Ironside*)

1952 Lawrence Tarrow (a.k.a. Mr. T),
bodyguard, actor

## Events

1832 First Democratic party national
convention.

1881 The American Red Cross is founded by
Clara Barton.

1927 Lindbergh lands in Paris, after first
solo across Atlantic.

# May 22

## Birthdays

1813 Richard Wagner, composer

1828 Albrecht Grafe, pioneer eye surgeon,
founded modern ophthalmology

## Events

1807 Townsend Speakman begins making
and selling fruit-flavored carbonated
drinks, Philadelphia.

1947 First ballistic missile fired.

# May 23

## Birthdays

1883 Douglas Fairbanks, first of Hollywood's
swashbucklers

1910 Artie Shaw, band leader

1928 Rosemary Clooney, singer

1933 Joan Collins, actress

## Events

1873 Canada's North West Mounted Police
force was established.

1903 First automobile trip across U.S. from
San Francisco to New York (ended
April 1).

1934 Bonnie and Clyde shot in Louisiana
ambush.

# May 24

### Birthdays

1686 Gabriel Daniel Fahrenheit, invented the thermometer

1819 Queen Victoria, British ruler

1943 Gary Burghoff, actor (M*A*S*H*)

### Events

1844 Samuel F.B. Morse taps out "What Hath God Wrought" on telegraph.

1899 The first auto repair shop opens in Boston, MA.

# May 25

### Birthdays

1803 Ralph Waldo Emerson, philosopher

1889 Igor Sikorsky, developed a working helicopter

1898 Bennett Cerf, publisher

### Events

1721 John Copson becomes America's first insurance agent.

1787 Constitutional Convention convenes in Philadelphia.

1953 First noncommercial educational television station, Houston, TX.

# May 26

### Birthdays

1886 Al Jolson, jazz singer

1907 John Wayne, actor

### Events

1896 Dow Jones Industrial Average adopted.

1927 Henry Ford stops producing the Model T car (begins Model A).

1946 Patent filed in U.S. for the H-Bomb.

# May 27

### Birthdays

1837 Wild Bill Hickok, U.S. marshall

1907 Rachel Carson, ecologist

1911 Hubert Horatio Humphrey, U.S. Senator from Minnesota, vice president

1923 Henry Kissinger, former U.S. Secretary of State

### Events

1931 First full scale wind tunnel for testing airplanes, Langley Field, VA.

1941 German battleship *Bismarck* is sunk by a British naval force lead by the HMS Hood.

# May 28

### Birthdays

1738 Dr. Joseph Guillotin, inventor of the ultimate amputation device

1886 Jim Thorpe, Olympic athlete

1908 Ian Fleming, writer (James Bond series)

### Events

1530 Hernando de Soto lands in Florida.

1742 First indoor swimming pool opens at Goodman's Fields, London.

1929 First all color talking picture *On With The Show* exhibited, New York City.

# May 29

### Birthdays

1736 Patrick Henry, patriot

1826 Ebenezer Butterick, inventor of the tissue paper dress pattern

1903 Leslie Townes (Bob) Hope, entertainer, famous profile

1917 John F. Kennedy, 35th President

## Events

1912 Fifteen young women fired by Curtis Publishing for dancing the "Turkey Trot" during their lunch break.

1953 Sir Edmund Hillary and Norgay of New Zealand become the first to reach the top of Mt. Everest.

# May 30

## Birthdays

1908 Mel Blanc, the voice of Bugs Bunny, Elmer Fudd, Daffy Duck, Porky Pig, Tweety Bird, Sylvester the Cat, Barney Rubble, and many, many more

1909 Benny Goodman, bandleader, king of swing

## Events

1431 Joan of Arc burned at the stake in Rouen, France, at age 19.

1911 Indianapolis 500 car race run for first time. Winning driver Ray Harroun takes it with a blazing 75 mph.

# May 31

## Birthdays

1819 Walt Whitman, poet

1898 Norman Vincent Peale, author, minister

1930 Clint Eastwood, actor (*Dirty Harry, Heartbreak Ridge, City Heat*)

1943 Joe Namath, New York Jets quarterback

## Events

1879 Madison Square Garden opens its doors.

1889 Two thousand people perished in a dam break in Johnstown, PA flood.

# June 1

## Birthdays

1801 Brigham Young, Mormon prophet

1926 Andy Griffith, actor (*Matlock, Mayberry RFD*)

1926 Norma Jean Baker (Marilyn Monroe), actress

## Events

1495 First written record of scotch whiskey appears in the Exchequer Rolls of Scotland. Friar John Cor is the distiller.

1813 Captain John Lawrence utters what became the U.S. Navy motto: "Don't give up the ship."

# June 2

## Birthdays

1904 Johnny Weismuller, swimmer, actor (Tarzan)

1944 Marvin Hamlisch, pianist, composer

1948 Jerry "the Beaver" Mathers, actor

## Events

1835 P.T. Barnum and his circus begin their first tour of the U.S.

1851 First Prohibition law enacted in Maine.

1924 U.S. citizenship granted to all American Indians.

# June 3

## Birthdays

1808 Jefferson Davis, President of the Confederacy

1864 Ransom Eli Olds, auto (Oldsmobile) and truck (REO) manufacturer

1925 Tony Curtis, actor

**Events**

1539 Hernando De Soto claims Florida for Spain.

1621 Dutch West India Company receives charter for "New Netherlands."

1942 Battle of Midway—turning point in war in Pacific—began.

1989 Chinese government puts down student democracy protest in Beijing; thousands die in Tiananmen Square.

# June 4

**Birthdays**

1924 Dennis Weaver, actor (*Gunsmoke, McCloud*)

1936 Bruce Dern, actor (*Coming Home*)

**Events**

1896 Henry takes his first Ford through the streets of Detroit.

1940 British complete miracle of Dunkirk by evacuating 300,000 troops.

1985 Supreme Court strikes down Alabama "moment of silence" law.

# June 5

**Birthdays**

1883 John Maynard Keynes, economist

1934 Bill Moyers, news commentator

**Events**

1783 Joseph Jaques Montgolfier becomes the first to fly (10 minutes) in a hot-air balloon.

1967 Israel, Syria, Jordan, Iraq, and Egypt begin Six-Day War.

1968 Senator Robert F. Kennedy assassinated at the Ambassador Hotel in Los Angeles by Sirhan Sirhan.

# June 6

**Birthdays**

1755 Nathan Hale, patriot

1875 Thomas Mann, author

1935 Dalai Lama, religious leader

**Events**

1844 The Young Men's Christian Association founded in London.

1925 Walter Percy Chrysler founded the Chrysler Corporation.

1932 U.S. federal gasoline tax enacted.

1933 First drive-in theatre opens, Camden, NJ.

1944 D-Day. Invasion of Europe; Allies storm Normandy, France.

# June 7

**Birthdays**

1778 Beau Brummel, English fancy dresser

1848 Paul Gauguin, French post-impressionist painter

1909 Jessica Tandy, actress (*Driving Miss Daisy, Cocoon*)

1922 Rocky Graziano, boxer

**Events**

1769 Daniel Boone begins to explore the Bluegrass State of Kentucky.

1776 Richard Lee of Virginia calls for Declaration of Independence.

1860 First American "dime novel" is published: *Malaseka, The Indian Wife of the White Hunter*, by Mrs. Ann Stevens.

1955 First President to appear on television in color— Dwight D. Eisenhower.

# June 8

## Birthdays

0570 Mohammed, prophet of Islam

1869 Frank Lloyd Wright, master builder

1918 Robert Preston, actor (*The Music Man*)

1933 Joan Rivers, comedian

## Events

1786 First commercially made ice cream sold in New York.

1869 Ives W. McGaffey patents his vacuum cleaner.

1953 Segregated lunch counters in D.C. forbidden by Supreme Court.

# June 9

## Birthdays

1893 Cole Porter, composer, lyricist

1916 Robert McNamara, former Ford Motor Co. President, former U.S. Secretary of State, head of World Bank

1934 Donald Duck

1961 Michael J. Fox, actor

## Events

1869 Charles Elmer Hires sells his first Root Beer, Philadelphia.

1991 Mt. Pinatubo, Philipines, erupts. Over the next several days, ash covers the surrounding area including Clark Air Force Base (U.S.).

# June 10

## Birthdays

1921 Prince Phillip, husband of Queen Elizabeth II

1922 Frances Gumm (a.k.a. Judy Garland), singer, actress

1933 F. Lee Bailey, lawyer

## Events

1639 First American log cabin at Fort Christina (Wilmington, DE).

1935 Alcoholics Anonymous formed in Akron, OH, by Dr. Robert Smith.

1944 Joe Nuxhall, at 15 years old, became youngest major league baseball player.

1977 Apple Computer ships its first Apple II.

# June 11

## Birthdays

1910 Jacques Yves Cousteau, marine explorer

1918 Nelson Mandela, South African civil rights leader & politician

1956 Joe Montana, football player

## Events

1859 Claim laid to the Comstock (silver) Lode, Nevada. The mine eventually produces more than $300 million in silver.

1919 Sir Barton becomes the first horse to win the Triple Crown.

1963 George Wallace blocks an Alabama schoolhouse door.

# June 12

## Birthdays

1924 George Herbert Walker Bush, 41st President

1929 Anne Frank, diarist

1932 Jim Nabors, actor (*Gomer Pyle, USMC; Mayberry RFD*), singer

## Events

1665 English rename New Amsterdam "New York" after Dutch pull out.

1939 Baseball Hall of Fame opens in Cooperstown, NY.

# June 13

## Birthdays

1865 William Butler Yeats, writer

1903 Harold "Red" Grange, the "Galloping Ghost" of football

1951 Richard Thomas, actor (*The Waltons*)

## Events

1927 Charles Lindbergh honored in New York City for his transatlantic flight—750,000 pounds of ticker-tape shower down.

1944 Nazi Germany begins V-1 (Fieseler Fi-103) buzz-bomb attacks against Britain.

1966 Supreme Court hands down *Miranda v. Arizona* decision. Declares a suspect must be informed of rights.

1967 Thurgood Marshall nominated as first black Supreme Court justice.

# June 14

## Birthdays

1909 Burl Ives, folk singer, actor

1946 Donald Trump, entrepreneur

1958 Eric Heiden, Olympic ice skater

1969 Steffi Graf, tennis player

## Events

1623 Rev. Gerville Pooley of Virginia files first breach-of-promise lawsuit against Cicely Jordan. He loses.

1775 U.S. Army founded.

1954 President Eisenhower signs order adding words "under God" to the Pledge of Allegiance.

# June 15

## Birthdays

1922 Morris K. Udall, Democratic Congressman from Arizona

1932 Mario Cuomo, New York governor

1937 Waylon Jennings, singer, actor

## Events

1215 King John signs the Magna Carta at Runnymede, England.

1752 Ben Franklin's kite is struck by lightning.

1844 Goodyear patents the vulcanization of rubber.

1986 *Pravda* announces high-level Chernobyl staff fired for incompetence.

# June 16

## Birthdays

1895 Stan Laurel, comedian (Laurel and Hardy)

1917 Katharine Graham, newspaper publisher, *Washington Post*

1937 Erich Segal, author

## Events

1775 The Battle of Bunker Hill (actually Breed's Hill).

1903 The Ford Motor Company is started.

1947 First network news—Dumont's "News from Washington."

# June 17

## Birthdays

1882 Igor Stravinsky, composer (*Firebird Suite, The Rite of Spring*)

1917 Dean Martin, singer, actor

## Events

1579 Sir Francis Drake lands on the coast of California.

1856 Republican Party opened its first convention in Philadelphia.

1885 Statue of Liberty arrived in New York City.

1963 Supreme Court strikes down rule requiring recitation of the Lord's Prayer or reading of Biblical verses in public schools.

# June 18

## Birthdays

1901 Jeanette MacDonald, singer

1913 Sylvia Porter, financial writer

1942 Paul McCartney, musician (Beatles)

## Events

1583 Richard Martin of London takes out first life insurance policy, on William Gibbons. The premium is 383 pounds.

1812 War of 1812 begins as U.S. declares war against Britain.

1815 Battle of Waterloo—British and Prussians defeat Napoleon.

1873 Susan B. Anthony fined $100 for attempting to vote.

1981 Sandra Day O'Connor becomes first woman justice on U.S. Supreme Court.

# June 19

## Birthdays

1886 Duchess of Windsor

1903 Henry Louis Gehrig, baseball player, the "Iron Horse" of the Yankees

1978 Garfield, famed cat

## Events

1862 Slavery is abolished in the U.S. territories.

1910 Father's Day is celebrated for the first time in Spokane, WA.

1964 Civil Rights Act of 1964 survived an 83-day filibuster in Senate.

# June 20

## Birthdays

1923 Chet Atkins, guitar picker

1931 Olympia Dukakis, actress (*Moonstruck*)

1942 Brian Wilson, singer, songwriter (Beach Boys)

## Events

1632 Britain grants second Lord Baltimore rights to Chesapeake Bay area.

1782 The U.S. Congress approves the Great Seal of the United States and the Eagle as its symbol.

1837 Queen Victoria at age 18 ascends British throne following death of uncle King William IV. Ruled for 63 years (ending 1901).

1893 Lizzie Borden found not guilty of murdering her parents.

# June 21

## Birthdays

1732 Martha Washington, the First Lady

1921 Jane Russell, actress (The Paleface)

1982 William Montbatten, Prince of Wales

## Events

1788 U.S. Constitution goes into effect as New Hampshire becomes the ninth state to ratify it.

1834 Cyrus Hall McCormick received a patent for his reaping machine.

1879 F. W. Woolworth opens his first store (failed almost immediately, so he started another one!).

1893 The first Ferris wheel is premiered at Chicago's Columbian Exposition.

# June 22

## Birthdays

1922 Bill Blass, fashion designer

1937 Kris Kristofferson, singer-songwriter

1941 Ed Bradley, CBS newscaster

1949 Meryl Streep, actress

## Events

1847 The doughnut is invented.

1910 First airship passengers fly aboard the zeppelin in Deutscheland.

1970 President Nixon signs the 26th Amendment, making voting age 18.

# June 23

## Birthdays

1846 Antoine J. "Adolphe" Sax, inventor of the saxophone

1894 Alfred Kinsey, sex researcher

1911 David Ogilvy, advertising guru

## Events

1683 William Penn signs friendship treaty with the Lenni Lenape Indians in Pennsylvania; only treaty "not sworn to, nor broken."

1868 Christopher Latham Sholes patents typewriter.

1889 First issue of *The Wall Street Journal*.

# June 24

## Birthdays

1839 Gustavus Franklin Swift, founder of Swift and Company

1842 Ambrose Bierce, author and cynic

1895 Jack Dempsey, boxer, "The Manassa Mauler"

## Events

1948 The Berlin Blockade and Berlin Airlift begin.

1949 Hopalong Cassidy becomes first network western.

1986 U.S. Senate approves "tax reform."

# June 25

## Birthdays

1925 June Lockhart, actress (*Lassie, Lost in Space*)

1945 Carly Simon, singer

1949 Phyllis George, former Miss America

## Events

1876 Lt.-Col. George Custer and 7th Cavalry wiped out by Sioux and Cheyenne Indians.

1950 Korean conflict begins; North Korea invades South Korea.

1951 First color TV broadcast—CBS's Arthur Godfrey from New York City.

# June 26

## Birthdays

1819 Abner Doubleday, credited with inventing American baseball

1892 Pearl S. Buck, author (*The Good Earth*)

## Events

1797 Charles Newbold patents the first iron plow. Farmers don't buy it; they're scared of the effects of iron on soil.

1900 Dr. Walter Reed begins research that beats yellow fever.

1934 FDR signs Federal Credit Union Act, establishing Credit Unions.

# June 27

## Birthdays

1880 Helen Keller, blind-and deaf author,-lecturer

1927 Bob Keeshan (a.k.a. Captain Kangaroo)

1930 H. Ross Perot, billionaire

## Events

1693 The first woman's magazine, *The Ladies' Mercury*, published in London and features the first advice column.

1955 U.S.'s first automobile seat belt legislation is enacted in Illinois.

1977 Supreme Court decides lawyers may advertise—a 5-4 decision.

# June 28

## Birthdays

1926 Mel Brooks, comedian, actor, director

1946 Gilda Radner, comedian, actor

1960 John Elway, football quarterback

## Events

1914 Austrian Archduke Francis Ferdinand and his wife Sofia assassinated.

1919 The Treaty of Versailles, ending World War I, was signed.

1939 Pan Am begins transatlantic air service (Dixie Clipper).

# June 29

## Birthdays

1577 Peter Paul Rubens, artist

1858 George Washington Goethals, engineer who built the Panama Canal

1919 Slim Pickens, singer

## Events

1854 Congress ratifies Gadsden Purchase, adds parts of New Mexico, Arizona.

1863 The very first First National Bank opens, in Davenport, IA.

1916 A Boeing aircraft flies for first time.

# June 30

## Birthdays

1917 Buddy Rich, drummer

1917 Lena Horne, singer

1966 Mike Tyson, boxer

## Events

1870 Ada Kepley becomes the first female law-college graduate.

1936 *Gone With the Wind* by Margaret Mitchell is published.

1936 Forty hour work week law approved in U.S. (federal law).

1948 Transistor demonstrated, Murray Hill, NJ.

# July 1

## Birthdays

1936 Jamie Farr, actor (M*A*S*H*)

1937 "Wolfman Jack," radio disk jockey

1952 Dan Ackroyd, comedian, actor

1961 Carl Lewis, U.S. track and field star

1961 Princess Diana Spencer, Prince Charles's ex-wife

## Events

1847 First adhesive U.S. postage stamps go on sale.

1898 Teddy Roosevelt charges up San Juan Hill.

1943 First withholding tax from paychecks.

1966 Medicare established to help elderly with health care costs.

# July 2

## Birthdays

1877 Hermann Hesse, Swiss novelist, poet (*Siddhartha*) (Nobel Prize, 1946)

1908 Thurgood Marshall, first black Supreme Court Justice

1937 Richard Petty, auto race driver

## Events

1890 Sherman Antitrust Act prohibits industrial monopolies.

1937 Amelia Earhart and Fred Noonan disappeared over the Pacific Ocean.

1964 President Johnson signs the Civil Rights Act.

# July 3

## Birthdays

1567 Samuel de Champlain, explorer

1883 Franz Kafka, author (*The Trial*, "Metamorphosis")

1943 Geraldo Rivera, newsman

## Events

1608 City of Quebec founded by Samuel de Champlain.

1819 First savings bank in U.S. (Bank of Savings, NYC) opens its doors.

1984 Supreme Court rules Jaycees may be forced to admit women as members.

# July 4

## Birthdays

1804 Nathaniel Hawthorne, author (*The Scarlet Letter*)

1826 Stephen Foster, composer ("Oh, Susanna," "Swanee River")

1872 Calvin Coolidge, 30th President

1900 Louis Armstrong, trumpet player

1918 Abigail Van Buren and Ann Landers, twin sisters, advice columnists

## Events

1776 American colonies declare their independence from England.

1802 U.S. Military Academy officially opened at West Point, NY.

1884 Statue of Liberty was presented to U.S. in Paris.

# July 5

## Birthdays

1794 Sylvester Graham, inventor of the Graham cracker

1810 Phineas T. Barnum, showman and circus promoter

## Events

1935 President Franklin Delano Roosevelt signs into law the National Labor Relations Act.

1946 Louis Reard's bikini swimsuit design debuts at a fashion show, Paris.

# July 6

## Birthdays

1747 John Paul Jones, U.S. naval officer ("I have not yet begun to fight")

1923 Nancy Davis Reagan, actress, former First Lady

1946 Sylvester Stallone, actor (Rocky, Rambo)

**Events**

1885 First inoculation (for rabies) of a human being, by Louis Pasteur.

1886 Horlick's of Wisconsin offers first malted milk to the public.

1933 First All-Star baseball game. American League won 5-2.

# July 7

**Birthdays**

1906 Satchel Paige, baseball pitcher

1907 Robert A. Heinlein, science-fiction author (*Stranger in a Strange Land*)

1922 Pierre Cardin, fashion designer

1940 Ringo Starr, musician (Beatles)

**Events**

1891 A patent was granted for the travelers' cheque.

1930 Construction began on Boulder Dam (later renamed Hoover Dam).

1987 Kiwanis Clubs end men-only tradition—vote to admit women.

# July 8

**Birthdays**

1838 Count Ferdinand Graf von Zeppelin, inventor

1931 Jerry Vale, singer

1931 Roone Arledge, TV executive (ABC)

1935 Steve Lawrence, singer, actor

**Events**

1796 First American passport issued by the U.S. State Department.

1889 Vol. 1, No. 1, of *The Wall Street Journal* published.

1907 Florenz Ziegfeld staged first "Follies" on the roof of the New York Theater.

# July 9

**Birthdays**

1802 Thomas Davenport, invented the first commercially successful electric motor

1819 Elias Howe, sewing machine inventor

1956 Tom Hanks, actor

**Events**

1776 Declaration of Independence is read aloud to General George Washington's troops in New York.

1850 Zachary Taylor, 12th President of U.S., died in White House; served 16 months.

1953 First helicopter passenger service, New York City.

# July 10

**Birthdays**

1871 Marcel Proust, novelist (*Remembrance of Things Past*)

1915 Saul Bellow, novelist (*Herzog, Dangling Man*) (Nobel Prize, 1976)

1920 David Brinkley, newscaster (NBC, ABC)

**Events**

1892 First concrete-paved street built, Bellefountaine, OH.

1940 The Battle of Britain began as Nazi forces attacked by air.

1985 Coca-Cola Co. announces it will resume selling old formula Coke.

# July 11

## Birthdays

1767 John Quincy Adams, 6th President

1899 E. B. White, writer (*Charlotte's Web, The Elements of Style*)

1920 Yul Brynner, actor (*The King and I, The Ten Commandments*)

## Events

1798 U.S. Marine Corps was created by an act of Congress.

1936 Triborough Bridge linking Manhattan, the Bronx, and Queens, opened.

1955 New U.S. Air Force Academy dedicated at Lowry Air Base, Colorado.

# July 12

## Birthdays

1817 Henry David Thoreau, naturalist, author

1854 George Eastman, inventor of the Kodak camera

1895 R. Buckminster Fuller, architect, inventor, philosopher, inventor of the geodesic dome

1908 Milton Berle, comedian, "Uncle Miltie," "Mr. Television"

1917 Andrew Wyeth, American painter

1937 Bill Cosby, comedian, actor

## Events

1862 Congress authorizes the Medal of Honor.

1933 Congress passes first minimum wage law ($0.33 per hour).

1957 First President to fly helicopter—Dwight Eisenhower.

# July 13

## Birthdays

1935 Jack Kemp, New York congressman

1942 Harrison Ford, actor (*Star Wars, Indiana Jones, Witness*)

1946 Cheech Marin, comedian (Cheech and Chong)

## Events

1787 Congress establishes Northwest Territory.

1865 Horace Greeley advises his readers to "Go west."

1898 Marconi is granted a patent for the radio.

# July 14

## Birthdays

1903 Irving Stone, author

1904 Isaac Bashevis Singer, Yiddish novelist (*The Penitent*, "Yentl," *Enemies*) (Nobel Prize, 1978)

1912 Woody Guthrie, folk singer

1913 Gerald R. Ford, 38th President

## Events

1789 The citizens of Paris storm the Bastille prison.

1850 First public demonstration of ice made by refrigeration.

1966 Richard Speck kills eight nurses in a Chicago dormitory.

# July 15

## Birthdays

1606 Rembrandt van Rijn, Dutch painter

1779 Clement Clarke Moore, poem ("'Twas the Night Before Christmas")

1946 Linda Ronstadt, singer

## Events

1869 Margarine is patented in Paris, for use in the French Navy.

1929 First airport hotel opens—Oakland, CA.

1954 The first commercial jet transport airplane built in U.S. is tested (Boeing 707).

# July 16

## Birthdays

1821 Mary Baker Eddy, founder of Christian Science movement

1872 Roald Amundsen, Norwegian explorer, discoverer of South Pole

1907 Orville Redenbacher, popcorn king

## Events

1769 Father Junipero Serra founds Mission San Diego, first mission California.

1790 Congress establishes the District of Columbia.

1935 First automatic parking meter in U.S. installed, Oklahoma City, OK.

1945 First atomic blast, Trinity Site, Alamogordo, New Mexico.

# July 17

## Birthdays

1889 Erle Stanley Gardner, writer, created Perry Mason

1900 James Cagney, actor

1912 Art Linkletter, TV host

## Events

1938 Douglas "Wrong Way" Corrigan leaves New York for Los Angeles.

1954 Construction begins on Disneyland....

1955 Disneyland opens its doors in rural Orange County.

# July 18

## Birthdays

1913 Red Skelton, comedian

1918 Nelson Mandela, human rights activist, former political prisoner

1921 John Glenn, Jr., first American in orbit, Ohio senator

## Events

1872 Britain introduced the concept of voting by secret ballot.

1938 Douglas "Wrong Way" Corrigan arrives in Ireland—left New York for Los Angeles.

1969 Mary Jo Kopechne and Teddy Kennedy plunge off Chappaquiddick bridge.

# July 19

## Birthdays

1814 Samuel Colt, invented the Colt Revolver

1834 Edgar Degas, French impressionist painter

1865 Charles Horace Mayo, American surgeon, co-founder of Mayo Clinic

## Events

1848 First Women's Rights Convention, Seneca Falls, NY

1877 First Wimbledon tennis championships held.

1961 First in-flight movie is shown (on TWA).

# July 20

## Birthdays

1919 Sir Edmund Hillary, explorer, one of first two men to scale Mt. Everest

1933 Nelson Doubleday, publisher

1938 Natalie Wood, actress

## Events

1872 Mahlon Loomis receives patent for wireless—the radio is born.

1969 During the Apollo 11 mission, Neil Armstrong and "Buzz" Aldrin become the first humans to step on the moon (4:18 p.m. EDT)

# July 21

## Birthdays

1899 Ernest Hemingway, writer (*A Farewell to Arms, The Old Man and the Sea*) (Nobel Prize, 1954)

1899 Hart Crane, American poet ("The Bridge")

1924 Don Knotts, comedian, actor

1952 Robin Williams, actor, comedian

## Events

1873 World's first train robbery, by Jesse James.

1925 John Scopes found guilty in Tennessee for teaching evolution.

1976 "Legionnaire's Disease" kills 29 in Philadelphia, PA.

# July 22

## Birthdays

1822 Gregor Mendel, geneticist who discovered laws of heredity

1849 Emma Lazarus, whose poem was inscribed on the Statue of Liberty

1890 Rose Kennedy, mother of a president, an attorney general, and a senator

## Events

1933 Wiley Post completes first round-the-world solo flight.

1934 John Dillinger shot and killed in Chicago movie theatre.

# July 23

## Birthdays

1936 Don Drysdale, baseball pitcher

1961 Woody Harrelson, actor

## Events

1866 Cincinnati Baseball Club (the Reds) established.

1904 The ice cream cone is invented.

1947 First (U.S. Navy) air squadron of jets, Quonset Point, RI.

# July 24

## Birthdays

1783 Simon Bolivar, freed six Latin American republics from Spanish rule

1895 Robert Graves, poet, historical novelist (*Goodbye to All That*)

1898 Amelia Earhart, avaitor

1920 Bella Abzug, New York representative

1947 Arnold Schwarzenegger, former Mr. Olympia and Mr. World, actor

1951 Lynda Carter, Miss USA, actress (Wonder Woman)

## Events

1701 French make first landing at site of Detroit.

1824 The *Harrisburg Pennsylvanian* newspaper publishes results of first public opinion poll. Clear lead for Andrew Jackson.

1925 John Scopes, found guilty of teaching evolution at a Tennese high school, fined $100 and costs.

1940 Courts rule it is legal for radio stations to broadcast recorded music.

1959 Vice President Nixon argued with Khrushchev; known as the "Kitchen Debate."

# July 25

## Birthdays

1902 Eric Hoffer, longshoreman, author (*The True Believer*)

1954 Walter Payton, NFL running back

1978 Louise Brown, world's first "test tube baby"

## Events

1866 U.S. Grant named General of the Army, the first officer ever to hold that rank.

1956 Italian liner *Andrea Doria* sank off Nantucket Island after it collided with the *Stockholm*.

# July 26

## Birthdays

1856 George Bernard Shaw, dramatist (Nobel Prize, 1925)

1875 Carl Jung, founded analytic psychology

1894 Aldous Huxley, author (*Brave New World*)

1943 Mick Jagger, musician (Rolling Stones)

## Events

1775 Benjamin Franklin becomes first U.S. Postmaster General.

1908 Federal Bureau of Investigation established.

1947 Department of Defense established.

# July 27

## Birthdays

1906 Leo Durocher, baseball manager

1916 Keenan Wynn, actor

1922 Norman Lear, TV writer, producer (*All in the Family*)

1932 Jerry Van Dyke, actor

## Events

1586 Sir Walter Raleigh brings first tobacco to England from Virginia.

1866 Atlantic telegraph cable successfully laid (1,686 miles long).

1917 Ford introduces the Model TT truck.

1940 *Billboard* magazine starts publishing best-seller's charts.

# July 28

## Birthdays

1901 Rudy Vallee, band leader, singer ("My Time Is Your Time")

1907 Earl S. Tupper, inventor of Tupperware

1929 Jacqueline Bouvier Kennedy Onassis, former first lady

## Events

1868 14th Amendment ratified; due process of law, citizenship to ex-slaves.

1900 The hamburger is created by Louis Lassing of Connecticut.

1933 First singing telegram is delivered (to Rudy Vallee), New York City.

# July 29

## Birthdays

1871 Grigori Rasputin, Russian monk

1883 Benito Mussolini (Il Duce), Italian fascist dictator

1892 William Powell, actor (the Thin Man movies)

1905 Clara Bow, silent screen actress (*It, Saturday Night Kid*)

## Events

1858 First commercial treaty between U.S. and Japan is signed.

1899 First motorcycle race, Manhattan Beach, NY.

1914 First transcontinental phone link made between New York City and San Francisco.

## July 30

### Birthdays

1863 Henry Ford, automobile manufacturer

1889 Vladimir Zworykin, electronics engineer, inventor, father of TV

1890 Casey Stengel, New York Yankees and Mets manager

### Events

1619 The House of Burgesses in Virginia is formed. First elective governing body a British colony.

1733 Society of Freemasons opens its first American lodge in Boston.

1956 Motto of U.S., "In God We Trust," authorized.

## July 31

### Birthdays

1912 Milton Friedman, economist

1951 Evonne Goolagong, tennis player

### Events

1777 Marquis de Lafayette, 19, made major-general of the Continental Army.

1789 The U.S. Customs Service is started.

1922 Eighteen-year-old Ralph Samuelson rides world's first water skis at Lake City, MN.

## August 1

### Birthdays

1770 William Clark, explored Pacific Northwest with Meriwether Lewis

1779 Francis Scott Key, wrote the "Star-Spangled Banner"

1819 Herman Melville, author (*Moby Dick*, "Billy Budd")

### Events

1790 First U.S. census.

1903 First coast-to-coast automobile trip (San Francisco-New York) completed.

1953 California introduces sales tax (for education).

## August 2

### Birthdays

1924 Carroll O'Connor, actor (*All in the Family, In the Heat of the Night*)

1924 James Baldwin, novelist

1926 Betsy Bloomingdale, department-store mogul

### Events

1776 Formal signing of the Declaration of Independence.

1858 First street mailboxes, Boston, MA.

1876 Wild Bill Hickok is shot dead (from behind) by Jack McCall. The poker hand he held has since been known as the dead man's hand: a pair of aces and a pair of eights.

## August 3

### Birthdays

1811 Elisha Graves Otis, inventor of the safe elevator

1900 John T. Scopes, Tennessee teacher convicted of teaching evolution

1923 Anne Klein, fashion designer

### Events

1492 Columbus sets sail from Palos, Spain for "Indies."

1678 Robert LaSalle builds the first ship in America, the *Griffon.*

# August 4

## Birthdays

1755 Nicolas-Jacque Conte, invented the modern pencil

1792 Percy Bysshe Shelley, poet

1958 Mary Decker Tabb Slaney, track star

## Events

1693 Champagne is invented by Dom Perignon.

1777 Retired British cavalry officer Philip Astley establishes the first circus.

1790 United States Coast Guard founded.

# August 5

## Birthdays

1899 Conrad Aiken, American poet, short story writer, critic

1906 John Huston, film director, writer, actor

1930 Neil Armstrong, X-15 pilot, first moonwalker (*Gemini 8, Apollo 11*)

## Events

1861 To finance the war, the U.S. Congress passes the first income tax law (3 percent of incomes more than $800).

1884 Cornerstone for the Statue of Liberty laid.

1945 Atom Bomb dropped on Hiroshima by the "Enola Gay" (Pacific Time).

1962 Marilyn Monroe dies at age 36.

# August 6

## Birthdays

1809 Alfred Lord Tennyson, poet laureate of England

1881 Sir Alexander Fleming, discovered penicillin (Nobel Prize, 1954)

1917 Robert Mitchum, actor

1945 Ken Norton, heavyweight boxer

## Events

1926 New York's Gertrude Ederle becomes first woman to swim the English Channel.

1965 Federal Voting Rights Act guarantees black voting rights.

# August 7

## Birthdays

1876 Mata Hari, dancer, courtesan, spy

1923 Esther Williams, swimmer, actress

1937 Dustin Hoffman, actor

1942 Garrison Keillor, humorist

## Events

1782 George Washington creates the Order of the Purple Heart.

1789 U.S. War Department established.

1888 Theophilus Van Kannel of Philadelphia receives a patent for his revolving door—described as a storm door structure.

# August 8

## Birthdays

1763 Charles Bullfinch, first U.S. professional architect

1879 Emiliano Zapata, Mexican revolutionary, peasant leader

1922 Rudi Gernreich, designed first women's topless swimsuit and the miniskirt.

## Events

1709 First known ascent in a hot-air balloon, by Father Bartolomeu de Gusmao of Portugal (indoors).

1900 First Davis Cup tennis matches, held in Boston. The U.S. defeats Britain.

1963 Great Train Robbery, England.

# August 9

## Birthdays

1928 Jimmy Dean, actor

1930 Betty Boop, animated cartoon

1957 Melanie Griffith, actress

1963 Whitney Houston, singer

## Events

1638 Jonas Bronck of Holland becomes the first European settler what is now known as the Bronx.

1945 U.S. drops second atomic bomb on Japan destroying part of Nagasaki. An estimated 74,000 people died. The original target was Kokura.

1974 President Richard Nixon resigns in the wake of the Watergate scandal.

# August 10

## Birthdays

1874 Herbert Hoover, 31st President

1933 Jerry Falwell, evangelist

## Events

1846 Smithsonian Institute established.

1866 Transatlantic cable laid—President Buchanan speaks to Queen Victoria.

1945 Japan surrenders, one day after second atom bomb dropped by the U.S.

# August 11

## Birthdays

1921 Alex Haley, American author (*Roots*)

1950 Steve Wozniak, co-founded Apple Computer

1953 Hulk Hogan, professional wrestler

## Events

1866 The world's first roller rink opens its doors, Newport, RI.

1919 Green Bay Packers founded.

1965 Watts riots in Los Angeles, $200 million in damages in six days.

# August 12 .

## Birthdays

1881 Cecil B. deMille, director

1939 George Hamilton, actor

## Events

1851 Isaac Singer granted a patent for his sewing machine.

1955 President Eisenhower raises minimum wage from 75 cents to $1 an hour.

# August 13

## Birthdays

1655 Johann Christoph Denner, invented the clarinet

1860 Annie Oakley, frontier woman

1899 Alfred Hitchcock, director (*Psycho, The Birds*)

## Events

1831 Nat Turner leads uprising of slaves in Virginia.

1847 English astronomer J.R. Hind discovers asteroid Iris.

# August 14

## Birthdays

1903 John Ringling North, circus director

1925 Russell Baker, newspaper columnist

1958 Earvin "Magic" Johnson, basketball star

## Events

1248 Construction of Cologne Cathedral is begun.

1846 Henry David Thoreau jailed for tax resistance.

1848 The Oregon Territory established.

1880 Construction of Cologne Cathedral is completed.

1893 France issues first driving licenses, including a required test.

1935 Social Security Act became law.

# August 15

## Birthdays

1769 Napoleon Bonaparte, emperor

1771 Sir Walter Scott, novelist, poet (*Lady of the Lake, Ivanhoe*)

1888 T. E. Lawrence (a.k.a. Lawrence of Arabia), writer

1912 Julia Child, chef

## Events

1620 Mayflower sets sail from Southampton with 102 Pilgrims.

1914 The Panama Canal opened to traffic.

1939 "The Wizard of Oz" premieres at Grauman's Chinese Theater, Hollywood.

1961 East German workers began building the Berlin Wall.

1969 Woodstock Music and Art Fair opened in New York State.

# August 16

## Birthdays

1894 George Meany, labor leader

1925 Fess Parker, actor (Davy Crockett, *Gunsmoke*)

1930 Frank Gifford, football star, sportscaster

## Events

1829 Siamese twins Chang and Eng Bunker arrived in Boston to be exhibited.

1863 Emancipation Proclamation signed.

1977 Elvis Presley dies of heart ailment at Graceland at age 42.

# August 17

## Birthdays

1786 Davy Crockett, American frontiersman, adventurer, soldier

1892 Mae West, actress

1943 Robert De Niro, actor

## Events

1807 Robert Fulton's steamboat *Clermont* begins first trip up Hudson River from New York to Albany (150 miles, 32 hours).

1870 Mrs. Esther Morris becomes the first woman magistrate—appointed Justice of the Peace, South Pass, WY.

1896 Gold discovered at Bonanza Creek, Klondike region of the Yukon.

# August 18

## Birthdays

1587 Virginia Dare, first child born in America of English parents

1774 Meriwether Lewis, searched the Louisiana territory

1834 Marshall Field, founder of a Chicago-based store chain

1937 Robert Redford, actor (*The Sting, The Natural, The Great Gatsby*)

## Events

1960 First photograph bounced off a satellite, Cedar Rapids, IA.

1963 James Meredith became first black graduate from University of Mississippi.

# August 19

## Birthdays

1785 Seth Thomas, pioneer in mass production of clocks

1871 Orville Wright, aviator

1902 Ogden Nash, American humorous poet ("I'm a Stranger Here Myself")

## Events

1848 The *New York Herald* announced the discovery of gold California

1888 The first beauty contest is held, Spa, Belgium.

1950 ABC begins the tradition of Saturday morning kid shows.

# August 20

## Birthdays

1833 Benjamin Harrison, 23rd President

1921 Jacqueline Susann, writer *(Valley of the Dolls)*

1946 Connie Chung, TV newscaster

## Events

1920 U.S.'s first commercial radio, 8MK (later WWJ), Detroit, began daily broadcasting

1940 British Prime Minister Churchill said of the Royal Air Force, "Never on the field of human conflict was so much owed by so many to so few," referring to the Battle of Britain.

# August 21

## Birthdays

1660 Hubert Gautier, engineer, wrote first book on bridge building

1906 Count Basie, musician

1930 Don King, boxing promoter, hair style trend-setter

1936 Wilt Chamberlain, basketball great

1938 Kenny Rogers, singer

## Events

1841 John Hampson patents the venetian blind.

1858 First debate between senatorial contenders Abraham Lincoln and Stephen Douglas. Lincoln lost the election, but gained visibility.

1878 American Bar Association founded at the Saratoga, NY town hall.

# August 22

## Birthdays

1920 Ray Bradbury, science-fiction author *(Fahrenheit 451)*

1940 Valerie Harper, actress *(Mary Tyler Moore Show, Rhoda)*

1948 Cindy Williams, director, actress *(Laverne and Shirley)*

## Events

1851 The yacht *America* wins the first Royal Yacht Squadron Cup, now known as the America's Cup, at a regatta in England.

1864 Geneva Convention signed, by 12 nations.

# August 23

## Birthdays

1785 Oliver Hazard Perry, American commander at Battle of Lake Erie

1869 Edgar Lee Masters, American poet (*Spoon River Anthology*)

1912 Gene Kelly, dancer, actor, singer

## Events

1617 The first one-way streets are established, London.

1833 Britain abolishes slavery in colonies; 700,000 slaves freed.

1919 "Gasoline Alley" cartoon strip premieres in *Chicago Tribune*. It was the first cartoon in which the characters aged.

# August 24

## Birthdays

1816 Sir Daniel Gooch, laid first successful transatlantic cables

1960 Cal Ripken, Jr., baseball's other Iron Man

## Events

0079 Mt. Vesuvius erupts; Pompeii and Herculaneum are buried.

1814 British sack Washington, D.C.; White House burned.

1853 The first potato chips are prepared by Chef George Crum, Saratoga Springs, NY.

1869 The waffle iron is invented.

1960 Temperaure drops to -88 degrees Celsius (-127 degrees Fahrenheit) at Vostok, Antarctica (world record).

# August 25

## Birthdays

1819 Allan Pinkerton, founder of the famous Chicago detective agency

1913 Walt Kelly, cartoonist, creator of "Pogo"

1918 Leonard Bernstein, conductor, composer, pianist

## Events

1875 Matthew Webb becomes first to swim the English Channel.

1919 First scheduled passenger service by airplane (Paris-London).

1944 Paris is liberated from Nazi occupation, WWII.

# August 26

## Birthdays

1873 Lee De Forest, invented the Audion vacuum tube (radio tube)

1921 Benjamin C. Bradlee, *Washington Post* executive editor, journalist

1935 Geraldine Ferraro, first female major-party vice-presidential candidate

## Events

55 B.C. Roman forces under Julius Caesar invaded Britain.

1973 University of Texas at Arlington becomes the first accredited school to offer a course in belly dancing.

# August 27

## Birthdays

1871 Theodore Dreiser, novelist (*Sister Carrie, An American Tragedy*)

1908 Lyndon B. Johnson, 36th President

1910 Mother Teresa of Calcutta (Nobel Prize, 1979)

**Events**

1912 Edgar Rice Burroughs publishes *Tarzan.*

1921 Green Bay Packers granted NFL franchise.

## August 28

**Birthdays**

1774 Elizabeth Ann Bayley Seton, first American-born saint

1828 Leo Tolstoy, writer, social philosopher (*War and Peace, Anna Karenina*)

1925 Donald O'Connor, comedian, actor, dancer

**Events**

1837 Pharmacists John Lea and William Perrins of Worcester, England begin manufacture of worcestershire sauce.

1907 United Parcel Service begins service, Seattle.

1963 Martin Luther King, Jr., gives "I have a dream" speech at Lincoln Memorial; 200,000 demonstrate for equal rights.

## August 29

**Birthdays**

1632 John Locke, philosopher

1915 Ingrid Bergman, actress (*Casablanca*)

1938 Peter Jennings, ABC anchor

1958 Michael Jackson, singer

**Events**

1885 Gottlieb Daimler receives German patent for a motorcycle.

1896 Chop suey invented in New York City by chef of visiting Chinese ambassador.

## August 30

**Birthdays**

1797 Mary Shelley, author (*Frankenstein*)

1908 Fred MacMurray, actor (*The Caine Mutiny, My Three Sons*)

1918 Ted Williams, baseball great

**Events**

1961 First black judge of a District Court confirmed—J.B. Parsons.

1979 First recorded occurrence of a comet hitting the sun (the energy released was about equal to 1 million hydrogen bombs).

## August 31

**Birthdays**

1870 Maria Montessori, educator

1903 Arthur Godfrey, radio, TV host

1924 Buddy Hackett, comedian, actor

**Events**

1842 U.S. Naval Observatory is authorized by an act of Congress.

## September 1

**Birthdays**

1875 Edgar Rice Burroughs, novelist (*Tarzan*)

1923 Rocky Marciano, boxer

1939 Lily Tomlin, comedian, actress (*9 to 5, All of Me*)

**Events**

1864 Sherman's march through Georgia begins.

1878 First woman telephone operator starts work (Emma Nutt Boston).

1914 Martha, last known passenger pigeon, dies at Cincinnati Zoo.

1977 First TRS-80 Model I computer sold.

1985 *Titanic*, sunk 1912, found by French and American scientists.

# September 2

## Birthdays

1937 Peter Ueberroth, baseball commissioner

1948 Terry Bradshaw, football quarterback, sportscaster

1952 Jimmy Connors, tennis player

## Events

490 B.C. Phidippides runs first marathon, to announce the victory of Sparta over Persia.

1789 U.S. Treasury Department established by Congress.

1963 CBS and NBC expand network news from 15 to 30 minutes.

# September 3

## Birthdays

1860 Edward A. Filene, merchant, established U.S. credit union movement

1965 Charlie Sheen, actor

## Events

1783 Treaty of Paris, ending the Revolutionary War, is signed.

1916 The Allies turned back the Germans in World War I's Battle of Verdun.

1935 First automobile to exceed 30 mph— Sir Malcolm Campbell.

# September 4

## Birthdays

1908 Richard Wright, author (*Native Son, Uncle Tom's Children*)

1917 Henry Ford II, businessman

1918 Paul Harvey, news commentator

## Events

1609 Navigator Henry Hudson discovered the island of Manhattan.

1781 Los Angeles founded in the Valley of Smokes (Indian name).

1882 First district lit by electricty (New York's Pearl Street station).

1885 The first cafeteria opens for business, New York City.

1888 George Eastman patents first roll-film camera and registers "Kodak."

# September 5

## Birthdays

1847 Jesse James, outlaw

1897 Arthur C. Nielsen, developer of Nielsen ratings for television

1902 Darryl F. Zanuck, Hollywood producer and motion picture executive

1940 Raquel Welch, actress

## Events

1882 10,000 workers marched in the first Labor Day parade in New York City.

1958 First color video recording on magnetic tape presented, Charlotte, NC.

# September 6

## Birthdays

1757 Marquis de Lafayette, American patriot, French revolutionary

## Events

1716 First lighthouse in U.S. built, Boston.

1901 President William McKinley shot and critically wounded in Buffalo, NY. He died eight days later.

1966 *Star Trek* appears on TV for the first time (on NBC.)

# September 7

## Birthdays

1860 Anna Mary Robertson (a.k.a. Grandma Moses), American primitive painter

1923 Peter Lawford, actor, (*Mrs. Miniver, Little Women, Ocean's Eleven*)

1936 Buddy Holly, singer ("Peggy Sue," "That'll Be the Day")

## Events

1896 First closed-circuit auto race, at Cranston, RI.

1980 32nd Emmy Awards shown despite actors' boycott.

# September 8

## Birthdays

1922 Sid Caesar, comedian, actor

1925 Peter Sellers, actor

1940 Frankie Avalon, singer, actor

## Events

1920 First U.S. Air Mail service begins.

1974 President Gerald Ford pardons former president Richard Nixon.

# September 9

## Birthdays

1754 William Bligh, mean ship's captain

1919 Jimmy "the Greek" Snyder, oddsmaker

## Events

1776 Continental Congress authorizes the name "United States."

1839 John Herschel takes the first glass plate photograph.

1850 California becomes the 31st state.

1926 NBC created by the Radio Corporation of America.

# September 10

## Birthdays

1839 Isaac Kauffman Funk, publisher (Funk and Wagnalls)

1907 Fay Wray, actress (*King Kong*)

1929 Arnold Palmer, golfer

## Events

1846 Elias Howe receives patent for his sewing machine.

1913 Lincoln Highway opens as the first paved coast-to-coast highway.

1953 Swanson sells its first TV dinner.

1963 20 black students entered public schools in Alabama.

# September 11

## Birthdays

1862 O. Henry (pen name of William Sidney Porter), short-story writer

1885 D.H. Lawrence, author (*Lady Chatterley's Lover*)

1913 Bear Bryant, football coach

1932 Robert Packwood, Oregon senator

## Events

1928 First TV drama—WGY's *The Queen's Messenger*.

1946 First mobile long-distance car-to-car telephone conversation.

1950 "Dick Tracy" TV show sparks uproar concerning violence.

# September 12

## Birthdays

1818 Richard Jordan Gatling, inventor of hand-cranked machine gun

1888 Maurice Chevalier, actor, singer

1892 Alfred A. Knopf, publisher

## Events

1609 English explorer Henry Hudson enters the Hudson River

1959 *Bonanza* premieres—in color.

1966 *The Monkees* premieres.

# September 13

## Birthdays

1851 Walter Reed, proved mosquitoes transmit yellow fever

1857 Milton S. Hershey, chocolate manufacturer, philanthropist

1925 Mel ("Velvet Fog") Torme, singer

## Events

1788 New York City becomes capitol of U.S.

1906 First airplane flight in Europe.

1977 First TV viewer-discretion warning— *Soap.*

# September 14

## Birthdays

1849 Ivan Pavlov, Russian physiologist, pioneer in psychology

1879 Margaret Sanger, feminist, nurse, birth control proponent

1914 Clayton Moore, actor (the Lone Ranger)

## Events

1814 Francis Scott Key inspired to write "The Star-Spangled Banner."

1848 Alexander Stewart opens the first department store in the U.S.

1886 The typewriter ribbon is patented.

1899 While in New York, Henry Bliss becomes first automobile fatality.

# September 15

## Birthdays

1789 James Fenimore Cooper, first major American novelist

1857 William Howard Taft, 27th President, Supreme Court chief justice

1890 Dame Agatha Christie, mystery writer

## Events

1789 Department of Foreign Affairs renamed the Department of State.

1935 Nuremberg Laws deprived German Jews of citizenship and made the swastika the official symbol of Nazi Germany.

1963 Four children are killed in bombing of a black Baptist church in Birmingham.

# September 16

## Birthdays

1914 Allen Funt, "Candid Camera" creator

1924 Lauren Bacall, actress, whistler (*Dark Passage, Key Largo, Always*)

1925 B. B. King, singer, musician

## Events

1630 Massachussetts village of Shawmut changed its name to Boston.

1782 Great Seal of the United States is used for first time.

# September 17

## Birthdays

1907 Warren E. Burger, Supreme Court chief justice

1923 Hank Williams, country singer ("Cold, Cold Heart," "Hey Good Lookin' ")

## Events

1630 City of Boston founded.

1776 The Presidio of San Francisco was founded as Spanish fort.

1787 U.S. Constitution adopted and signed.

1920 National Football League formed in Canton, OH.

# September 18

## Birthdays

1905 Greta Garbo, actress

1933 Robert Blake, actor

1940 Frankie Valli, singer

## Events

1851 *The New York Times* goes on sale at two cents a copy.

1895 D.D. Palmer of Davenport, IA, becomes the first chiropractor.

1927 The Columbia Broadcasting System goes on the air.

# September 19

## Birthdays

1926 Duke Snyder, baseball player

1932 Mike Royko, syndicated columnist

## Events

1849 First commercial laundry established, Oakland, CA.

1881 President James Garfield dies of gunshot wound.

# September 20

## Birthdays

357 B.C. Alexander III the Great, king of Macedonia, emperor

1878 Upton Sinclair, novelist (*The Jungle*)

1934 Sophia Loren, actress (*Desire Under the Elms, Black Orchid*)

## Events

1519 Magellan starts first successful circumnavigation of the world.

1850 Slave trade abolished in District of Columbia, but slavery allowed to continue.

1859 Patent granted on the electric range.

# September 21

## Birthdays

1866 H. G. (Herbert George) Wells, futurist, writer (*War of the Worlds*)

1931 Larry Hagman, actor (*I Dream of Jeannie, Dallas*), son of Mary Martin

## Events

1895 First auto manufacturer opens—Duryea Motor Wagon Company.

1930 Johann Ostermeyer patents his invention, the flashbulb.

1970 *Monday Night Football* on ABC premieres—New York Jets vs. Cleveland Browns.

# September 22

## Birthdays

1791 Michael Faraday, discovered principle of the electric motor

1902 John Houseman, actor

1927 Tom Lasorda, baseball manager

## Events

1776 Nathan Hale is executed as a spy by the British.

1789 The U.S. Post Office was established.

1862 President Lincoln makes his Emancipation Proclamation speech.

1893 First auto built in U.S. runs in Springfield (built by Duryea brothers).

1903 Italo Marchiony granted a patent for the ice-cream cone.

# September 23

## Birthdays

1800 William H. McGuffey, educator (*McGuffey Readers*)

1930 Ray Charles, musician

1949 Bruce "The Boss" Springsteen, musician ("Born in the U.S.A.")

## Events

1780 John Andre reveals Benedict Arnold's plot to betray West Point.

1862 Lincoln's Emancipation Proclaimation published in Northern newspapers.

1962 ABC's first color TV series—*The Jetsons.*

# September 24

## Birthdays

1755 John Marshall, Supreme Court chief justice

1870 Georges Claude, inventor of the neon light

1896 F. Scott Fitzgerald, writer *(The Great Gatsby)*

1931 Barbara Walters, first network news anchorwoman

1936 Jim Henson, creator of the Muppets, "our era's Charlie Chaplin, Mae West, W.C. Fields, and Marx Brothers"

## Events

1853 First round-the-world trip by yacht (Cornelius Vanderbilt).

1895 First round-the-world trip by a woman on a bicycle (took 15 months).

1934 Babe Ruth made his farewell appearance as a baseball player.

# September 25

## Birthdays

1725 Nicolas-Joseph Cugnot, designed and built first automobile

1897 William Faulkner, U.S. author (*Sound and the Fury*) (Nobel Prize, 1949)

1952 Christopher Reeve, actor (*Superman, Somewhere in Time*)

## Events

1513 Vasco Nunez de Balboa is the first European to see the Pacific Ocean.

1639 First printing press in America.

1926 Henry Ford announces the five-day work week.

1956 First transatlantic telephone cable goes into operation.

# September 26

## Birthdays

1774 John Chapman, alias Johnny Appleseed

1888 T.S. Eliot, playwright, poet (*The Waste Land*) (Nobel Prize, 1948)

1898 George Gershwin, composer (*Rhapsody in Blue*)

## Events

1789 Jefferson is appointed first Secretary of State; John Jay, first chief justice; Samuel Osgood, first Postmaster; and Edmund J. Randolph, first Attorney General.

1914 Federal Trade Commission formed to regulate interstate commerce.

1960 First of four TV debates between Richard Nixon and John F. Kennedy took place in Chicago.

# September 27

## Birthdays

1722 Samuel Adams, revolutionary hero

1840 Thomas Nast, political cartoonist of late 1800s America

1957 Cheryl Tiegs, model

## Events

1825 Railroad transportation is born with first track England.

1919 Democratic National Committee voted to admit women.

1964 Warren Commission decides that Lee Harvey Oswald acted alone.

# September 28

## Birthdays

0551 Confucius (as celebrated in Taiwan)

1909 Al Capp, cartoonist (*Li'l Abner*)

## Events

1920 In baseball's biggest scandal, a grand jury indicts eight Chicago White Sox for throwing the 1919 World Series with the Cincinnati Reds.

1982 First reports appeared of death from cyanide-laced Tylenol capsules.

# September 29

## Birthdays

1907 Gene Autry, cowpoke, singer, actor, California Angels owner

1935 Jerry Lee Lewis, singer ("Great Balls of Fire," "Breathless")

1948 Bryant Gumbel, talk-show host

## Events

1829 Scotland Yard formed in London.

1892 First night football game was played, Mansfield, PA.

1982 Cyanide-laced Tylenol capsules killed seven in Chicago.

# September 30

## Birthdays

1924 Truman Capote, author (*In Cold Blood*)

1931 Angie Dickinson, actress

## Events

1452 First book published—Johann Gutenberg's *Bible*.

1846 William Morris first uses ether in the first tooth extraction under anesthesia at Charlestown, MA.

1927 Babe Ruth hits 60th homer setting the record off Tom Zachary.

# October 1

## Birthdays

1881 William Edward Boeing, founded aircraft company

1920 Walter Matthau, actor (*The Odd Couple, The Bad News Bears*)

1927 Tom Bosley, actor (*Happy Days, Murder She Wrote*)

1935 Julie Andrews, actress, singer (*Sound of Music, Mary Poppins, Victor/Victoria*)

## Events

1896 Yosemite becomes a national park.

1903 First World Series starts between the National and American Leagues.

1908 Henry Ford introduces the Model T car.

1962 Johnny Carson hosts his first "Tonight Show."

1971 Walt Disney World, Orlando, FL, opens.

# October 2

## Birthdays

1895 Groucho Marx, comedian

1904 Graham Greene, prolific English novelist (*Brighton Rock*)

## Events

322 B.C. Aristotle dies of indigestion.

1942 First self-sustaining nuclear chain-reaction demonstrated in one of the squash courts under Stagg Field, University of Chicago.

1950 First *Peanuts* comic strip featuring Charlie Brown and Snoopy appears in nine newspapers.

# October 3

## Birthdays

1803 John Gorrie, invented cold-air process of refrigeration

1925 Gore Vidal, writer (*Myra Breckinridge, Lincoln*)

1941 Chubby Checker, singer

## Events

1789 Washington proclaims the first national Thanksgiving Day on November 26.

1863 Lincoln designates the last Thursday in November as Thanksgiving Day.

1913 Federal income tax is signed into law (at 1 percent).

1920 National Football League (then American Pro Football Association) plays first games.

# October 4

## Birthdays

1822 Rutherford B. Hayes, 19th President

1880 Damon Runyon, writer

1895 Buster Keaton, silent-movie actor (*The Navigator, Steamboat Bill, Jr.*)

1923 Charlton Heston, actor (*The Ten Commandments, Ben Hur, Planet of the Apes*)

## Events

1648 Peter Stuyvesant establishes America's first volunteer fire department.

1883 The Orient Express begins its first run, linking Turkey to Europe by rail.

1931 The comic strip *Dick Tracy* debuts.

1957 *Leave It to Beaver* debuts on CBS.

# October 5

## Birthdays

1829 Chester A. Arthur, 21st President

1905 Ray Kroc, founder of McDonald's

## Events

1892 Dalton Gang ends in shoot-out in Coffeville, Kansas bank holdup.

1921 First radio broadcast of the World Series—New York Yankees beat New York Giants 3-0.

1931 First nonstop transpacific flight, Japan to Wenatchee, WA.

# October 6

## Birthdays

1846 George Westinghouse, pushes for alternating current in U.S.

1912 Thor Heyerdahl, anthropologist, explorer, author (*Kon-Tiki, Aku-Aku*)

1956 Stephanie Zimbalist, actress (*Remington Steele*)

## Events

1863 Dr. Charles H. Sheppard opens the first public bath, Brooklyn, NY.

1889 Thomas Edison shows his first motion picture.

1927 *The Jazz Singer*, first movie with a sound track, premieres.

# October 7

## Birthdays

1849 James Whitcomb Riley, American poet ("The Raggedy Man")

1879 Joe Hill, songwriter, IWW organizer, martyr

1885 Niels Bohr, physicist, expanded quantum physics (Nobel Prize, 1922)

## Events

1931 First infrared photograph, Rochester, NY.

1968 Motion Picture Association of America adopts film rating system.

# October 8

## Birthdays

1869 J. Frank Duryea, with his brother, invented first auto built and operated in the U.S.

1890 Eddie Rickenbacker, aviator

1943 Chevy Chase, comedian, actor

## Events

1896 Dow Jones starts reporting an average of industrial stocks.

1918 Sgt. Alvin York single-handedly kills 25, captures 132 Germans.

1956 Don Larsen's perfect World Series game beats Dodgers 2-0.

1995 O.J. Simpson acquitted of double murder of his ex-wife Nicole Brown Simpson and Ronald Goldman.

# October 9

## Birthdays

1547 Miguel de Cervantes, novelist (*Don Quixote*)

1940 John Lennon, musician (Beatles)

## Events

1000 Leif Ericson discovers "Vinland" (possibly New England).

1876 First two-way telephone conversation.

# October 10

## Birthdays

1830 Emily Dickinson, poet

1924 James Clavell, author (*Shogun, Tai Pan, King Rat, Noble House*)

1930 Adlai Stevenson III, Illinois senator

## Events

1845 U.S. Naval academy opens at Annapolis, Maryland.

1886 Griswold Lorillard wears the first dinner jacket to the Autumn Ball in Tuxedo Park. Thus the name 'tuxedo.'

1957 President Eisenhower apologized to finance minister of Ghana, Komla Agbeli Gbdemah, after he was refused service in a Dover, DE restaurant.

# October 11

## Birthdays

1844 Henry John Heinz, founded a prepared-foods company

1884 Eleanor Roosevelt, first lady, crusader

## Events

1890 Daughters of the American Revolution founded.

1975 Saturday Night Live premieres.

1984 Kathy Sullivan becomes first American woman to walk in space.

# October 12

## Birthdays

1860 Elmer Sperry, inventor of the gyrocompass

1928 Spanky McFarland, actor (Little Rascals)

1933 Joan Rivers, comedian

1935 Luciano Pavarotti, operatic tenor

## Events

1492 Christopher Columbus and crew sighted land present-day Bahamas.

1823 Charles Macintosh of Scotland begins selling his raincoats.

# October 13

## Birthdays

1853 Lillie Langtry (the Jersey Lily), actress, singer

1925 Margaret Thatcher (Tory), British PM

1941 Paul Simon, musician

## Events

1775 Continental Congress establishes a navy.

1953 Burglar alarm—ultrasonic or radio waves—patented—Samuel Bagno.

1987 First military use of trained dolphins by U.S. Navy, Persian Gulf.

# October 14

## Birthdays

1890 Dwight D. Eisenhower, 34th President

1894 e e cummings, poet

## Events

1884 George Eastman patents paper-strip photographic film.

1947 Chuck Yeager pilots the world's first supersonic flight (Mach 1.015 at 12,800m) at Muroc, CA.

# October 15

## Birthdays

1844 Friedrich Nietzsche, philosopher

1858 John L. Sullivan, famed boxer

1908 John Kenneth Galbraith, economist

1921 Mario Puzo, author (*The Godfather*)

1924 Lee A. Iacocca, CEO of Chrysler Corp

## Events

1860 Grace Bedell writes to Lincoln, tells him to grow a beard.

1939 LaGuardia Airport opened in New York City.

1951 *I Love Lucy* premieres.

# October 16

## Birthdays

1758 Noah Webster, lexicographer

1888 Eugene O'Neill, playwright (*Desire Under the Elms*) (Nobel Prize, 1936)

1925 Angela Lansbury, actress (*Sweeney Todd; Murder, She Wrote*)

## Events

1829 The Tremont Hotel, the first modern hotel in the U.S., opens in Boston, featuring washbowls in each room, and eight bathrooms in the basement!

1846 Dentist William T. Morton demonstrated effectiveness of ether.

1859 Abolitionist John Brown leads group of 20 in a raid on the U.S. armory at Harper's Ferry, VA.

1916 Margaret Sanger opens the first public birth control clinic, Brooklyn, NY.

1923 Disney Company founded.

# October 17

## Birthdays

1915 Arthur Miller, playwright (*Death of a Salesman, The Crucible*)

1919 Rita Hayworth, actor

1930 Jimmy Breslin, newspaperman

1938 Robert "Evel" Knievel, daredevil

## Events

1931 Al Capone convicted of tax evasion, sentenced to 11 years in prison.

1933 Albert Einstein arrives in the U.S., a refugee from Nazi Germany.

1973 The Arab oil embargo begins. It will last until March, 1974.

1979 Mother Teresa of India was awarded the Nobel Peace Prize.

1985 Lou Pinella named New York Yankees manager.

# October 18

## Birthdays

1926 Chuck Berry, rock 'n' roll star

1927 George C. Scott, actor (*Patton, The Exorcist, Scrooge*)

1928 Keith Jackson, sportscaster

## Events

1776 The back of a bar in New York is decorated with birds' tail feathers. Customer jokingly asks for glass of "cock tails," and a tradition is born!

1892 First commercial long-distance phone line opens (Chicago-New York).

# October 19

## Birthdays

1922 Jack Anderson, columnist

1931 John Le Carre, English spy novelist (*Little Drummer Girl*)

1967 Amy Carter, daughter of President Jimmy Carter

## Events

1781 Cornwallis surrenders at Yorktown at 2 p.m., U.S. wins American Revolution.

1872 World's largest gold nugget (215 kg) found in New South Wales.

# October 20

## Birthdays

1632 Sir Christopher Wren, astronomer, greatest English architect of his time, built many of the cathedrals in London.

1859 John Dewey, philosopher

1931 Mickey Mantle, home-run slugger

## Events

1820 Spain sells (east) Florida to U.S. for $5 million.

1906 Dr. Lee DeForest gives a demonstration of his radio tube.

1944 During WWII, MacArthur leads U.S. forces landing at Leyte, Phillipines, stating "I have returned."

# October 21

## Birthdays

1833 Alfred Bernhard Nobel, creator of dynamite and Nobel Prizes

1917 Dizzy Gillespie, trumpeter, pioneer of modern jazz

## Events

1879 Thomas Edison commercially perfects the light bulb.

1918 Margaret Owen sets world typing speed record of 170 wpm for one minute.

# October 22

## Birthdays

1920 Timothy Leary, psychologist, drug testing advocate

1922 John Chafee, Rhode Island senator

1938 Christopher Lloyd, actor (*Taxi, Star Trek III, Back to the Future*)

1942 Annette Funicello, Mouseketeer, actress

## Events

4004 B.C. Universe created at 8:00 p.m., according to the 1650 pronouncement of Anglican archbishop James Ussher.

1797 Andres-Jacques Garnerin makes the first parachute jump from a balloon (Paris, France).

1962 JFK imposes naval blockade on Cuba, beginning missile crisis.

# October 23

## Birthdays

1752 Nicolas Appert, inventor of food canning, bouillon tablet

1925 Johnny Carson

## Events

1915 25,000 women marched in New York City, demanding the right to vote.

1956 First video recording on magnetic tape televised coast-to-coast.

1973 President Nixon agrees to turn over White House tape recordings.

# October 24

## Birthdays

1904 Moss Hart, playwright

1911 Clarence M. Kelley, FBI head

1926 Y.A. Tittle, football quarterback

## Events

1836 The match is patented.

1861 First transcontinental telegram sent.

1901 Anna Taylor, first to go over Niagara Falls, in a barrel and live.

1945 United Nations Charter goes into effect.

# October 25

## Birthdays

1881 Pablo Picasso, artist

1888 Richard E. Byrd, polar explorer

1912 Sarah Ophelia Colley (a.k.a. Minnie Pearl), entertainer (Grand Old Opry, Hee-Haw)

## Events

1415 Battle of Agincourt; Welsh longbow defeats the armored knight.

1854 The Light Brigade charges—Battle of Balaklava (Crimean War).

1930 First scheduled transcontinental air service began.

1939 Nylon stockings go on sale in the U.S.

1960 First electronic wrist watch placed on sale, New York City.

# October 26

## Birthdays

1855 Charles Post, creator of Post cereals

1917 Felix the Cat, cartoon character

## Events

1774 First Continental Congress adjourns in Philadelphia.

1861 Telegraph service inaugurated in U.S. (end of Pony Express).

1881 Shootout at OK Corral, Tombstone, AZ.

1949 President Truman increases minimum wage—from 40 cents to 75 cents.

1984 "Baby Fae" gets a baboon heart in an experimental transplant, Loma Linda, CA. She lives for 21 days with the animal heart.

# October 27

## Birthdays

1728 Captain James Cook, discovered the Sandwich Islands

1858 Theodore Roosevelt, 26th President (Nobel Prize, 1906)

## Events

1858 R.H. Macy and Co. opens first store, on 6th Avenue, New York City. First day's gross receipts: $1,106.

1954 Walt Disney's first TV show, *Disneyland*, premieres on ABC.

# October 28

## Birthdays

1914 Dr. Jonas Salk, inventor of the polio vaccine

1936 Charlie Daniels, country-music star

1949 Bruce Jenner, decathlon champ

## Events

1790 New York gives up claims to Vermont exchange for $30,000.

1793 Eli Whitney applies for patent for the cotton gin.

1886 President Grover Cleveland dedicates the Statue of Liberty.

1904 St. Louis Police try a new investigation method—fingerprints.

# October 29

## Birthdays

1884 Bela Lugosi, horror actor (*Dracula, The Body Snatcher*)

1921 Bill Mauldin, political cartoonist

1947 Richard Dreyfuss, actor (*Jaws, Close Encounters of the Third Kind*)

## Events

1682 Pennsylvania granted to William Penn by King Charles II.

1863 International Committee of the Red Cross is founded (Nobel Prize, 1917, 1944, 1963).

1904 The first intercity trucking service goes into business with route between Colorado City and Snyder, TX.

# October 30

## Birthdays

1735 John Adams, 2nd President

1885 Ezra Pound, poet (*Cantos*)

1945 Henry Winkler, actor (*Happy Days*)

## Events

1775 U.S. Navy is created.

1938 Orson Welles panics nation with broadcast of "War of the Worlds."

1945 U.S. government announces end of shoe rationing.

# November 1

## Birthdays

1798 Sir Benjamin Lee, Baronet Guinness, Irish brewer, Dublin mayor

1871 Stephen Crane, poet, author *(Red Badge of Courage)*

## Events

1834 First published reference to the game of poker; describes it as a Mississippi riverboat game.

1870 U.S. Weather Bureau begins operations.

# November 2

## Birthdays

1734 Daniel Boone, explorer, pioneer

1755 Marie Antoinette, advocate of cake eating

1795 James Knox Polk, 11th President

1815 George Boole, mathematician, father of boolean logic

## Events

1920 KDKA (Pittsburgh) on the air as first commercial radio station.

1947 Howard Hughes's flying boat flies for first (and last) time.

1948 Truman beats Dewey, confounding pollsters and newspapers.

1959 Charles Van Doren confesses TV show *21* is rigged.

# November 3

## Birthdays

1718 John Montague, 4th Earl of Sandwich, inventor of same

1918 Bob Feller, pitcher

1933 Ken Berry, actor, dancer

## Events

1900 The first national automobile show opens at Madison Square Garden in New York City.

1952 Clarence Birdseye markets frozen peas.

# November 4

## Birthdays

1879 Will Rogers, humorist

1916 Walter Cronkite, newsman

1918 Art Carney, actor *(The Honeymooners, Harold and Maude)*

1937 Loretta Swit, actress *(M\*A\*S\*H\*)*

## Events

1879 James Ritty patents the first cash register, to combat stealing by bartenders in his Dayton, Ohio saloon.

1922 Howard Carter discovers the tomb of Tutankhamen.

1924 Nellie Tayloe Ross elected first U.S. female governor (Wyoming).

1939 First air-conditioned automobile (Packard) exhibited, Chicago, IL.

# November 5

## Birthdays

1885 Wil Durant, writer, historian *(Story of Civilization)*, poet

1912 Roy Rogers, cowboy, singer

1913 Vivien Leigh, actress *(Gone With The Wind)*

1941 Art Garfunkel, singer, songwriter

## Events

1605 Plot to blow up British Parliament fails—first Guy Fawkes Day.

1875 Susan B. Anthony arrested for attempting to vote.

1895 First U.S. patent granted for the automobile, to George B. Selden.

1911 First coast-to-coast airplane flight (New York-Pasadena, many stops).

1935 The Parker Brothers launch the game of Monopoly.

# November 6

## Birthdays

1771 Aloys Senefelder, inventor of lithography

1851 Charles Henry Dow, co-founder of Dow Jones, first editor of *The Wall Street Journal*

1854 John Phillip Souza, march king ("Stars and Stripes Forever")

1861 James A. Naismith, inventor of basketball

1887 Walter Johnson, Hall of Fame pitcher

## Events

1860 Abraham Lincoln is elected 16th President of the United States.

1869 First intercollegiate football game (Rutgers 6, Princeton 4).

1939 WGY-TV (Schenectady, NY), is the first commercial-license station to begin service.

1952 U.S. explodes world's first hydrogen bomb at Eniwetok Atoll.

# November 7

## Birthdays

1867 Madame Marie Sklodowska Curie, discovered radium (Nobel Prize, 1903, 1911)

1918 Billy Graham, evangelist

1922 Al Hirt, trumpet player

## Events

1805 Lewis and Clark first sighted the Pacific Ocean.

1874 First cartoon to use the elephant as the symbol of the Republican Party appears in *Harper's Weekly*. It is drawn by Thomas Nast.

1885 Canada completes its own transcontinental railway.

1962 Richard Nixon's first time quitting politics—"You won't have Nixon to kick around anymore," he tells the press.

# November 8

## Birthdays

1656 Sir Edmond Halley, astronomer, first to calculate a comet's orbit

1900 Margaret Mitchell, author (*Gone With the Wind*)

1909 Katherine Hepburn, actress

1922 Dr. Christiaan Barnard, performed first human heart transplantation

## Events

1789 Bourbon Whiskey is first distilled from corn by Reverend Elijah Craig, Bourbon County, Kentucky.

1793 The Louvre, Paris, opened to public.

1837 Mount Holyoke Seminary, Massachusetts, is the first U.S. college founded for women.

1970 Tom Dempsey of New Orleans Saints kicks NFL-record 63-yard field goal.

# November 9

## Birthdays

1903 Gregory Pincus, birth-control-pill inventor

1918 Spiro Agnew, 39th Vice President

1926 Hugh Hefner, publisher

1932 Carl Perkins, musician

1934 Carl Sagan, astronomer, author
(*Cosmos, Broca's Brain*)

## Events

1924 Miriam (Ma) Ferguson becomes first elected woman governor (of Texas).

1965 Massive power failure New England and Ontario, Canada at 5:16 p.m.

# November 10

## Birthdays

1819 Cyrus West Field, financier known for the success of the first transatlantic cable

1827 Lewis Wallace, soldier, diplomat, novelist (*Ben Hur*)

1847 Joseph Pulitzer, journalist, publisher

1925 Richard Burton, Welsh actor (*Cleopatra, Who's Afraid of Virginia Woolf?*)

## Events

1775 U.S. Marine Corps established by Congress.

1891 First Women's Christian Temperance Union meeting held (Boston).

1945 Nazi concentration camp at Buchenwald liberated by U.S.

1951 First Long Distance telephone call without operator assistance.

1960 Senate passes landmark Civil Rights Bill.

1969 "Sesame Street" premieres.

# November 11

## Birthdays

1821 Fyodor Dostoevsky, author (*Crime and Punishment*)

1885 George S. Patton, U.S. military leader

1922 Kurt Vonnegut, Jr., author (*Slaughterhouse-Five, Sirens of Titan*)

1925 Jonathan Winters, comedian, actor

## Events

1918 Armistice Day—WW I ends (at 11 a.m. on Western Front).

1921 President Harding dedicates Tomb of the Unknown Soldier.

1939 Kate Smith first sang Irving Berlin's "God Bless America."

# November 12

## Birthdays

1840 Auguste Rodin, sculptor

1929 Grace Kelly, actress, Princess of Monaco

## Events

1859 Jules Leotard performs the first Flying Trapeze circus act in Paris. He also designed the garment that bears his name.

1933 First Sunday football game, Philadelphia (previously illegal).

1946 The first "autobank" (banking by car) was established, Chicago.

1987 Van Gogh's "Irises" sells for $53,900,000 —record amount for a painting.

# November 13

## Birthdays

1850 Robert Louis Stevenson, writer (*Treasure Island*)

1856 Louis Brandeis, Supreme Court justice

1916 Jack Elam, actor

1934 Garry Marshall, producer

## Events

1849 Peter Burnett is elected first governor of California.

1875 Harvard-Yale game is first college football contest with uniforms.

1927 The Holland Tunnel, first underwater vehicular tunnel, opened between New York and New Jersey.

1942 Minimum draft age lowered from 21 to 18.

1970 Cyclone kills 300,000 in Bangladesh.

1982 Vietnam War Memorial dedicated Washington, D.C.

# November 14

## Birthdays

1765 Robert Fulton, built first commercial steamboat

1840 Claude Monet, impressionist painter

1896 Mamie Doud Eisenhower, former First Lady

1948 Charles, Prince of Wales

## Events

1851 *Moby Dick*, by Herman Melville, is published.

1910 First airplane flight from the deck of a ship.

# November 15

## Birthdays

1887 Georgia O'Keeffe, painter

1929 Ed Asner, actor (Lou Grant)

1932 Petula Clark, singer

## Events

1763 Charles Mason and Jeremiah Dixon begin surveying the Mason-Dixon Line—the southern boundary of Pennsylvania.

1806 Zebulon Pike sights Pike's Peak.

1869 Free postal delivery inaugurated.

1881 American Federation of Labor (AFL) founded, Pittsburgh, PA.

1926 National Broadcasting Company goes on the air, with 24 stations.

1939 Social Security Administration approves first unemployment check.

# November 16

## Birthdays

1873 William Handy, blues musician

1896 Jim Jordan, radio comic (Fibber McGee of Fibber McGee and Molly)

1908 Burgess Meredith, actor (*Rocky*)

## Events

1864 William Tecumseh Sherman begins his "march to the sea" through Georgia.

# November 17

## Birthdays

1925 Rock Hudson, actor

1938 Gordon Lightfoot, folk singer

1942 Martin Scorsese, director (*Mean Streets, Taxi Driver*)

1944 Danny DeVito, actor

1944 Tom Seaver, Hall of Fame pitcher

## Events

1800 Congress convened for its first Washington, D.C. session.

1869 The Suez Canal opens.

1940 Green Bay Packers become first NFL team to travel by plane.

1968 The Heidi Bowl: NBC cuts off broadcast of lengthy New York Jets-Oakland Raiders football game to begin *Heidi*. Jets lose 10-point lead, and game, in final two minutes.

1973 President Nixon told Associated Press "...people have got to know whether or not their president is a crook. Well, I am not a crook."

# November 18

## Birthdays

1901 George H. Gallup, pollster

1923 Alan B. Shepard, Jr., first American space (*Freedom 7, Apollo 14*)

## Events

1820 Antarctica discovered by U.S. Navy Captain Nathaniel B. Palmer.

1883 U.S. and Canada begin the use of standard time zones (standard time zones established by the railroads, both countries).

1913 Lincoln Deachey performs first airplane loop-the-loop.

1928 Walt Disney's Mickey Mouse debuts in New York—*Steamboat Willie.*

# November 19

## Birthdays

1831 James A. Garfield, 20th President

1905 Tommy Dorsey, band leader

1933 Larry King, radio talk show host

1938 Ted Turner, broadcasting mogul

1942 Calvin Klein, clothes designer

## Events

1493 Christopher Columbus discovers Puerto Rico.

1620 Pilgrims reach Cape Cod on the Mayflower.

1863 President Lincoln delivers *The Gettysburg Address.*

1915 Union organizer and folk singer Joe Hill is executed by firing squad in Utah.

1959 Ford cancels the Edsel.

1978 Reverend Jim Jones leads 911 people in suicide in Jonestown, Guyana.

# November 20

## Birthdays

1925 Robert Kennedy, senator and U.S. Attorney General

1939 Dick Smothers, comedian

## Events

1888 William Bundy invents the first time-card clock.

1914 The State Department starts requiring photographs for passports.

1967 At 11 a.m., census clock at Department of Commerce ticks past 200 million.

# November 21

## Birthdays

1694 Voltaire, philosopher

1920 Stan Musial, baseball player

1938 Marlo Thomas, actress (*That Girl*)

1945 Goldie Hawn, actress

## Events

1620 Mayflower Compact signed by Pilgrims, Provincetown, MA harbor.

1959 Jack Benny (violin) and Richard Nixon (piano) play their famed duet.

1964 The Verranzano Narrows Bridge (Brooklyn to Staten Island) opens, becoming the world's longest suspension bridge.

# November 22

## Birthdays

1888 Tarzan of the Apes, according to Edgar Rice Burroughs's novel.

1890 Charles de Gaulle, president of France, general

## Events

1906 International Radio Telegraphic Convention adopts "SOS" as new call for help.

1963 Kennedy assassinated in Dallas, TX.

# November 23

## Birthdays

1804 Franklin Pierce, 14th President

1859 Billy the Kid (William H. Bonney), criminal

1887 Boris Karloff, actor (*Frankenstein, Isle of the Dead*)

## Events

1863 Patent granted for a process of making color photographs.

1889 The first jukebox is installed, at a saloon in San Francisco.

1980 Mae West dies at age 88.

# November 24

## Birthdays

1632 Baruch Spinoza, philosopher

1784 Zachary Taylor, 12th President

1864 Henri de Toulouse-Lautrec, painter

1868 Scott Joplin, musician, composer

1888 Dale Carnegie, author (*How to Win Friends and Influence People*)

## Events

1874 A patent is granted to Joseph Glidden for barbed wire.

1963 First and only live murder on TV—Jack Ruby shoots Lee Harvey Oswald.

1971 "D.B. Cooper" parachutes from a Northwest Airlines 727 with $200,000 and passes into legend.

# November 25

## Birthdays

1835 Andrew Carnegie, steel industrialist, philanthopist

1846 Carry Nation, scourge of barkeepers and drinkers

## Events

1783 Britain evacuated New York, their last military position in U.S.

1867 Alfred Nobel invents dynamite.

# November 26

## Birthdays

1607 John Harvard, English clergyman, scholar, founder of Harvard University.

1922 Charles M. Schulz, cartoonist (*Peanuts*)

## Events

1789 First national celebration of Thanksgiving.

1865 *Alice in Wonderland* is published.

1940 Nazis force 4.5 million Warsaw Jews to live in walled ghetto.

# November 27

## Birthdays

1701 Anders Celsius, scientist

1942 Jimi Hendrix, guitarist

## Events

1095 Pope Urban II preaches first Crusade.

1895 Alfred Nobel establishes Nobel prize.

1910 New York's Penn Station opens as world's largest railway terminal.

# November 28

## Birthdays

1628 John Bunyan, English cleric, author (*Pilgrim's Progress*)

1757 William Blake, poet (*Songs of Innocence and Experience*)

1937 Gary Hart, Colorado senator

1949 Paul Schaffer, musician (*Saturday Night Live, David Letterman*)

## Events

1520 Magellan begins crossing the Pacific Ocean.

1776 Washington and his troops cross the Delaware River.

1895 America's first auto race starts; six cars, 55 miles, winner averages a blazing 7 mph.

# November 29

## Birthdays

1803 Christian Doppler, discovered Doppler effect (color shift)

1832 Louisa May Alcott, author (*Little Women*)

1849 Sir Ambrose Fleming, inventor of the diode

1927 Vin Scully, sportscaster

## Events

1890 First Army-Navy football game. Score: Navy 25, Army 0.

1922 King Tut's Tomb is discovered in Egypt.

1929 Richard Byrd and crew flies over the South Pole.

1986 Cary Grant, dies in Davenport, Iowa, at 82.

# November 30

## Birthdays

1667 Jonathan Swift, satirist (*Gulliver's Travels*, "A Modest Proposal")

1810 Oliver Fisher Winchester, rifle maker

1835 Samuel Clemens (a.k.a. Mark Twain), author (*Tom Sawyer, Huckleberry Finn*)

1874 Sir Winston Churchill, British Prime Minister (Nobel Prize, 1953)

## Events

30 B.C. Cleopatra died.

1954 First meteorite known to have struck a woman—Sylacauga, AL.

1958 First guided missile destroyer launched, the *Dewey*, Bath, ME.

# December 1

## Birthdays

1899 Robert Welch, founded John Birch Society

1911 Walter Alston, baseball manager

1913 Mary Martin, actress (*Peter Pan*)

1935 Allen Stuart Konigsberg (a.k.a. Woody Allen), actor, producer (*Zelig, Annie Hall*)

## Events

1887 Sherlock Holmes first appears in print: "A Study in Scarlet."

1913 First drive-up gasoline station opens, Pittsburgh, PA.

1929 Bingo invented by Edwin S. Lowe.

1955 Rosa Parks arrested for refusing to move to back of the bus.

1959 First color photograph of Earth from outer space.

# December 2

## Birthdays

1859 Georges Seurat, painter, pointillist

1906 Peter Carl Goldmark, developed color TV and LP records

1915 William Randolph Hearst, publisher

# Events

1927 First Model A Fords sold, for $385.

1982 First permanent artificial heart successfully implanted.

# December 3

## Birthdays

1755 Gilbert Stuart, painted Washington

1857 Joseph Conrad, novelist (*Lord Jim, Heart of Darkness*)

1930 Andy Williams, singer ("Moon River")

## Events

1621 Galileo invents the telescope.

1954 Joseph McCarthy condemned by U.S. Senate.

1984 Two thousand die in Union Carbide subsidiary in Bhopal, India.

# December 4

## Birthdays

1795 Thomas Carlyle, essayist, historian

1835 Samuel Butler, author (*Erewhon, The Way of All Flesh*)

1949 Jeff Bridges, actor

## Events

1674 Father Marquette builds first dwelling in what is now Chicago.

# December 5

## Birthdays

1782 Martin Van Buren, 8th President

1839 George Armstrong Custer, U.S. general

1901 Walter Elias Disney

## Events

1791 Wolfgang Amadeus Mozart dies.

1955 AFL and CIO labor unions merge.

# December 6

## Birthdays

1822 John Eberhard, built first large scale pencil factory in U.S.

1886 Joyce Kilmer, poet ("Trees")

1896 Ira Gershwin, lyricist

## Events

1768 First edition of *Encyclopaedia Brittanica* is published in Scotland.

# December 7

## Birthdays

1873 Willa Cather, author (*My Antonia*)

1956 Larry Bird, basketball player

## Events

1787 Delaware is the first state to ratify the Constitution.

1941 Japan attacks Pearl Harbor in the Hawaiian Islands.

# December 8

## Birthdays

1765 Eli Whitney, inventor

1886 Diego Rivera, Mexican muralist

1894 James (Grover) Thurber, writer

1925 Sammy Davis, Jr., actor

## Events

1886 American Federation of Labor (AFL) formed by 26 craft unions, in Columbus, OH.

1941 The United States declares war on Japan.

1980 John Lennon assassinated in New York by Mark David Chapman.

# December 9

## Birthdays

1608 John Milton, poet

1886 Clarence Birdseye, frozen vegetable king

1898 Emmett Kelly, circus clown

1918 Kirk Douglas, actor (*Gunfight at the OK Corral, 7 Days in May*)

## Events

1793 Noah Webster establishes New York's first daily newspaper (*American Minerva*).

1907 First Christmas Seals sold in the Wilmington, DE post office.

# December 10

## Birthdays

1787 Thomas H. Gallaudet, pioneer of educating the deaf

1830 Emily Dickinson, poet

1851 Melvil Dewey, created the Dewey Decimal System for libraries

## Events

1869 Women granted right to vote in Wyoming Territory.

1896 Alfred Nobel dies; Nobel Prize ceremony on this date.

# December 11

## Birthdays

1781 Sir David Brewster, physicist, inventor of kaleidoscope

1882 Fiorello La Guardia, mayor of NYC

1918 Aleksandr Solzhenitsyn, writer (*The Gulag Archipelago, Cancer Ward*) (Nobel Prize, 1970)

## Events

1936 King Edward VIII of England abdicates for the woman he loves.

1946 U.N. Children's Fund (UNICEF) established (Nobel Prize, 1965).

1961 JFK provides U.S. military helicopters and crews to South Vietnam.

# December 12

## Birthdays

1805 Henry Wells, founded American Express Co. and Wells Fargo and Co.

1852 Henri Becquerel, discoverer of radioactivity (Nobel Prize, 1903)

1863 Edvard Munch, artist (*The Scream*)

1915 Frank Sinatra, singer, "Old Blue Eyes"

## Events

1899 George F. Grant patents golf tee.

1901 Marconi receives the first transatlantic radio signal from England to U.S.

1925 Arthur Heinman coins the term "motel"—opens one in San Luis Obispo, CA.

# December 13

### Birthdays

1818 Mary Todd Lincoln, former First Lady

1925 Dick Van Dyke, actor

### Events

1577 Sir Francis Drake sets sail from England to go around the world

1918 Woodrow Wilson becomes first to make a foreign visit while President.

1978 Susan B. Anthony dollar, first U.S. coin to honor a woman, issued.

# December 14

### Birthdays

1503 Nostradamus, astrologer, physician, "prophet"

1895 George VI, king of England

1932 Charlie Rich, singer

### Events

1962 Mariner 2 makes first U.S. fly-by of another planet (Venus)

1989 Andrei Sakharov, Soviet dissident and physicist, dies.

# December 15

### Birthdays

1832 Alexandre-Gustave Eiffel, built the Eiffel Tower.

1892 J. Paul Getty, business tycoon

### Events

1791 Bill of Rights ratified when Virginia gave its approval.

1877 Patent granted to Thomas Edison for the phonograph.

1939 World premiere of *Gone With The Wind*, Atlanta, GA.

# December 16

### Birthdays

1770 Ludwig von Beethoven, composer

1775 Jane Austen, novelist (*Pride and Prejudice*)

1899 Sir Noel Coward, playwright

### Events

1773 Boston Tea Party, Boston Harbor

1905 *Variety*, covering all phases of show business, first published.

# December 17

### Birthdays

1807 John Greenleaf Whittier, poet

1894 Arthur Fiedler, Boston Pops conductor

### Events

1843 "A Christmas Carol" by Charles Dickens published in London.

1903 At 10:35 a.m., for 12 seconds, first sustained motorized aircraft flight (36 meters) by Wright Brothers at Kitty Hawk, N.C.

# December 18

### Birthdays

1886 Ty Cobb, baseball great

1916 Betty Grable, actress

1942 Muhammad Ali, boxer

1947 Steven Spielberg, director (*Schindler's List, E.T., The Color Purple, Jaws*)

### Events

1898 Auto speed record set—63 kph.

1899 George Grant wins patent for golf tee.

1932 Chicago Bears beat Portsmouth Spartans 9-0 in first NFL playoff game.

# December 19

## Birthdays

1790 Sir William Parry, Arctic explorer

1849 Henry Clay Frick, industrialist

1933 Cicely Tyson, actress

1946 Robert Urich, actor (*Vega$, Spencer for Hire, Ice Pirates*)

## Events

1732 Benjamin Franklin begins publication of *Poor Richard's Almanack*.

1957 *The Music Man*, starring Robert Preston, opens on Broadway.

# December 20

## Birthdays

1868 Harvey S. Firestone, tiremaker

1928 Joyce Brothers, doctor

## Events

1820 Missouri imposes a $1 bachelor tax on unmarried men between 21 and 50.

1879 Tom Edison privately demonstrated incandescent light at Menlo Park.

1880 New York's Broadway lighted by electricity, becomes known as the "Great White Way."

1892 Pneumatic automobile tire patented.

# December 21

## Birthdays

1911 Josh Gibson, professional baseball player, the "Negro Babe Ruth"

1935 Phil Donahue, talk-show host

1937 Jane Fonda, actress, activist

## Events

1620 The Pilgrims land at Plymouth Rock, MA.

1913 First crossword puzzle (with 32 clues), printed in *New York World*.

1937 First feature-length cartoon with color and sound, premieres: *Snow White and the Seven Dwarfs*.

# December 23

## Birthdays

1790 Jean-Francois Champollion, deciphered Egyptian hieroglyphics

## Events

1947 Transistor invented by Bardeen, Brattain, and Shockley, Bell Labs.

1975 Congress passes Metric Conversion Act.

# December 24

## Birthdays

1809 Kit Carson, Western scout

1905 Howard Hughes, billionaire

## Events

1814 Treaty of Ghent signed, ending War of 1812 (this news did not arrive until after the Battle of New Orleans).

1906 First known radio program in U.S. is broadcast from Brant Rock, MA: Reginald A. Fessenden became first to broadcast music over radio.

# December 25

## Birthdays

0000 Jesus Christ, savior, philosopher

1642 Isaac Newton, scientist

1821 Clara Barton, philanthropist, American Red Cross founder

1899 Humphrey Bogart, actor (*The Maltese Falcon, The African Queen*)

## Events

1776 Washington crosses the Delaware and surprises the Hessians.

1939 Montgomery Ward introduces Rudolph, the ninth reindeer.

# December 26

## Birthdays

1893 Mao Tse-tung, Chinese leader, revolutionary, author

1921 Steve Allen, comedian, jazz musician

## Events

1492 First Spanish settlement New World founded, by Columbus.

# December 27

## Birthdays

1571 Johannes Kepler (at Weil-der-Stadt, Germany), astronomer, discovered that planets travel in elliptical orbits.

1822 Louis Pasteur, French chemist and bacteriologist

## Events

1825 First public railroad using steam locomotive completed in England

1831 Darwin begins his voyage on board the *HMS Beagle.*

1932 Radio City Music Hall in New York City opens.

# December 28

## Birthdays

1856 Woodrow Wilson, 28th President (Nobel Prize, 1919)

1905 Earl "Fatha" Hines, jazz pianist

## Events

1669 William Semple patented chewing gum.

1890 Battle of Wounded Knee, SD—Last major conflict with Indians.

# December 29

## Birthdays

1776 Charles MacIntosh, chemist, patented waterproof fabric

1800 Charles Goodyear, invented vulcanization process for rubber

1937 Mary Tyler Moore, actress

## Events

1851 First Young Men's Christian Association chapter opened in Boston.

1952 First transistorized hearing aid offered for sale, Elmsford, NY.

# December 30

## Birthdays

1865 Rudyard Kipling, poet and novelist

1928 Bo Diddley, bluesman, rock 'n' roll pioneer

## Events

1903 More than 600 die as flames sweep through the Iroquois Theater, Chicago.

# December 31

## Birthdays

1869 Henri Matisse, impressionist painter

1943 John Denver, singer, actor

## Events

1890 Ellis Island opened as a U.S. immigration depot.

# Index